PRAISE FOR CATHY GLASS

'Poignant and revealing … real-life stories such as these have helped to move and inspire a generation'   *Sunday Mirror*

'A true tale of hope'   *OK!* Magazine

'Heartbreaking'   *Mirror*

'A life-affirming read … that proves sometimes a little hope is all you need'   *Heat* Magazine

'A hugely touching and emotional true tale'   *Star* Magazine

'Foster carers rarely get the praise they deserve, but Cathy Glass's book should change all that'   *First* Magazine

'Cannot fail to move those who read it'   Adoption-net

'Once again, Cathy Glass has blown me away with a poignant story'   The Writing Garnet,
book blogger

'Brilliant book. I'd expect nothing less from Cathy … I cried, of course'   Goodreads review

'… gripping page-turner from start to finish … emotive and heart-wrenching ..'   Kate Hall,
…ok blogger

Unsafe

ALSO BY CATHY GLASS

THE MULTI-MILLION COPY BESTSELLING AUTHOR

CATHY GLASS

Unsafe

**Damian longs for home,
but one man stands in his way**

Certain details in this story, including names, places and dates, have been changed to protect the family's privacy.

HarperElement
An imprint of HarperCollins*Publishers*
1 London Bridge Street
London SE1 9GF

www.harpercollins.co.uk

HarperCollins*Publishers*
Macken House, 39/40 Mayor Street Upper
Dublin 1, D01 C9W8, Ireland

First published by HarperElement 2023

1 3 5 7 9 10 8 6 4 2

© Cathy Glass 2023

Cathy Glass asserts the moral right to be
identified as the author of this work

A catalogue record of this book is
available from the British Library

ISBN 978-0-00-864053-8

Printed and bound in the UK using 100%
renewable electricity at CPI Group (UK) Ltd

ACKNOWLEDGEMENTS

A big thank-you to my family; my editors, Kelly and Holly; my literary agent, Andrew; my UK publisher HarperCollins, and my overseas publishers, who are now too numerous to list by name. Last, but definitely not least, a big thank-you to my readers for your unfailing support and kind words. They are much appreciated.

CHAPTER ONE

ALLEGATION

Cathy, are you free to talk? the text message read.

It was from Tash, a friend and, like me, a foster carer. Her full name was Natasha, but we all knew her as Tash, and she lived about a five-minute drive away. Normally I would have seen her every few months, either at foster-carer training or our monthly support-group meetings, which included time to talk over a coffee, but that hadn't happened since before the pandemic.

I assumed she was phoning for a chat or to arrange a get-together. The country was gradually coming out of lockdown and restrictions on mixing were easing. I also assumed the reason she'd texted first rather than just phoning was because of the time. It was nearly 10 p.m., when most of us with children were winding down after a busy day or on our way to bed. I'd been about to switch off the television and go up to bed, but I was happy to hear from her. Rather than reply to her text, I decided to call. She answered straight away.

'Oh, Cathy, just a minute,' she said, sounding flustered.

It went quiet, as though she might have been going to another room, and I thought I should have texted first. Tash lived with her husband, Jamal, their fifteen-year-old son, Ryan, thirteen-year-old daughter, Evie, and a looked-after child. They often fostered teenagers, which seemed to work well with their own children. I didn't know who she was fostering at present as I hadn't seen or spoken to her for some time. Although we were friends, I wouldn't say we were close friends. She was younger than me and it was fostering that had brought us together.

I heard a door close, then Tash came on the phone.

'Oh, Cathy, thank you for calling,' she said, her voice trembling.

'What is it, Tash? Are you OK?'

'No.'

'Are you hurt?'

'No,' she said and began to cry.

'Tash, please tell me what's wrong. Is it one of your family? Is someone ill?' Please don't say a loved one has died, I silently prayed.

'No, no one's ill.' She stifled another sob.

'Is everything all right with Jamal?' I tried.

'He's in the other room. I had to come out as he can't bear to talk about what's happened. But I need to talk. I thought you might understand as you've been fostering for so long.'

'I'll help if I can,' I said. My heart was racing, and any thought of sleep had gone. What could possibly have happened to make Tash so upset? She was usually confident, vibrant and very able to cope.

She gave another sob. 'It's Becks,' she said.

'Who's Becks?'

'The young person we were fostering. You didn't meet her. She arrived after lockdown and was here for six months. She's accused Ryan of sexually abusing her.'

'Oh no.' I knew then Tash had every reason to be distraught – her son had been accused of abusing their foster child.

'It's a living nightmare,' Tash said. 'We've had the police here and …' She dissolved into tears again.

'Take your time,' I said gently. I waited for her to recover. My adult daughter, Paula, was upstairs in her room, and Damian, the seven-year-old I was fostering, was asleep in his room.

'I can't believe this is happening to us,' Tash said at last. 'The police have interviewed all of us separately – Ryan, Evie, Jamal and me – like criminals. And all because Becks was angry with me. They even contacted the school to see if they had any concerns about us, so they all know now.' Her voice trembled with emotion.

'What happened for Becks to make the claim?' I asked.

I heard Tash sniff and say to someone there, 'I won't be long.' Then to me she said, 'That was Jamal wondering where I was. This is destroying us.'

'I can imagine.'

'We're getting no support from the social services. They say they can't talk to us or comment about the case until the investigation is complete. Their first priority is with the looked-after child, but what about us?' Tash said, her voice rising. 'We're the victims here.'

I knew of other carers who'd been put in a similar position, where an allegation had been made by a looked-after child, and that the social services followed a strict procedure. Often not even the carer's supervising social worker (SSW) contacted the carer until the investigation was complete.

'What about Joy?' I asked. We shared the same supervising social worker – Joy Philips.

'She phoned once when it first happened and that's it. She's not allowed to discuss it with me either.'

All foster carers in the UK have a supervising social worker and their role is to support, monitor, advise and guide the carer and their family in every aspect of fostering. Clearly Joy was now bound by the same procedure.

'She gave us the number of a telephone helpline, but that's all,' Tash said. 'I can't believe we're being investigated by the safeguarding team as if we'd actually abused Becks! We're not allowed to attend the meetings. They're behind closed doors. I know what the parents of children in care feel like now.'

'When did all this happen?' I asked.

'It began two weeks ago. It was Sunday and we'd gone for a walk. Jamal is still working from home and he needed to catch up on some stuff. It's never quiet in the house with three teenagers, and Becks often played her music very loudly rather than using headphones. Sometimes I'm sure it was just to annoy us. So we went for a walk in the woods – you know, the ones near us. We've been there a lot during lockdown. Although my children are teenagers, they enjoy playing hide-and-seek around the bushes and trees. We were there for about an hour and everything seemed fine, nothing was said, then we returned home. Becks poured herself a drink of juice and went to her bedroom, where she started playing her music very loudly again. I went up and asked her to turn it down or use her headphones as Jamal was still working. She did, but as soon as I was downstairs she turned it up again. Ryan shouted at her from his room to stop being so selfish as he couldn't concentrate either. She yelled back and an argument started, so I went up. Becks was in a really bad mood – I think because of what Ryan had said about her being selfish. She was never an easy child, volatile and unpredictable. She shouted at me. Jamal told her to calm down, but she yelled she hated us all and stormed off out of the house. She often did that if she couldn't get her own way or was angry, and usually came back within a couple of hours, when we all forgave her and carried on as normal.

'But this time she didn't come back. I tried calling her phone, but she didn't answer. Eventually I called the duty social worker as we're supposed to and he said if she wasn't back within two hours we should phone him again and then report her missing to the police.

'So at seven o'clock I phoned him again and he gave me the go-ahead to report Becks missing to the police, which I did. An hour later the duty social worker phoned and said Becks had been found and to cancel the missing person report, but that she wouldn't be return-ing to us. He wouldn't say why and seemed very guarded. It was the following afternoon when we were told that Becks was claiming Ryan had sexually abused her. She said he'd grabbed her breast when they'd been playing hide-and-seek.' Tash's voice broke and I heard her stifle a sob.

'I am so sorry,' I said, appreciating the seriousness of this.

'I blame myself, Cathy. I should never have let them out of my sight. But Becks seemed to be settling. She was supposed to be with us long term. Yes, she could be very challenging at times, and we still don't know what really happened at home with her mum's boyfriend. But never in a million years would I have imagined she'd do this to us. And just because her music was too loud!'

'How old is Becks?' I asked.

'Sixteen, a year older than Ryan, but she's a lot more mature and streetwise. He's like a little boy by comparison, trusting and naive. You should have seen his face when he was told what she'd said. He didn't understand to begin with.' Tash's voice broke again.

'To make matters worse,' Tash continued after a moment, 'when Ryan was interviewed he said he might have accidently touched her breast when he grabbed her. They were playing hide-and-seek and when he discovered where she was hiding he crept up from behind and grabbed her, with the intention of just scaring her. Of course he knows he shouldn't have touched her at all, but he and his sister rough and tumble sometimes and he just forgot in the moment. We believe him, but I'm not sure the police do. It's destroying us, Cathy, the waiting and not knowing.'

'Yes, I can understand that.' I sympathized deeply.

'Jamal is furious and says we won't ever foster again. I agree with him.'

'I don't blame you. How is Ryan coping?'

'He's not, really. He's quiet and withdrawn. He's got schoolwork to do, but he can't concentrate. The police took away his laptop and phone to begin with, but they've returned them now. Of course there was nothing on them other than ordinary teenage stuff. He's close to tears a lot of the time and keeps apologizing, saying he's let us down. I've told him he's got nothing to be sorry about. He made an error of judgement and Becks has blown it out of all proportion.' Tash paused. 'Have you ever had to face anything like this?'

'Yes, although it didn't become a police matter. Some years ago a child I was fostering told her mother that my son, Adrian, and his friends had kissed her on the lips. Fortunately, I was there and saw what happened.' (I cover this in my book *Another Forgotten Child*.) 'As a single parent I had to deal with it alone. I can still remember the worry.'

'It happens a lot,' Tash said. 'The person I spoke to on the helpline said one in four foster carers has a false allegation made against them at some point in their fostering career, and most of them stop fostering as a result.'

'We are in a very vulnerable position,' I said. 'Is there anything I can do to help?'

'Not really. I just needed to talk, and it helps knowing you came through something similar. And you didn't stop fostering?'

'No. Although I did consider it.'

'We are not allowed to contact Becks, and the social worker who collected all her belongings said she couldn't discuss it with us as the investigation was ongoing. We've been dropped just like that. Never mind all the years of fostering. Whyever did we bother?'

'Because you made a big difference to the lives of many children,' I said.

'Maybe, but I can't think like that at present. The damage this is doing to my family …' Her voice fell away.

There wasn't really much more I could say. Tash thanked me again for listening and we said goodnight.

CHAPTER TWO

TOO MUCH RESPONSIBILITY

As the call from Tash ended I felt low and worried for her. I stayed where I was on the sofa in the living room, deep in thought. What she and her family were going through was truly horrendous – every foster carer's worst nightmare: being accused of sexually abusing their looked-after child.

I appreciated the allegation had to be thoroughly investigated, just as it did with any child or young person claiming they'd been abused. Ryan had admitted he might have accidently touched Becks's breast during the game of hide-and-seek, but the police and social services would need to be sure it was accidental and that he didn't intentionally grope her. It was going to be difficult to prove one way or the other. There were no witnesses and ultimately the decision might be based on the balance of probabilities – what had most likely happened. And even if it was an accident, there could still be safeguarding concerns.

The incident highlighted just how vulnerable foster carers and their families are. Unlike teachers, nursery assistants, staff in children's homes and most others working with children, we are alone in our homes, isolated, with no colleagues nearby to uphold our version of events when something goes wrong or to support us when we need it. Yet we work with society's most vulnerable children, those who have often been neglected and abused. We are classified as self-employed and, at the time of writing, trade union representation for foster carers is in its infancy, so any foster carer facing an investigation is effectively alone, and on the receiving end of a process that is far from straightforward and transparent – not something you think about when you start fostering, full of hope and goodwill, unless, like Tash, you find your family accused. Some foster carers install CCTV in their homes, but, like most, I rely on safer caring practices.

Foster carers in the UK have a 'safer caring policy', which is designed to keep all family members feeling safe. It includes rules on privacy (for example, not going into someone else's bedroom, and wearing clothes in communal areas), advises carers not to leave a foster child in a room with someone with the door closed, and to avoid teasing, suggestive remarks and rough play, and offers guidance on how to stay safe online. The carer will also keep detailed log notes. Ryan would have been aware of the safer caring policy and may have attended foster carer training for birth children. There is also training specifically for men.

Sadly, many of the children we foster have been abused, some sexually, and they bring with them the memories and fallout of that dreadful time, sometimes subconsciously. An event or object can act as a trigger, reminding them of the abuse, so their reaction is based on what they suffered before rather than the present situation. An incident which might go unnoticed or be laughed off by another person can be very distressing for those who are dealing with past trauma. Had Ryan accidently touched his sister's breast while playing, he would have very likely been embarrassed, apologized and been more careful next time, not found himself the subject of police and social services investigations. There was also the possibility that, as Tash had said, Becks was angry and had retaliated by making the allegation, which she knew would hurt the family. Sometimes when a looked-after child feels settled and cared for, which Becks would have done after six months of being part of Tash's family, they decide they've got close enough and it's time to test the boundaries or even leave. Making an allegation of this type is a sure way out.

The average person has little idea of the issues foster parents face, especially when dealing with difficult behaviour in abused children. One of the reasons I write my fostering memoirs is to try to raise awareness about this and other matters connected with our care system. With that in mind, a last word on the subject before I move on: when an allegation is made against a foster carer, it stays on the family's case file at the social services forever, even if it's proved false.

It was time to go to bed, I thought, and with a heavy heart I hauled myself from the sofa. Sammy, our cat, aware it was his bedtime too, stretched, jumped down from the chair and followed me into the kitchen-diner, where his bed was. I checked that the back door was locked and his water bowl was full, and came out.

Upstairs, I went to Damian's bedroom where the door was partly open as he liked it. I looked in and could see he was fast asleep. I went to Paula's room to say goodnight. My son, Adrian, was married and living with his wife, Kirsty. My other daughter, Lucy, was living with her partner, Darren, and they had given me my first grandchild – Emma. Paula was propped up in bed with her laptop open.

'Everything all right?' I asked, going in.

'Yes, fine, I'm watching a film.'

'OK, night, love.'

'Night, Mum.'

We hugged, I kissed her goodnight and then came out. Paula had been furloughed from work until the end of July. It was now May. Furlough was a government scheme to allow businesses that were closed or couldn't run at full capacity as a result of the pandemic to keep staff on their payroll rather than making them redundant. But like many others, she worried there might not be a job at the end of it. The economy had slowed as a result of the pandemic and orders at her company were low. Earlier in the year, during lockdown, she'd got a bit depressed and since then I'd kept a close eye on her, but she seemed to be coping better now.

I got into bed, still thinking about what Tash had told me. On top of all the other bad stuff we'd had to deal with since the start of the pandemic, it weighed heavily on my mind. Adrian was of the opinion that I should cut down on fostering and it was at moments like this that I considered it. My husband had left us when my family was very young, so I'd faced all the ups and downs of fostering for thirty years alone. Perhaps Adrian was right and I should cut back, but then again …

It was another day tomorrow and I'd start it afresh. It was going to be a busy day. After taking Damian to school I'd do the weekly shop, then in the afternoon I'd look in on Lara. I'd fostered Lara, now aged twenty-one, and her nineteen-month-old son Arthur, before Damian. Although she was doing all right, I visited every so often to give her a bit of extra support and because I liked to see her, as I do all the children I've fostered. They are part of my extended family.

It seemed I'd no sooner dropped off to sleep than it was time to get up. Friday, and Damian was spending the weekend at home with his mother as he had been doing every weekend, which gave me a chance to spend time with my family.

But first I had to face the ordeal of breakfast with Damian, which I knew wasn't going to be easy.

I showered and dressed and then woke him, preparing myself for the conversation I knew would follow.

'Good morning, love,' I said brightly. 'Time to get up.' I opened his curtains. 'It's a lovely sunny day out there.'

Damian rubbed his eyes, yawned and sat upright in bed. 'Am I seeing my mummy?' he asked, slightly anxiously.

'Yes, love, for the weekend as usual.'

'I don't want any breakfast.'

'But you're going to try to have a little something,' I reminded him. 'You can choose what it is.'

'I feel sick,' he said, getting out of bed.

'I think you will feel better once you are up and about. You did last time.'

'I might be sick if I have breakfast.'

'I don't think so.' I handed him his clean clothes. 'Go to the bathroom and I'll wait here while you get ready.'

I always give the child I'm looking after age-appropriate responsibility for washing, toileting and dressing. Damian had good self-care skills. As the eldest of three, he'd had to grow up quickly. I waited on the landing while he used the toilet, washed and dressed. Five minutes later he was ready.

'Well done, that was quick,' I said.

'I'm not hungry,' he said. 'I don't want any breakfast. Mummy says I don't have to.'

'I know, love, but your social worker and the doctor want you to have a little. You can choose what you want.'

I offered him my hand, but he walked downstairs behind me, looking sullen and a bit annoyed with me. I was acting on advice from the paediatrician and with the knowledge I'd received from Damian's social worker, Korin Elrod, that he should be offered regular meals, and if he had some responsibility for choosing and preparing them it could help ease some of his anxiety around food. At just seven years old, Damian was showing all the signs of an eating disorder, which it was thought he'd learnt from his mother. It's not unusual for children of Damian's age to be 'fussy' or 'selective' eaters, and they usually grow out of it, but Damian seemed to be copying his mother to the point of making himself sick. It was worrying and upsetting to watch.

Damian's mother, Rachel, had spent some of her life in a children's home and had struggled with an eating disorder since becoming a teenager. She was the only role model Damian had. Aged twenty-four, she was a single parent, and after the birth of her last baby she had agreed that Damian should go into care, as long as she could have him home every weekend. The social services had drawn up a care plan so that I looked after him during the week and he stayed with his mother from Friday after school to Sunday evening. Rachel knew she could phone me to collect him earlier if necessary, but so far that hadn't happened. I'd already noticed that Damian's attitude to food worsened on a Friday just before the weekend. He loved his mother and seeing his younger siblings, and I'm sure his mother loved him, but there was a lot of anxiety in their home as she struggled to cope.

Downstairs, Damian opened the door to the kitchen-diner, as he liked to do first thing each morning, then petted Sammy. We'd got into a little routine, him and me. As Damian made a fuss of Sammy, I rinsed the cat's bowl, refilled the water compartment and set it on the floor, then Danny added the dry cat food. Sammy knew this and now meowed at Damian for breakfast rather than me. Damian would have loved a pet of his own, but his mother had bought a puppy some months before and had then had to have it rehomed when it kept messing on the floor and she couldn't cope.

'Good boy,' I said to Damian as he put away the scoop and bag of dry cat food. 'Now, what would you like to drink?'

Drinking wasn't a problem for Damian. 'Blackcurrant,' he said. He took the bottle of blackcurrant juice from the cupboard and handed it to me. I poured a little into a glass and added water. Damian took it to his place at the table.

'What would you like to eat?' I asked him lightly.

He didn't reply but sipped his drink.

'Cereal, toast or yoghurt?' I suggested. He'd had these before.

'I don't want toast,' he replied.

'No, OK. What would you like?'

As I waited for him to reply I filled the kettle and popped a slice of bread in the toaster for my breakfast.

'Cereal?' I suggested.

He shrugged, put down his glass, came into the kitchen and began opening and closing cupboard doors. I had most things he liked within his reach so they were easily accessible and he didn't have to use a stool. He eventually took out the packet of Bitesize Shredded Wheat and a bowl, then carefully counted out five. He returned the packet to the cupboard and took the bowl to the table.

'Would you like milk and sugar on them?' I asked. Although I could guess his reply, I still offered them.

He shook his head.

I poured my coffee, buttered the toast, spread on marmalade and joined Damian at the table. He picked up one piece of Shredded Wheat and nibbled on it first before putting it into his mouth. He spent a long time chewing it while I set about my breakfast. I liked my food, I always have, and it pained me to see Damian so reluctant to enjoy his. Interestingly, while eating in the home environment was a challenge for Damian and problematic, he ate school dinners. This was probably what kept him going and the reason he wasn't underweight like his mother. I had been asked to keep a food diary and the school also let me know what he'd had to eat.

As I ate, I could see Damian out of the corner of my eye. He had a drink, swallowed with a rather loud, dramatic gulp, then picked up another Shredded Wheat and nibbled on that. I always kept my presence relaxed and low key when he was eating, unlike his mother, who apparently reacted to Damian's refusal to eat – becoming distraught and bribing him. While this was understandable, it didn't improve Damian's relationship with food. It had been suggested that some of his behaviour around food was to gain attention.

Eventually, one by one, he nibbled and then ate the five small Shredded Wheat.

'What fruit shall we have?' I asked. I always offered fruit at breakfast and he often ate a little if I had some too. 'Tangerine, like yesterday?'

'No. I don't like tangerines.' I didn't point out that he had liked them yesterday and the day before.

'What shall we have then?' I asked.

'Banana,' he said.

I left the table, sliced up a banana and set the plate between us. He ate two slices and I eventually ate the rest. Breakfast had taken half an hour, but he had eaten. I was following strategies suggested by the paediatrician as well as some that had worked for me in the past.

'Time to brush your teeth and then we'll leave for school,' I said.

Damian rushed from the table and then upstairs, where he began gagging into the sink in the bathroom. I hurried after him. He'd done this before.

'No,' I said firmly, going into the bathroom. 'You know you don't do that. Brush your teeth, good boy, then we can go to school.'

He stopped retching, squirted toothpaste onto his toothbrush and began cleaning his teeth. When he'd first arrived and tried to make himself sick it had shocked me, although I'd been warned by his mother that he did this. In the first week after he'd moved in he did it every day, but now it was only every so often, usually on a Friday when he would be going home for the weekend, or on a Monday after he'd just returned. I'd informed his social worker as well as entering it in my log notes, as foster carers are supposed to. It seemed likely Damian had learnt this behaviour from his mother, although she claimed she always closed the bathroom door when she was being sick so he couldn't have seen her. In my experience children don't miss much, and even if Damian hadn't seen his mother trying to be sick, he'd very likely heard her through the bathroom door. Rachel's eating disorder had become significantly worse during lockdown due to all the anxiety caused by the pandemic. She was receiving help from an eating disorder clinic, but at present all the sessions were still online because of the restrictions on mixing.

'Good boy,' I said as Damian finished cleaning his teeth. He patted his mouth dry on the towel.

As we went along the landing I could hear Paula moving around in her bedroom, so I called goodbye and that I'd see her later.

'Don't forget my bag,' Damian told me as we left the house.

'I won't. I'll bring it with me when I collect you from school,' I reassured him.

I took a bag containing what he needed for the weekend with me in the car when I collected him from school on a Friday and took him to his mother's. I hadn't forgotten his bag yet, but that didn't stop Damian worrying. Prior to coming into care, he'd arrived at school dirty and smelly and had told his teacher they didn't have enough money for the launderette. If I didn't pack fresh clothes to last the weekend, it was likely he wouldn't have any. Plenty of his belongings had remained at home, but his mother's life was chaotic.

Damian liked going in my car – Rachel didn't drive – but before we got in we had our usual conversation about why he couldn't sit in the front passenger seat. He wasn't old enough, but he still asked, hoping I'd relent, although I had explained that it was the law, not me. He then sat in the back and as I drove made *vroom-vroom* noises that were supposed to mimic the engine accelerating. He also made the sounds of gears clashing (which I never did) and tyres screeching (not often). He asked questions about cars, which I answered as best I could, and said he was going to learn to drive when he was old enough.

Damian was a cute kid; some would say cheeky and challenging, but I liked him a lot. He spoke his mind and had character. It was just such a pity he'd had so much responsibility so young. When he'd first arrived he'd wanted to assume all the responsibility he had at home, including cooking for all of us – chicken nuggets and chips in the oven – putting out the rubbish, shopping and being in charge of me. I'd given him age-appropriate tasks like making his bed, putting away his toys and taking his washing to the linen basket, but I'd explained that as his foster carer I liked to do the rest. That didn't stop him from asking, though, and worrying about what was happening at home: did his mother have enough money? Had his younger brother, Nathan, been fed? Had baby Liam had his nappy changed? And so on. I'd seen it before in children I'd fostered who'd had to assume some of their parent's role. As well as causing the child anxiety, it puts them in the position of being in charge, so setting boundaries for good behaviour and sanctioning negative behaviour then becomes very difficult, as Rachel had found out. She saw Damian as 'hard work', which he could be, but he'd responded to my clear and consistent boundaries. Although, of course, I'd had the benefit of years of bringing up children and foster-carer training, which Rachel had not.

There was a lot of noise from Damian as I approached the school, gently braked and then parked the car.

'Well done, you didn't hit the kerb,' he said.

'That happened once,' I said indignantly. And it had been because I was concentrating on him rather than parking.

'Have you put the handbrake on?' he asked.

'Yes, love,' I replied with a smile.

I got out and opened the rear door, which was child-locked. I put on my face mask, as adults were expected to do, and we entered the playground. The start and end times of school were still being staggered to help reduce contact and the spread of coronavirus, so there was only one class going in or coming out at this time. Breaks and lunchtime were staggered too. Damian's teaching assistant (TA), Mrs Halas, was in the playground to greet us. I said goodbye to him, wished him a good day and told him I'd see him later.

'Don't forget my bag!' he called as he went in.

'I won't.'

I returned to my car, tucked my face mask into my pocket and then texted Lara.

Going to the supermarket. Do you need anything?

By the time I arrived at the supermarket she'd replied with her list.

CHAPTER THREE

LARA AND ARTHUR

I tell Lara's story in *Unwanted*, so I'll not say too much here, other than this: her mother had died when she was a child, and with no family to look after her she'd gone into care. This hadn't been a good experience for Lara. She'd had a lot of moves and generally didn't have a good word to say about foster carers. With no role model and little help, she'd struggled to bring up her son, Arthur, as a single parent and had found herself in an abusive relationship. I'd fostered her and Arthur in a mother-and-child placement, at the end of which Lara had been allowed to keep her son. However, they were still being monitored by the social services, so Lara knew it was important she didn't fall into bad ways. Parenting doesn't have to be perfect but 'good enough'. It's a term the social workers use when assessing parenting capacity.

It was nearly 1.30 when I parked outside the block of flats where Lara lived with Arthur. It was a three-storey brick building fronted by a grass verge on an estate that was a mixture of private and social housing, about a twenty-minute drive away from my house. Lara would have had time to collect Arthur from nursery, which he attended in the mornings only, and given him lunch. I took the carrier bag containing her shopping from the passenger seat and got out. It was another lovely May day with the sun shining and birds singing from the rooftops.

I put on my mask and went in through the main door. There was no one in the communal hall so I took the mask off as I climbed the flight of stairs to Lara's flat, which was at the rear of the building and looked out over the lawn. I'd been here many times before, first helping her with the decorating and furnishing, then after she'd moved just to visit. I didn't want to ring the doorbell in case Arthur was having a nap, which he did sometimes after nursery. Lara was expecting me, so I tapped lightly on the door and said, 'It's Cathy.'

Arthur couldn't have been asleep for I heard his footsteps running towards the door, then he banged on it with his fists. 'Caffy, Caffy.'

'Yes. It's me,' I replied with a smile.

It was a few moments before Lara opened the door. She had her phone pressed to her ear. 'Speak later,' she said to whoever was on the phone. 'My foster carer is here.' She still referred to me as her foster carer, which I rather liked.

'How are you?' I asked, going in and taking off my shoes.

'OK.'

Arthur was trying to get into the carrier bag of shopping, aware that I usually bought something for him. He was collecting play animals to go in his farmyard/zoo set, and I often bought an animal to add to his collection or another small gift. I had a box of eggs in the bag today, so I didn't want those broken.

'Just a minute, love,' I told him. 'Let's take Mummy's shopping to the kitchen first.'

I took the few steps into the one main room of the flat and stopped dead.

'Good grief, Lara! What's happened here?'

'I know, it's a mess,' she said gloomily. 'I haven't had time to clear up.'

'You're not kidding! But what's the mattress doing in here?' I asked, aghast. The mattress from the double bed was on the floor, taking up most of the available floor space. On top of it were the pillows and duvet from the bed, various discarded clothes, some of Arthur's toys and empty cereal bowls. 'It looks like you're camping,' I added, with a weak smile.

'We couldn't all sleep in the bedroom,' she said. 'So Frazer helped me move the mattress in here last week-end.' Frazer was her boyfriend.

'It's been like this all week?' I asked.

'Yes.'

'Claudette hasn't been?' I checked, worried. Claudette was their social worker.

'No, she's not due until next week.'

'And supposing she made an unannounced visit and found it like this?' Lara knew, as I did, that social workers made unannounced visits in addition to their planned ones.

'I know,' Lara said dispiritedly. Arthur was still trying to get into the carrier bag.

'Here you are, love,' I said, and gave him the wrapped model of a roaring lion.

'Let's put away the shopping,' I said to Lara. 'Then I'll help you take the mattress back to the bedroom and have a tidy-up.'

'There's no point,' she said. 'Frazer will be back tonight. He can help me put it away before he leaves on Monday.'

It seemed Frazer was spending most weekends here. I hesitated. 'As long as you do. Why is it here?'

'When Frazer stays we either wake Arthur or he wakes us, so it works better if we sleep in here.'

I could see her problem. The flat was tiny, with one main living room, a kitchenette leading off it and one bedroom, where there was just enough room for a bed and a cot.

'All right, love. Let's put your shopping away.'

I trod carefully along the narrow space between the mattress and the sofa and went into the kitchenette. There was washing up in the sink and a musty smell coming from somewhere. I handed the carrier bag to Lara for her to unpack, as I set about doing the washing up.

'How much do I owe you?' Lara asked as she put away the items.

'Nothing.' I never charged her for the food I bought. She was living on benefit money and I could afford to help her out. I knew Frazer helped too.

'Thanks,' she said, but she sounded down.

'Are you OK, love?' I asked.

'I guess.'

'You don't sound it.'

I turned from what I was doing to look at her, in time to see Arthur pulling rubbish out of the bin, which was overflowing.

'No, love, yucky,' I said to him.

He paused, threw me a cheeky grin and continued. It wasn't really his fault as the bin looked like a treasure trove with all the different-coloured wrappers, tins, cardboard containers and general assortment of rubbish within his reach. I guessed that was where the smell was coming from too.

'Lara, why don't you empty the bin while I finish off here,' I said. 'Then we can have a chat over a cup of tea. I've bought a packet of your favourite biscuits.'

'Thanks,' she said, but without much enthusiasm, and moved Arthur away from the bin.

She carried the bin from the kitchenette, across the mattress and out of the flat. Arthur looked at her, disappointed.

'Mummy will be back soon,' I said. 'She's emptying the bin. Where's the lion I bought you?'

He ran into the living room, picked it up and brought it back to show me.

'Well done. What noise does a lion make?' I asked as I continued doing the dishes. Arthur was only a year and a half old, so I wasn't expecting him to know. 'It roars,' I said, and made the noise. He copied my roar and laughed.

'Yes, well done. Can you find me a cow?'

He returned to the living room and brought back a toy cow.

'Good boy. What noise does a cow make?' I asked, rinsing a dish. 'They moo.' I mooed and Arthur copied me. I'd played with him a lot while he and Lara had lived with me, and since visiting them, so he was very comfortable in my presence. 'What about a cat?' I asked, and meowed. Arthur chuckled and copied me.

'Well done. A horse?'

We were still making animal noises when Lara returned from emptying the bin.

'Sounds like you're having fun,' she said, setting down the bin. She opened the packet of biscuits I'd bought and began eating them. Arthur started agitating for one and Lara peeled off a couple for him. He ran off to eat them on the mattress in the living room.

'Have you both had lunch?' I checked.

'Yes.'

I finished the dishes as Lara filled the kettle and then made us a mug of tea each. It was a bit of ritual when I visited. I gave the kitchen a tidy, did any washing up, then we had tea with whatever treat I'd bought while we talked. Lara and I had done a lot of talking while she and Arthur had been living with me and since. I could read her moods and knew she got down sometimes. She was considering trying counselling again when the services were fully operational once lockdown was completely lifted.

We took our mugs of tea into the living room and sat side by side on the sofa, resting our feet on the edge of the mattress. Arthur was still on the mattress, the toy lion in one hand and a half-chewed biscuit in the other.

'Make sure Frazer helps you put the mattress away after this weekend,' I said. 'I am worried what Claudette will think.'

'I know. He had to leave in a hurry to get to work on Monday,' she said, her voice flat. Frazer worked for a small firm of builders I knew.

'Is everything all right between you two?' I asked, wondering if they'd argued and that was why she seemed low.

'Yes, we're good.'

'Excellent. So what's the matter?'

'I don't know.' She shrugged and cupped her mug in her hands. 'My life doesn't seem to be going anywhere. I'm stuck in the same old routine.'

'I think we all feel that way to some extent,' I said. 'It should start to get better once lockdown is over.'

'I was talking to Shell and Courtney last night and they are planning on going to Ibiza as soon as travel opens up. A week of clubbing. They assumed I couldn't go as I had Arthur.'

Shell and Courtney were good friends of Lara's, although their lifestyles were very different now as Lara had Arthur to look after.

'While I'm happy to babysit Arthur so you can have a night out or even a weekend away, I wouldn't offer for a whole week,' I said, thinking I should make that clear. 'It wouldn't be fair on Arthur, and I don't think Claudette would approve either.'

'I know, and I can't afford it anyway,' Lara said.

'Is that what's upsetting you?' I asked gently.

'Not really. I just feel it's the same old, same old, day after day. I look forward to seeing Frazer at the weekend, but that's it really.'

'Are you still managing to get out for a night?'

'Yes, Marg is babysitting.' Marg lived in the flat below Lara.

'Did you look into the college course you were interested in?' I asked, taking my feet off the mattress. Arthur was now jumping up and down on it, making my legs shake and my tea wobble.

'I'll need to do an entry course first. There is some funding available, but I don't think it covers all the costs. I don't want to get into debt again.'

'Look upon it as an investment in your future,' I said. 'If you want to do the course then find out the details and I'll help you with the cost.' I could afford it – not all foster carers can – and I felt it was the least I could do.

'Thanks. Frazer said he'd help too.'

'There you go then. A plan for the future. Is there anything else worrying you?'

'Not really.'

'A lot of us have struggled during the pandemic and lockdown, especially those with young children. I think you are doing very well.'

'You've always been my biggest fan,' she said, and finally smiled. 'I'll look into college again and let you know.'

'Good. Feeling a bit better?'

She nodded and I gave her a hug. A big one to make up for all those she hadn't had as a child. We then chatted about other matters as we finished our tea. I played with Arthur as Lara looked on, then it was time for me to leave to collect Damian from school. Lara seemed a bit brighter as she came to the door with Arthur at her side.

'I'm making Frazer dinner tonight, rather than ordering pizza,' she said. 'The stir-fry you showed me.'

'Great. I thought that might be so from the items on your shopping list. Phone me if you need any advice.' During Lara's stay with me I'd shown her how to cook simple dishes. (Many of the recipes are in my book *Happy Mealtimes for Kids*.)

We stood at her door and hugged goodbye. Lara returned indoors as I went downstairs. I was pleased Frazer would be arriving later and staying the weekend. I liked him. He was good with Arthur and a big source of comfort and support for Lara. Having been in care himself, he understood much of what Lara had been through and was patient when her mood dipped. Like her, he'd had to move from his last foster home and had found himself pretty much alone. Support for care leavers is improving, but it is often problematic and relies on the individual tracking it down, unlike good parents, who are usually there ready to help and advise as needed when their child leaves home.

CHAPTER FOUR

RACHEL AND HER CHILDREN

I drove to Damian's school and parked in a side road close by. Having put on my face mask, I turned the corner and joined a short, socially distanced queue feeding into the playground. I went to my usual spot to wait for Damian's class to come out and nodded to another parent I'd got to know by sight. Damian was one of the last children to appear, accompanied by his TA, Mrs Halas.

'Have you remembered my bag?' he asked straight away. Mrs Halas smiled, having heard this conversation before on a Friday.

'Yes, love, it's in my car,' I replied.

'Cathy doesn't forget your things,' Mrs Halas reassured him.

'She might,' Damian returned. 'I need to check.' Damian was used to checking up on his mother.

'We've had a reasonable day,' Mrs Halas said to me. 'Damian completed most of his work and ate most of his lunch. Fish fingers, mash and peas.'

'I ate it all!' Damian exclaimed indignantly. 'And did my work.'

'Most,' Mrs Halas mouthed to me.

'Thank you,' I said. I would enter what he'd had in the food diary later. The school published the full menus on their website.

'Have a nice weekend and see you on Monday,' Mrs Halas said to us both.

'Thanks, and you,' I said.

She and other relevant members of staff had information about Damian's background; they knew he was in foster care and were aware of the contact arrangements – that he went home at weekends.

Damian walked by my side as we crossed the playground, calling 'Bye!' and 'See ya!' to some of his friends. He was popular at school, sometimes getting into trouble when he entertained his peers during lessons; 'the class clown' his mother had called him. But I knew there was another side to Damian that worried and fretted and assumed far too much responsibility. I suspected that he used clowning to mask his fears and anxieties about what was happening in his family. I'd found before with other children I'd fostered that they could have one set of behaviours for school and another at home or with me.

'Mrs Halas said I don't have to do my homework,' Damian said as we approached my car.

'No, she didn't,' I replied lightly. 'She said that if you didn't have time to do your homework at the weekend, we could do it on Monday evening and hand it in on Tuesday.' I knew because that was the arrangement.

'That's what I meant,' he said, and scrambled into the back of the car.

The children had a little homework to do each evening and at the weekend, but Damian rarely did his weekend homework. The school were understanding and made allowances for children in care, so we handed his week-end homework in late. When he'd lived with his mother full-time he'd hardly done any homework at all. His mother claimed it was because they were overcrowded and there was nowhere for him to study. They lived in a two-bedroom flat. Baby Liam slept in a cot in his mother's room and Damian shared a bedroom with his younger brother, Nathan, aged three. Many families live in homes far more cramped than this, so finding a space for Damian to do his schoolwork shouldn't have been impossible. However, his mother struggled with this, as she did with many things in her life.

'You can take off your face mask now,' Damian told me as I fastened my seatbelt.

'Thank you, love,' I said with a smile.

'You're welcome,' he replied in his cheeky manner. 'And don't forget to indicate.'

'I won't.'

Damian was chatty to begin with, the after-effects of a good day at school, but as we drew closer to where he lived, he fell silent.

'You know you don't have to stay the whole weekend,' I reminded him. 'Tell your mum if you want to come back early and I'll collect you. She'll understand.'

'I know,' he said, but the spark had gone out of him.

I thought how confusing it must be for him and other children in care, and the many mixed emotions they had to deal with. Damian loved his mother and siblings and hadn't wanted to leave them, but I had given him the freedom to be a child, to play, to be cared for and to relax, knowing his needs would be met. It was a stark contrast to the constant chaos and source of worry that was his home. In the month he'd been with me his social worker, teacher, TA and even his poor mother had noticed a difference in him for the better.

I pulled into a free parking bay opposite the block of flats where Damian lived. Three boys, mid-teens, were standing by the entrance and glanced over as I parked. I saw Damian look at them through his side window.

'Do you know them?' I asked. I hadn't seen them before.

'Sort of,' he said.

I got out of the car and opened his door, and he joined me on the pavement. I reached in and took his schoolbag from where he'd left it in the footwell and handed it to him. He rolled his eyes. 'I won't have time to do it.'

'I know, but your mother likes you to have it with you.' I opened the boot and took out his weekend case, then we crossed the road together. As we passed the lads one of them said hello to Damian.

'Hello,' he replied in a quiet, flat voice. I smiled an acknowledgement at them, and we continued in.

Damian's flat was on the third floor of the eight-storey block. One of the lifts was taped off with an *Out of Order* sign and the other was on another level so we took the stairs.

'How do you know that boy?' I asked as we made our way up.

'They live around here. Mum says I mustn't talk to them as they're bad news.'

'Why?'

'Don't know,' he shrugged.

We continued up the second flight of stairs to Level 3, where a baby could be heard crying.

'That's Liam,' Damian said.

'Yes.'

At five months old, Damian's baby brother could often be heard crying, although it was thought he was generally being well cared for. The health visitor had reported that Rachel seemed to be coping with him, and he was putting on weight, and always in clean clothes when she saw him. Rachel hadn't been coping with Damian, which was why she'd put him in care. It was voluntary, so in theory she could remove him at any time. But if she did and the social services had concerns about him or her other children then they could apply to the court for a care order to remove them all. At present Rachel was cooperating with the social services, accepting help and promising to make the necessary changes to be able to parent all three children, so I was hopeful that at some point Damian would be able to return home.

I put on my mask and pressed the doorbell, and we waited. A dog barked from another flat and I heard the lift moving in the lift shaft. Rachel didn't answer the door straight away, so Damian banged loudly on the door.

'That won't help,' I said.

'It might. She can't hear when he's screaming.'

I waited, rang the doorbell again, and Rachel finally answered, Liam still wailing in her arms.

'Oh, is it that time already,' she asked, flustered. She was wearing a long-sleeved top, jogging bottoms and well-worn mule slippers, and was jiggling Liam up and down, trying to pacify him. 'Come in. I've got my mask somewhere.'

Damian sighed as he went in, dropped his schoolbag in the hall and continued into the living room. Rachel nearly tripped over his bag but didn't say anything. I picked it up and closed the front door. I could hear the television coming from the living room. It was on all day; Rachel said it was company. I guessed Nathan was in there too.

'I'll put his bags in his room, shall I?' I checked with Rachel. It was what I usually did.

'Yes,' she said, and went into the living room.

Damian and Nathan's bedroom was the second on the right. All the rooms led off a short hall with the living room at the end. I pushed open the door. There was just enough space in the room for the bunk bed and a chest of drawers. Damian slept on the top bunk and Nathan on the lower. The room was tidier than usual, as though someone had cleared up. I doubted it was for my benefit. I put Damian's bags by the end of the bunk beds and came out. I took the few steps into the living room where Rachel was sitting on the sofa, beside Damian and Nathan. Liam was sucking on a dummy, and they were all facing the television. This room, too, was tidier than usual, but I didn't comment.

I looked at Rachel, sitting with her family, her thin frame only partly disguised by her loose clothing. She always wore her hair tied back in a ponytail with a fringe, which made her look even younger. My heart went out to her. At twenty-four, she'd spent most of her adult life having, and then struggling to raise, her children. She had a gentle manner, was quietly spoken and had been diagnosed with mild learning difficulties. She was naive, trusted too easily, and with no family to support her – apart from an aunt who phoned occasionally – she was at the mercy of those who came into her life. I didn't know all the details of her past, but her social worker described her as vulnerable and easily taken advantage of. All three children had different fathers who had promised her the world and then disappeared once she was pregnant. Damian had no contact with his father and as far as anyone knew Liam's and Nathan's fathers weren't in touch either. Rachel had had social services involvement for most of her life – as a child in care and then as a mother. It seemed set to continue indefinitely.

'Have you got everything you need for the weekend?' I asked her, as I usually did when I dropped off Damian on a Friday.

'I think so,' Rachel said, and she stood. 'Wera was here this morning.' Wera was a support worker who visited Rachel two mornings a week. As well as putting in place practical and emotional support, she fed back to the social worker. 'Have a look,' Rachel said, going into the kitchen. 'I've got lots of food.' Any thought of her putting on a mask had been forgotten but I'd had both my Covid injections, so I felt reasonably safe.

Rachel opened and closed a cupboard door and then the fridge. The cupboards were well stocked. 'I've got Damian chicken nuggets – he likes those – and the ready-meals are for Troy and me.'

'Whose Troy?' I asked.

'My friend. He lives on the estate. He's been really good to me and the kids and gives me money. I wanted to do something for him and Wera suggested a meal, so we bought those.'

'I see. So Wera knows about Troy?'

'Yes.'

'Mum!' Damian cried from the living room. 'Nathan has pooed.'

35

Nathan was still in nappies.

'I'm coming,' Rachel called back anxiously. Baby Liam began to cry.

'Shall I take him while you see to Nathan?' I asked.

'Yes, please.'

She passed baby Liam to me, collected Nathan from the living room and took him into the bathroom to change him. I waited in the living room and gently rocked Liam until Rachel reappeared carrying a nappy bag. 'Can you take it down when you go?' she asked.

'Yes, of course. Is there anything else I can do?'

Although I was here simply to bring Damian, Rachel always asked me in, and then I found it difficult to leave. She had the air of someone who was only just about coping, someone you felt sorry for and wanted to help. There was no secret side to her, no hidden agenda, and as far as I knew she always told the truth. I don't think she had the guile to lie.

'I think I'm good,' she said with a small, child-like smile.

'Excellent. Your flat looks nice.'

'Thank you. Wera helped me tidy it.'

I said goodbye to Damian, and to Nathan, who at three years old was showing signs of developmental delay. I then passed baby Liam back to Rachel.

'Have a good weekend,' I said. 'Remember to give me a ring if you want me to collect Damian.'

'I will, thank you. What time is school on Monday? They keep changing it.'

'Damian's class has to go in at eight-fifty.'

'Remember that!' she called to Damian. 'Eight-fifty.'

I heard him sigh. Saying another goodbye, I saw myself out.

Rachel had so much on, I suppose I should have been pleased she had a new friend, someone in her life to help and support her, but cynical me heard alarm bells ringing. How old was Troy? How had they met? It wasn't for me to question Rachel, but as I dropped the nappy bag into the communal bin outside, I wondered what Troy wanted with her – a single mother with three children, one in care, living on benefits and the food bank. Perhaps I was doing him a grave injustice. Wera saw more of Rachel than I did; she was with her for at least two mornings a week and sometimes popped in at other times. Presumably Rachel had talked to her about Troy and she had passed it on to the social worker, Korin. Not because Rachel wasn't allowed a new boyfriend, if that was what he was, but to make sure her children were safe. If Troy was spending a lot of time with Rachel and maybe staying the night, then it was likely the social services would want to carry out a DBS check (a police check) on him, to make sure there was nothing in his past that could mean his presence would be detrimental to her children. Foster carers are regularly DBS checked, including all adult family members and partners who stay over.

I drove home, hoping my concerns were unfounded.

It was strange not having Damian in the house at weekends. He was such a character, but he could also be very loud, and you needed to keep an eye on him to make sure he wasn't up to mischief. So I intended to put this quiet time to good use.

After dinner, Paula went out to meet a friend she hadn't seen since before lockdown, while I went to my computer in the front room. First, I completed my log notes for the week, then I emailed Korin a résumé of Damian's week, including school, his behaviour, his eating, and that I'd taken him home for the weekend. I mentioned that Rachel's flat was clean and tidy and there was plenty of food in the cupboards, and that Wera had visited in the morning. I said Rachel was expecting Troy to dinner, and finished by saying that Rachel would take Damian to school on Monday unless she wanted me to collect him early. I was up to date with my foster-carer training, most of which was still online, so I then turned my attention to my social media accounts.

Since publishing my fostering memoirs I've received thousands of messages and emails from around the world. Many simply say how much they've enjoyed my books, which I greatly appreciate. However, a significant number tell me of abuse they've suffered as a child, young person or adult, sometimes disclosing it for the first time. I feel the responsibility of their disclosure and it's made me aware that abuse is far more widespread than most of us realize. The horror that some go through, suffering in silence for years, is unbelievable. I always answer their messages and emails – a confidante as surely as if I was in the same room as them. I think the anonymity of the internet sometimes allows us to talk about painful experiences when we wouldn't otherwise. As well as offering sympathy and understanding, I advise them where to get help if needed. It isn't a role I anticipated when I first started writing my fostering memoirs, but it's one I take very seriously. I know I've helped when I hear from them – sometimes many years later – thanking me and saying they've been able to report the abuse they suffered as a child, or have left a violent partner, or have moved on with their lives. At least three who have contacted me were able to draw back from the brink of suicide due to our online friendship, and while I've never met them they will always hold a place dear in my heart.

It was after 10 p.m. when I finally logged off. I'd been online for nearly three hours. Paula was still out; she'd let herself in later. I went into the kitchen, settled Sammy in his bed for the night, checked the back door was locked and went upstairs. Tash and all her worries weren't far from my mind, so before I got into bed I texted her.

Thinking of you all. Let me know if there is anything I can do. xx

She replied, *Thank you. x*

CHAPTER FIVE

FAMILY

The following morning when I checked my phone I found a text from Lara, sent late the night before.

The stir-fry was great! Frazer says hi.

Well done, I replied. *I hope you both have a nice weekend.* x

It was a fine morning and Paula and I were going to meet Lucy and family later. I was looking forward to seeing them again. Lucy was going to let me know where we were meeting and at what time.

At 9.30 I was in the kitchen loading the washing machine thinking how lovely it was to be able to see my family again now the lockdown rules were lifting when my phone rang. It was Lucy's number, so I assumed she was calling to tell me about the arrangements for later.

'Hello, love,' I said brightly. 'It's a nice day.'

'Yes, but, Mum, I've got a problem. The nursery assistant I was working with yesterday has tested positive for Covid.'

'Oh,' I said, immediately concerned and realizing the implications. Darren and Lucy worked at the same nursery – it was where they'd first met – and they'd only recently returned from being furloughed.

'We've just been told. We have to test, but the thing is, we only have one lateral flow test left and we both have to do one. We should have got some more yesterday but we forgot.'

The UK government had begun issuing free lateral flow tests to everyone as a means of identifying and controlling the spread of coronavirus. It involved taking a swab from the tonsils and nose using a long cotton bud and placing the sample in a solution. The result appeared after thirty minutes.

'I've got plenty here, love,' I said. 'Shall I drop off a box?'

'Please. That would be great. To be safe, leave them outside the door.'

'All right, love. I'll be there in about half an hour. But it's worrying that your colleague has coronavirus. Is she very ill?'

'I don't know. She said she had a headache yesterday but that was all. We worked together for most of the day. We had the window open so hopefully that will have helped. If we do get together later, we should stay outside.'

'Yes. I'll bring the tests now.'

Having said goodbye to Lucy, I took a box of lateral flow tests from the cupboard. There were seven kits in each box, and I had two spare boxes. Paula and I were testing at least twice a week, as we'd been advised. The kits were a precautionary measure, and if someone was showing symptoms of coronavirus or the test was positive then a PCR (polymerase chain reaction) test had to be done. I was worried that Lucy had spent a lot of time close to someone who had Covid. Neither she nor Darren had been vaccinated yet; they, like Paula, were in the next age group to be called. Adrian and Kirsty had just had their first jabs.

I went upstairs to tell Paula what was happening. She was awake, in bed and listening to music on her phone. She took out her earpieces as I went in. I explained about Lucy and Darren needing the test kits.

'Be careful. Don't go into their flat,' she warned. 'Just in case.'

'No, I won't, love.'

I said goodbye and headed out. My children worried about me catching coronavirus, in a way they hadn't worried about my health before. I worried about them too. This was unprecedented, and despite the infection and death rate from Covid falling, we were continually being reminded that the pandemic wasn't over yet, and that another wave could follow. I'd feel a lot happier once all my family had been fully vaccinated, as I was.

As I drove to Lucy and Darren's flat I thought what a strange and different world we now inhabited where words like lateral flow test, PCR, self-isolating and social distancing were part of the norm. Sadly, so was the graph depicting the daily number of infections and deaths shown on the news most nights.

I shrugged off the encroaching feeling of gloom that sometimes came from nowhere, and parked outside the small block of flats where Lucy and Darren lived. I got out and breathed in the fresh spring air. Inside, I propped the box of lateral flow testing kits by their front door, then rang the bell. I could hear my granddaughter, Emma, shout, 'Doorbell, Mummy, doorbell.'

I smiled and stood back as Lucy opened the door. 'Thanks so much,' she said. 'I did the test we had and it's negative.'

'That's a relief.'

'So, assuming Darren's is negative too, are you happy to meet up later?' she asked.

'Yes, love. I'm looking forward to it.'

'I'll text you as soon as we know.' Emma appeared at the door and Lucy picked her up. 'Say bye to Nana. Hopefully we'll see her later.'

'Bye, Nana,' she said cutely, and waved.

I waved back and blew her a kiss. At nearly three years old, Emma was adorable and lifted all our hearts.

'Bye, love,' I said, and came away.

I drove home. Paula was up now, still in her dressing gown, and making her breakfast.

'Coffee?' she asked.

'Yes, please.'

Five minutes later a text message arrived from Lucy saying Darren had tested negative. *We'll see you at 1 p.m. at …* and she named a local park.

Great. See you there x, I texted back.

I told Paula the good news and she went upstairs to shower and dress.

My family meant everything to me and I felt very lucky to have them. Adrian and Paula were my birth children, and Lucy had come to me as a foster child and I'd adopted her. She couldn't be more loved if she'd been born to me. I tell her story in *Will You Love Me?*

Relieved that Lucy and Darren hadn't tested positive for Covid, I unloaded the washing machine and hung the washing on the line. I then went to my computer in the front room. Because of the high number of emails and large files I receive and work on, I use my PC rather than my phone. I write my books early in the morning when the house is quiet, and in any free time during the day I check emails and messages. I wanted to see if Paige had replied to my last email. I was very concerned about her.

I'd never met Paige and only knew her through the emails we'd exchanged. She was fifteen and had gone into care a year ago. She'd been emailing me for the past month because she felt her foster carers didn't understand or care about her. She usually emailed every few days with a new grievance, many of which were about the rules in the house (there hadn't been any boundaries at home) or her belief that the carers didn't listen to her, preferred the other young person there and were only 'in it for the money'. The last of these complaints I'd heard before from young people in foster care who were feeling rejected. While fostering allowances are generally far more generous now than when I first started fostering nearly thirty years ago, I challenge anyone to go into fostering for the money. It's a vocation where you have to be 100-per-cent committed, to love children regardless of how testing they are and be on call twenty-four-seven without any time off. If you are not fully committed and don't love working with children then I guarantee you won't last long in fostering.

I'd been encouraging Paige to talk to her carers and social worker about all the things that were bothering her. She hadn't, and I knew the tension in the house was building. In her last message three days before she had threatened to run away. I'd written that it wouldn't help and she needed to talk to someone. If she really couldn't talk to her carers or social worker then perhaps there was a teacher at school she could confide in? I was worried and I now saw there was an email from her. I opened it with some trepidation.

Thankfully she hadn't run away, but the situation in the house had deteriorated, and it had led to a big argument between her and her carers two days before. The carers had phoned the social worker, who'd spoken to Paige on the phone for some time, then arranged a meeting for them all on Monday.

At last I am being listened to! Paige wrote. *We had a good evening last night, all together ... They were upset that I was unhappy and thought I'd just been testing the boundaries ... The argument cleared the air. They had no idea how bad I'd been feeling. I probably should have told them sooner ...* and so the email continued. I could hear her relief just as I felt relieved.

I replied, telling her she'd done well and to keep the communication going. I told her to say hi to her foster carers from me. If a young person messages with problems, I always like them to tell their parents or carers they are in contact with me. Sometimes it helps them to discuss their issues and it's right that they know.

With time to spare before we had to leave to meet Lucy, I replied to a few other emails, and then the comments posted on my Facebook page. Readers of my books are wonderful people, so kind and supportive. Over the years their words have helped raise my spirits, especially when they took a dip after my father and then my mother died, and during lockdown. I think the threat of the pandemic, limited social interaction and constantly being made aware of our mortality took its toll on many. It certainly made me more reflective and encouraged me to take stock of my life, as I'm sure it did for many. Life is so precious, but fragile, and we were being held hostage by a virus, something so small we couldn't see it, but deadly. I think it reinforced for many that we owe it to ourselves to make the best of life. I felt I had in the past and I wanted to make sure I did in the future, and that my life was on track. Like many others, I found myself re-evaluating.

Shortly before one o'clock Paula and I set off in her car to meet Lucy and family. Since Paula had been furloughed and didn't have to go to the office each day, she'd hardly used her car so liked to take it out when the opportunity arose. I knew that she, too, had spent time during the pandemic thinking about what she wanted to do in the future. She'd told me she'd like to travel and see faraway countries with different cultures, such as India, Thailand and South America.

Lucy and family arrived at the park at the same time we did. Emma was very excited and wanted to hold hands with both Paula and me, so we took a hand each and swung her between us as we walked, which she loved. It was wonderful to be out together again. The air was fresh in May, the trees were starting to turn green with new shoots and birds sang in their branches and the shrubbery. The café was open selling takeaways and had plenty of outdoor seating, so we had something to eat and drink. Once Paula and I had finished, we took Emma to the play equipment, leaving Lucy and Darren to finish their snacks. We pushed Emma on the swings, the roundabout, the rockers, then steadied her on the climbing frame. Once Lucy and Darren had eaten, they came to join us. Lots of other families were in the park making the most of the fine weather and enjoying the freedom that the easing of lockdown restrictions had allowed.

We talked about many things as we played with Emma, and invariably the conversation returned to the pandemic. It was impossible to avoid the subject and it came up in most conversations – those we knew who'd had Covid, the vaccine programme and so forth. Nevertheless, we spent a lovely three hours in the park and then said goodbye at the gates with the promise to do it again soon.

On the way home Paula said, 'Once everyone is vaccinated or has immunity from catching Covid, will the virus die out?'

'I hope so,' I replied.

'Do you think Adrian and Kirsty will have children?'

'I don't know. What made you think of that?' I asked, glancing at her as she drove.

'I just wondered. If they do, will we still foster?'

'I hadn't really thought about it. Why? Do you know something I don't?' I looked at her.

'No, but you looked after Emma when Lucy went back to work. Will you do the same if Adrian and Kirsty have a baby?'

'Yes, of course, if they want me to. Has Adrian been talking to you again?' Adrian thought I took on too much and I'd tried to reassure him.

'He might have mentioned you,' she said with a smile.

I smiled too. 'I'm fine, love. Really. If they do have a family and need my help, or Lucy and Darren have another child, then I can rethink fostering. Perhaps just do respite.'

'That's good to know,' Paula said. 'I mean, you can't foster forever.'

'No, I suppose not,' I agreed, although part of me had (unrealistically) thought I could.

The following day we were due to meet Adrian and Kirsty for a walk in our local woods. I was looking forward to the time when the remaining restrictions were lifted and all my family could sit around a dinner table again.

'No Damian?' Adrian asked as we met up.

'No, he goes home at the weekend,' I reminded him.

'That gives you a break,' Kirsty said.

'I suppose so, although he's a good lad. He's just had a lot to cope with.'

We talked as we walked, following the grassy path and then the trodden-down bracken path that led between the trees. We could only go in pairs here so Kirsty and Paula went in front and I fell into step beside Adrian. He'd been taller than me since the age of eleven, so I was used to looking up at him as I talked.

'Any indication of when you will be going back to the office?' I asked. Adrian worked for a firm of accountants and all the office staff had been working from home since the start of the first lockdown.

'September has been mentioned,' he said. 'But nothing is definite yet. It will depend on the infection rate and government guidelines. To be honest I rather enjoy working from home, although it would be nice to see some of my colleagues again. There's talk of us going into the office for two or three days a week and working from home the rest of the time.'

'I understand a lot of businesses are considering that.'

'Although it must be difficult if you have small children running around,' he added.

I looked at him carefully. 'But nice. I mean, to have children, when the time is right, of course.'

He gave a small laugh. 'Mum, you're as bad as Kirsty's parents. They asked us outright if we were planning on starting a family.'

'I see,' I said, quietly pleased they had. 'And what did you say?'

'That we are trying for a baby.'

'Oh, that's wonderful!' I cried, delighted. 'I am pleased. You will make great parents. I can picture it now. Nana would have been overjoyed.'

Ridiculously, a lump rose in my throat and I looked away to blink back tears. My little boy was all grown up and about to start a family of his own. My heart swelled with pride.

'No need to tell anyone yet,' Adrian added. 'Wait until we're actually expecting.'

'I won't,' I said, and continued walking, hoping my dear mum and dad were close enough to hear.

CHAPTER SIX

A MIXED WEEK

I suppose I could have had a lie-in on Monday morning as I didn't have to take Damian to school, but years of getting up early for children saw me out of bed at 6.30. I didn't immediately shower and dress, though, as I would normally have done; instead, I went downstairs in my dressing gown where I gave Sammy his breakfast and had a leisurely coffee.

Once showered and dressed, I did some housework and then worked at my computer. I wondered what sort of weekend Damian had had and hoped it was good. Mid-morning, Paula came to me with some good news.

'I've just received an email from work.'

'Oh yes?' I stopped what I was doing and looked at her.

'Now lockdown restrictions are easing their orders are starting to pick up so they're beginning to take staff off the furlough scheme and re-employ them.'

'Excellent.'

'Those of us who aren't needed yet will stay on the furlough scheme until we are required. It said that eventually they should be able to take us all on again.'

'That is good news.'

'I'm so relieved.'

Although Paula wasn't needed yet, it was a step in the right direction and suggested her job was safe.

I continued working at my computer and later Paula made us lunch. When it was time to collect Damian from school she said she'd come with me, as she did sometimes. She couldn't go into the playground as the Headteacher had asked that only one carer or parent go in, to help reduce the risk of transmitting the virus. She would wait outside. Damian was always pleased to see her. He told his friends and TA that she was his big sister, which Mrs Halas had queried with me, as Paula was older than his mother.

As I stood in the playground, mask on, waiting for Damian's class to come out, I prepared myself for him being in a bit of a mood. It would help having Paula waiting outside, but usually on a Monday, having spent the weekend with his family, he went through a period of readjustment. By Tuesday morning he was reasonably settled again. Most children in care are affected to some extent by seeing their family, even if the contact is only for a few hours, and they may not show it.

Mrs Halas came out carrying Damian's weekend bag, which his mother would have brought with her when she took him to school that morning. Mrs Halas looked rather serious and Damian was scowling.

'Not the best day, was it?' Mrs Halas said to Damian as she passed his bag to me.

Damian dutifully shook his head while looking as though he wasn't at all bothered if he'd had a good day or not.

'He was unsettled this morning,' Mrs Halas continued. 'He refused to do his work, then began stopping those around him from working, so we went out for some quiet time.'

'Oh dear,' I said, and looked at Damian. He was maintaining an air of someone who didn't care.

'I asked him what the problem was and he said he was hungry, so I got him a snack. I don't think that's the whole picture, though.'

'Thank you,' I said. 'I'll have a chat with him later.'

'On a positive note, he did his weekend homework,' Mrs Halas added.

'Fantastic,' I said to Damian, pleased and surprised. 'Well done.'

He shrugged dismissively, which Mrs Halas saw.

'There's definitely something bothering him,' she said. 'But I can't get to the bottom of it.' Teaching assistants often build up a close relationship with the children they support, so the child might confide something in them that they wouldn't tell their parent or carer.

'Thanks again,' I said. 'We'll have a talk.'

'No, we won't,' Damian said with attitude.

Mrs Halas threw me a knowing look and we said goodbye. Instead of walking beside me to cross the playground, Damian ran off. He knew he had to wait by the gate as there was a road outside. He didn't stop and I found him on the pavement.

'Damian, you know you don't leave the playground without me,' I said firmly.

'Paula was here,' he replied.

'You didn't know that when you ran out.'

'Yes, I did.'

There was no reasoning with him when he was in a mood like this.

'Next time, you wait for me in the playground,' I said. 'Now let's go home.' We crossed the road together. Damian was still looking very grumpy.

'Well done for doing your weekend homework,' I added.

'I'm going to rip it up,' he replied.

'That would be a waste,' Paula said.

'No, it won't.'

Neither Paula nor I replied as we got into the car and fastened our seatbelts.

Damian was unusually quiet to begin with as I drove, and I glanced at him in the rear-view mirror a couple of times. I knew him well enough to know there was something bothering him beyond having to readjust to me again.

'Did you have a nice weekend?' I asked him after a moment.

'It was OK,' he said, without any enthusiasm.

'Did you meet Troy?' I asked.

'Yes, but I've met him before.'

'And you like him?'

'No. He's the one who made me do my homework,' Damian said crossly.

I was starting to think I might have done Troy a disservice – surely someone who was concerned about their girlfriend's child doing their schoolwork couldn't be all bad. But Damian then said, 'He was there the whole weekend, although Mum pretended he wasn't. He kept bossing me about and telling Mum what to do. I hate him.'

'What did he tell you to do?' I asked, glancing at him in the rear-view mirror.

I'd found before that sometimes children I fostered could talk more easily in the car while I was driving, rather than when making eye-contact.

'He told me where to sit, when I could have the television on, and kept sending me to my room. He told Mum what meals to make him and she just did it. I didn't want what he had so I didn't get anything. Mum keeps doing what he says.'

'I see. So that's why you were hungry this morning. Did he stay the night?' I asked, my concerns growing.

'I think so. His things were there all weekend. He kept going out and coming back. Mum gave him a key and he bought her a new phone, so she thinks he's great. I think he's a silly arse.'

'Does Troy work?' I asked, ignoring that he'd used a word he wasn't supposed to.

'I don't know. He said if I was good he'd buy me a phone.'

Not if I have any say in the matter, I thought.

'I don't want to go next weekend if he's going to be there,' Damian said, scowling.

'Because?'

'I don't like him.'

'Any other reason?'

He shrugged.

As I parked outside my house Damian said, 'I do want to go and see Mum but not him.'

'I understand, love. I'll tell your social worker.' I couldn't make him any promises; it would be for his social worker to discuss contact with his mother.

I opened Damian's car door to let him out. Some of his usual humour returned and he threw me a cheeky grin. 'I don't think Troy will be there next weekend,' he said.

'No? Why's that?'

'I've got his key.' And he pulled a front-door key from his trouser pocket.

'How did you get that?'

'It was on the table when Mum and me left this morning.'

'And where was Troy?'

'In Mum's bed, I think.'

'I see. I'd better look after that.' I held out my hand and he gave me the key. 'Anything else you want to tell me.'

'No. Is Sammy in?'

I opened the front door and there was Sammy waiting for Damian. He greeted him with a fond purr and rubbed around his legs. Damian knelt to stroke and pet him. I am sure our cat knows when someone needs a little extra TLC. He wouldn't leave Damian alone for the rest of the evening, following him around and then jumping onto his lap as soon as he sat down.

Damian watched television while I made dinner; Paula was in the living room too. Once dinner was in the oven I took the opportunity to unpack Damian's weekend bag. As usual a lot of the items I'd sent were missing, including a nearly new towel of mine, Damian's toothbrush, his pyjamas and a sock from one of the pairs. One set of his casual clothes was unused, still neatly pressed and folded at the bottom of the bag, while the other was very grubby, so I guessed he'd been wearing the same clothes all weekend, which was normal in their home. The school uniform he'd worn on Friday was screwed up and unwashed. I sorted out what needed to be washed. The missing items would very likely be lost in the disorganization of his home, and I wasn't expecting to see them again. I'd once asked Rachel if she was selling goods on eBay but she hadn't understood my humour and had said, 'No.'

Most foster carers have experienced a child returning from contact minus items they've bought, and we just keep replacing them. There isn't really much else we can do. Rachel admitted that she struggled to find clean clothes for her and her family, as she struggled with many things, even with Wera's help. Korin, their social worker, had told me that when she'd made an unannounced visit once Rachel had still been in grubby pyjamas in the late afternoon. It was sad; I felt for her and hoped the situation would improve now Damian was in care and she just had Nathan and Liam to look after for most of the week. The last item I took from the bag was the food diary. I opened it but, as usual, Rachel hadn't added anything, so I had no idea what Damian had eaten over the weekend. I would continue it from today.

I'd made cottage pie for dinner and, once it was ready, I called Paula and Damian. I placed a little on a plate for Damian so he wouldn't feel overwhelmed. He knew he could have more if he wished. Sammy came with Damian and sat beside his chair hoping for a titbit. Paula and I began eating. Damian stared at his plate. I watched him from the corner of my eye. It was as though a battle raged inside him: the natural desire to eat versus the behaviour learnt from his mother. When he returned after the weekend it was as though, by enjoying his food, he was being disloyal to his mother. I waited and, thankfully,

A MIXED WEEK

after a while he picked up his fork and began to eat, vora-
ciously. Mrs Halas had said he'd been hungry that
morning, so I wondered just how much he'd had to eat
over the weekend. Probably not much.

'Mum wasn't allowed to be sick,' Damian suddenly
said as he ate. 'Troy said she was stupid as there were kids
in the world starving.'

It was difficult to know what to say so I just nodded.

'Troy kept going on at her and telling her what she
was doing wrong.'

'And what did your mother say?' I asked. Paula was
looking at Damian too.

'Nothing. She never does.'

I was thinking that Rachel's confidence was low
anyway without Troy criticizing her. It wasn't the way to
help her with her eating disorder.

Damian finished his meal, and I asked him if he'd
like seconds. He hesitated and then said, 'I don't mind if
I do.'

I smiled; this was an expression I used sometimes. He
was a great mimic. He came with me into the kitchen
where I held the dish as he helped himself to more cottage
pie.

'Some more broccoli?' I asked. Like many children he
wasn't so keen on vegetables.

'Don't push your luck,' he replied, and there was an
edge to his voice.

'I don't say that,' I said.

'Troy does.'

'Who to?'

'Mum, of course. He wouldn't dare say it to me if he
knows what's good for him.' This was bravado, but the

57

atmosphere in their home seemed to be changing with Troy there.

That evening Paula listened to Damian read his schoolbook and then helped him with his numeracy homework. He preferred her helping him to me – like a big sister, he said, adding cheekily that I was too old to be his big sister. After he'd finished his homework the three of us played a board game together, before I took him up to bed. It was a routine I'd established in the first week after he'd arrived, as he was used to sitting in front of the television until late at night, often pacifying baby Liam. He'd spent a lot of time looking after Liam and knew about bottles of formula, changing nappies and getting his own way.

Damian had been hard work to begin with, but then he'd settled into a routine and accepted that, while he was no longer in charge, he now had time to play – with all the games and toys in my cupboards. There wasn't much for him to do at home. There were very few toys and his mother just didn't have the time to sit and play with him, or crayon and paint, or even talk to him. At present Damian occupied two worlds: his home from Friday night to Monday morning and my home the rest of the week. I knew the social services wouldn't allow this situation to continue indefinitely. The care plan was that, once Rachel was managing better, Damian would return home, very likely with support.

Having seen Damian into bed, I spent some time chatting with Paula and then went to my computer where I emailed the social worker and typed up my log notes, including what Damian had said about Troy. I was objective and just kept to the facts. It wasn't for me to make judgements. There was an email from Joy, my supervising social worker, advising me she'd scheduled her next 'visit' for Thursday at 4.30 p.m. It would be online; most meetings and visits still were at present. I replied confirming the date and entered it in my diary.

Damian had a good day at school on Tuesday but there was an issue on Wednesday. He hit a boy during the lunch break. Damian was still at the same school he'd attended before coming into care, so some children (and parents) knew his family and that he was in foster care; some lived near Rachel. Mrs Halas told me what had happened when I collected Damian at the end of school. He'd had an argument with a lad he'd previously been friends with and at one point the boy had shouted that Damian's mother didn't want him and that's why she'd put him into care. It was wrong of Damian to hit the boy but understandable. Mrs Halas told me that the Headteacher had spoken to them both and talked about how we settle our differences, then made them apologize to each other. As we left the playground that afternoon Damian pointed out the boy and called a cheerful good-bye to him. The lad replied with a wave and 'See you tomorrow.'

'Friends again?' I asked Damian, and he nodded.

'Once all the restrictions are lifted, we could arrange a play date with him or another friend if you like.'

'Can we go bowling?'

'Yes, love. Just as soon as we can.'

* * *

Joy's virtual supervisory visit on Thursday took much the same format as if she'd visited in person. When the pandemic had first hit and we'd suddenly had to start using online conferencing apps like Zoom and Microsoft Teams it had been a learning curve for many of us, but now it was the norm. Joy and I discussed Damian's eating, routine, health and school life, and how contact was going. I told her what Damian had said about Troy, although Joy would have access to my online log notes, just as the social worker did. All this took about three-quarters of an hour. Paula was looking after Damian in the living room until he was needed. Joy and I discussed my future training, and I asked Joy how her brother was. Her whole family had caught Covid the year before (prior to a vaccine being available), and her brother had been very ill and was now suffering from Long Covid. She said he was gradually improving, although he might never regain full health. Previously he'd been fit and healthy with no underlying health concerns.

Joy asked if Damian had had any accidents or illnesses, which was a standard question during her 'visit'. I confirmed he hadn't apart from a couple of minor falls while playing, which I'd included in my log notes. She then asked to see Damian, after which she'd look around my house, as she did every visit. Aware of this, I was using my tablet rather than the computer and I carried it into the living room.

She said hello to Paula and then talked to Damian. I balanced the tablet on his lap so they could see each other as he answered her questions. How was he? she asked, and Damian replied, 'OK.' Did he have everything he needed living with me? He replied with a shrug and then said, 'Yes.' Did he like living with me? It was 'OK'. How was school? 'OK.' He was seeing his family at the weekend – how was that going? 'OK.' Then he suddenly said, 'Why do I have to talk to you?'

'You don't,' Joy said with a smile. 'I just want to make sure you're all right living with Cathy.'

'I am, so can I watch television now?'

'Yes. Tell Cathy if you need anything.'

I left Damian with Paula to watch some television while I took my tablet into the other rooms, showing Joy around the house, including a brief look outside and then upstairs. I returned to the front room where Joy wound up by asking if I had everything I needed to look after Damian, and I confirmed that I did. She asked me to check and sign online the minutes of her last visit and then she set the date for her next visit, which would still be online again. We said goodbye and I closed the app. I immediately regretted not asking about Tash. It was unlikely Joy would have been able to tell me anything, but at least it would have shown that others were concerned and thinking of her. It was nearly a week since I'd last texted Tash, so before I began dinner I messaged.

How are you all? Any news?

She replied almost immediately: *Nobody is telling us anything. It's a living nightmare.*

CHAPTER SEVEN

JOEL

It was Friday morning and Damian had slipped into his weekend mode: sullen, withdrawn and toying with the Bitesize Shredded Wheat in his bowl.

'Do I have to stay there all weekend?' he asked moodily, meaning home.

'No, love. You know you don't. Tell your mother if you want to come back early and I'll collect you.'

'I'm not staying if *he's* there,' he said, meaning Troy.

I hadn't heard from Damian's social worker other than an email acknowledging mine, so I had no idea if she had concerns about Troy being there or not.

'Do you think he knows I've got his key?' Damian asked, worried.

'I don't know, love, but I'll return it to your mother when we see her later.' I'd put it in my purse for safekeeping after Damian had produced it from his pocket.

'I hope he's not angry with me,' Damian said gloomily.

I looked at him carefully. 'Does Troy get angry?'

'Sometimes.'

'Has he been angry with you?'

'Don't know.' Which is the easiest response for a child to make to an issue they don't want to consider.

Damian pushed away his bowl of uneaten cereal, finished his drink, then went upstairs to brush his teeth ready for going to school. He had a water bottle in his schoolbag as all the children at his school did, and I knew if he told Mrs Halas he was hungry she would find him something to eat to see him through to dinnertime. She'd begun doing this when he'd lived at home and had often arrived at school not having had breakfast. Most schools now in the UK are good at identifying vulnerable children and supporting them – for example, by providing something to eat or a school uniform/PE kit, as well as an understanding ear. Damian had been one of the children who'd been allowed to attend school during lockdown as he'd been classified as vulnerable before coming into care.

Going to school in the car, Damian was so deep in thought that he forgot to remind me to remember his weekend bag when I collected him at the end of the day. Or possibly he was finally putting some faith in me. As I handed him over to Mrs Halas I mentioned he'd just had a drink for breakfast and she said she'd find him a snack. Saying goodbye and I'd see them at the end of school, I left the playground. As I did my phone sounded with a text message. It was from Lara telling me she was going out later so not to visit. I'd intended to drop by there after I'd been shopping.

Everything all right? I texted.

She replied with a thumbs-up emoji.

I wasn't obliged to visit Lara and Arthur as her social worker was; it was an informal arrangement where I offered some extra support. It was therefore largely up to Lara when and if she saw me, although if I ever had concerns I would tell her and her social worker. Many foster carers put in support when their care leaver moves to independence.

Having done a grocery shop, I drove home where Paula helped me unpack the bags. We had lunch and then I put in some time at my computer, reading and replying to emails. Some of them were upsetting. There was one from a woman in her forties who'd been abused as a child but had slipped through the net. She wrote that she remembered social workers coming to their home and how she'd prayed she would be rescued, but nothing happened. The abuse had continued until she was nearly sixteen, when she'd run away. Her life had descended into alcohol and bad relationships until her mid-twenties. She was now married to a good man and they had three children, but she was still tormented by her memories. She said reading my books had helped her come to terms with some of her past. I replied, empathizing with what she'd been through and praising her courage. She had done well to turn her life around, and I suggested she might benefit from counselling if she felt the time was right.

Another email was from a single mother whose children had been taken into care six weeks previously. Her anger was still raw and she claimed there was no reason to take them. She felt she was being targeted and victimized by the social services and wished the f***ing social worker would burn in hell. She claimed the foster carer wasn't looking after her children properly. There were very few details, but she wanted to know how to get her children back. I replied, sympathizing with the agony of her losing her children and suggesting she got legal representation if she didn't have it already. I always advised this to someone in her position, and also that they try to cooperate and work with the social services, difficult though they might find this. I suggested she kept a written record of anything relevant to her children's case, including phone calls to and from the social services. I said if she had genuine concerns about her children's care or the way she was being treated then she needed to raise them with the social services and her lawyer. This was the best I could offer. It was unlikely that the foster carer wasn't providing a good standard of care for her children. What was more likely was that the carer was doing things differently to her, but still, she should raise it.

These emails depicted two very different situations, but both women felt they had been let down by the system. In the first, the woman hadn't been removed from an abusive home as a child when she should have been, and in the second, a parent believed her children had been forcibly removed without good reason. Not for the first time in my fostering career, I thought how difficult it must be to decide when to bring a child into care – when the threshold had been reached and parenting was no longer 'good enough' and the children were in danger of neglect or abuse. Social workers are 'damned if they do and damned if they don't', as the saying goes.

'Have you got the key?' Damian asked in the playground that afternoon.

'He's been talking about a key all afternoon,' Mrs Halas said, puzzled.

'Yes, I've got it,' I said to Damian. Then to Mrs Halas, 'Damian accidently took a front-door key from his mother's flat. We're going to return it today.'

'He seemed to be a bit worried about it and thought he might be in trouble.'

'I'm sure it will be fine,' I said. 'I'll speak to Rachel.'

'There you go,' Mrs Halas told Damian. 'I said there was nothing to worry about.'

I thanked her, wished her a nice weekend and came away with Damian walking beside me.

He was quiet in the car as I drove.

'Good day at school?' I asked, glancing at him in the rear-view mirror.

'It was OK,' he said.

'Who did you play with?'

'Other kids.'

'No problems?'

'No.'

I parked in a bay opposite the block of flats where his mother lived and opened his car door to let him out. He stood on the pavement eyeing the two lads near the entrance as I took his weekend bag from the boot. They ignored us as we went in. Both lifts were working so we took one to the third floor. The lift doors opened and I took Rachel's key from my purse, ready to give to her. I rang her doorbell. No noise could be heard coming from inside as there often was, no sound of baby Liam crying or three-year-old Nathan.

'Hi, Rachel,' I said brightly as she opened the door.

'Hello,' she said in her small child-like voice.

I was expecting to be invited in, but she didn't offer. 'Shall I put Damian's bag in his room?' I asked.

'I can take it,' she said, and looked embarrassed.

'OK.' I passed her Damian's bag.

'Troy is here,' she said. 'So I can't ask you in.'

I nodded, although I didn't really understand the connection – how Troy being there stopped me from going in.

But then Rachel added in a quiet, apologetic voice, 'Troy says I don't have to let you in, only the social worker.'

'It's not a problem,' I said. I glanced at Damian, who was standing beside me, looking a bit unsure. 'Do you want Damian here for the weekend?' I checked with Rachel.

'Yes. You go in,' she said to him. 'Troy has a present for you.'

At the mention of a present, Damian disappeared down the hall.

'Is everything all right?' I asked Rachel.

'Yes.'

'Give me a ring if you want me to collect Damian earlier. And I think this is yours.' I handed her the key. 'Damian took it by mistake.'

'Oh, I wondered where that had gone. Troy blamed me,' she said with a nervous giggle. 'He had to get another one cut.'

'Sorry, I should have told you sooner. Well, have a good weekend then.'

'And you.'

I called goodbye to Damian, but he didn't reply. It sounded as though the television was on. I said goodbye to Rachel and came away, my feelings of unease about Troy growing.

Once home, I updated my log notes and emailed a résumé of the week to Korin, their social worker, including the fact that Troy had been at the flat when I'd ta

Damian and I hadn't been invited in. I put in quotes what Rachel had said. Korin replied saying she was due to visit Rachel next week.

At 5 p.m. Paula and I watched our prime minister's televised press conference in respect of the latest on Covid. Most of England was hoping that the final restrictions would be lifted as planned on 21 June, which had become known as 'Freedom Day'. But that largely depended on the infection rate. The address wasn't reassuring to begin with as there were growing clusters of the new strain of Covid (first seen in India), and it was thought to be more transmissible. How much more was, as yet, unknown. If it was only marginally more transmissible, our PM said we could continue with the easing of restrictions as planned. But if the virus was significantly more transmissible, we were likely to face some 'hard choices'. The good news was that there was no evidence to suggest our vaccines were any less effective against the new strain, and our vaccination programme was being accelerated. There was talk about surge testing, mobile testing units and the army being on the streets to hand out testing kits. The address ended as it had begun with a cautionary warning: that we were going to have to live with this new variant of the virus for some time, so we needed to exercise caution and common sense. Whether remaining restrictions would be lifted on 21 June remained to be seen.

Later, Paula and I cooked a stir-fry for dinner, after which we settled in front of the television to watch a film. It was the end of another busy week and it took a while before I felt myself starting to unwind. The weekend stretched before me, to do with as I wished. I could do some gardening, meet a friend, go out with Paula – whatever I chose.

'I could get used to this,' I said, resting my feet on the footstool.

'Mmm,' Paula agreed, involved in the film.

I was so relaxed I must have nodded off, for I suddenly heard Paula's voice gently waking me. 'Mum, your phone rang. I couldn't get to it in time. You've got a missed call from Lara.'

'Oh, OK, thanks, love,' I said, sitting more upright.

'I thought you'd want to know.'

'Yes.'

Paula paused the film. It was 8.40 p.m.

'I wonder what's the matter,' I said. It was unlikely Lara would just phone me for a chat at this time, especially when her partner was there.

I pressed to return her call and she answered straight away.

'Is everything all right?' I asked.

'Yes, but I'm wondering if you can help us out. Well, not us really, but Joel. He's the son of the woman who lives in the flat opposite. He needs a bed for the night. Can he come to you? We haven't got the room. He hasn't got anywhere to go.'

'Sorry, love, I don't understand. Why can't he stay with his mother?' Lara knew some of her neighbours, but I hadn't heard her mention Joel or his mother before.

'They've had an argument. We heard them shouting and we went out onto the landing and found Joel there. His mother had gone back into her flat and locked him out.'

'I see. How old is he?'

'Seventeen, I think. We don't really know him that well. We've just seen him coming and going a few times.'

'And he hasn't got anywhere else to go? No other family or friend?'

'I don't think so. Can you help him?'

I had a spare bedroom and my first instinct was to help. But this young man was a complete stranger to me and it seemed that Lara didn't know him either. When I fostered young people the social services gave me relevant background information, but I knew nothing of Joel. Lara had a big heart but could act impetuously at times.

'Lara, what do you know about Joel?'

'Nothing, really, we just say hi when we see him.'

I hesitated before I said, 'I'm sorry, I don't feel comfortable inviting someone I've never met and know so little about to stay here for the night. Where is he now?'

'Sitting on our sofa with a beer.'

'Perhaps there is a hostel that can take him?' I suggested.

'We'll try that. No worries.'

'Sorry, love,' I said again, and we said goodbye.

I felt bad, but I had my family and Damian to think about. True, he wasn't here at present, but what would happen on Monday? If Joel really was homeless and had nowhere to go then I could hardly just eject him onto the streets. I would feel even more responsible for him then – once I'd got to know him. In the past I'd had a desperate parent stop me in the street and ask me to look after her children. She knew I fostered and needed someone to take care of them for a few days. On another occasion a teacher of a teenage girl knocked on my door and asked if I could foster her. I'd had to explain that fostering was very tightly regulated and all the children and young people I looked after had been referred to me through the social services.

I told Paula why Lara had wanted to speak to me, although she'd caught the gist of it from hearing my one-sided conversation.

'Joel will probably make it up with his mother,' Paula said.

'I hope so.'

With no need to be up early in the morning, I stayed up later than usual and watched another film with Paula. It was after 11 p.m. when it finished. Paula and I were about to go upstairs to get ready for bed when my mobile rang. It was Lara again.

'You'll never guess what's happened!' she exclaimed as soon as I answered, her voice high with drama. 'We've had the police here! Joel has been arrested.'

'Oh no! What for?' Immediately I felt my heart start to race.

'Breaking into someone's house. The three of us were sitting here having a beer when suddenly there was a lot of banging on our front door, and shouting – "Police, open the door!" I was scared stiff. Frazer answered the door while Joel just sat on the sofa finishing his beer. Suddenly loads of police burst into the living room. They arrested Joel and took him away in handcuffs. They asked me and Frazer lots of questions, as if we knew him and could have been involved. Then his mother came over and told them we had nothing to do with it and explained what had happened. She said Joel had been in trouble with the police before and that's why she didn't want him to live with her any more.'

'What an awful experience,' I said, shocked. But I felt exonerated in my reluctance to take Joel. 'Are you all right?'

'Just a bit shaken.'

'I can imagine. Make sure you tell your social worker what's happened,' I said, 'so she knows you had nothing to do with it.'

'I will. I'm worried now. We were going to let him sleep on our sofa. He might have robbed us. Not that we've got much to take. But it's the thought of it. We trusted him.'

'Hopefully he'll get the help he needs now towards a better life,' I said. I wondered how someone so young had got into so much trouble with the police.

'His mother said Joel has stolen from her and she's had enough now,' Lara said. 'We felt sorry for her, but we feel a bit sorry for Joel too. I mean, he seems really nice.'

'I know, love, it's difficult.'

We continued talking. Lara wanted to go over everything that had happened step by step. She was clearly shaken and wanted to get it off her chest. It was nearly midnight before we said goodnight and I went to bed.

CHAPTER EIGHT

THE NEW BIKE

All too soon it was Monday again and my semi-relaxing weekend had passed. I was in my car heading for Damian's school and looking forward to seeing him again, although not to the period of readjustment that was likely to follow his weekend contact. I wondered how it had gone. Rachel hadn't phoned and asked me to collect Damian early so I assumed all was well. It needed to be if we were working towards him going home for good. I also wondered how Damian had got on with Troy and for how much of the weekend Troy had been there.

I parked the car and then waited in the playground in my usual place, mask on and socially distanced from the other parents and carers. Damian's class came out and I spotted Mrs Halas carrying Damian's weekend bag and Damian walking beside her, smiling. That bodes well, I thought as I went over.

'We've had a good day,' Mrs Halas said, also smiling, and she passed me his bag. 'He's completed most of his work and has been telling me he's had a really nice weekend.'

'Excellent,' I said, relieved.

'He's also got a new bike,' Mrs Halas added. 'But I'll let him tell you all about that.'

I glanced at Damian, who was beaming from ear to ear. I thanked Mrs Halas, and then Damian and I walked across the playground. He was bursting to tell me his news.

'Troy's bought me a new mountain bike! It's black and silver and really cool. I have to keep it at Mum's, but I can ride it outside with the other kids whenever I want. Troy wasn't upset about the key and laughed. I've been out on my bike all weekend!'

I could see how excited Damian was and I was pleased he was happy, but I had concerns. I would never have allowed a child of seven to play outside on a bike unsupervised. I felt it was far too dangerous. Many foster carers are placed in the position of having to deal with conflicting standards – when a parent does something very differently to how they would. I had no authority over the decisions that Rachel made while Damian was with her. She was in charge then. And while I appreciated there was a grass verge outside the block of flats that separated the path from the road, and older children did play and congregate there, I didn't think it was safe for a seven-year-old. But that was *my* feeling, and it was for Rachel to decide.

Damian continued to talk about his new mountain bike as we left the school and got into my car. I listened, nodded and smiled. I'd never seen him so animated. It was his first bike and my heart went out to him.

'Did you know how to ride the bike?' I asked as I drove.

'I fell off a few times, but then one of the older boys showed me what to do and I got the hang of it. Mum didn't want me to go outside by myself, but Troy said I could once I'd done my homework.'

'I see. Was he there all weekend?'

'I think so. I like Troy.'

I nodded.

I had another surprise when I arrived home and opened Damian's weekend bag. All his belongings were there, washed, ironed and neatly folded, just as I had packed them. Not only his clothes but his towel, flannel and toothbrush, all looking as though they hadn't been touched. The food diary wasn't filled in, but then it never was.

Damian was downstairs in the living room with Paula telling her all about his new mountain bike and how great Troy was. Sammy was rubbing around Damian's legs, purring and pleased to see him. I made dinner and as we ate – Damian tucking into his – I casually remarked, 'Did you change your clothes over the weekend?' For it was quite possible he'd been wearing Friday's school uniform all the time, although it didn't appear grubby.

Damian looked at me thoughtfully and then said, 'I've got my own clothes at Mum's now.'

'OK. Good.'

'Troy gave Mum money to buy us stuff.'

'I see.'

'He said to tell you we don't need your stuff any more.'

That may be, I thought, but I would still send Damian's weekend bag until Rachel or their social worker told me otherwise. Troy had only recently come into their lives and seemed to be making improvements, but if he left, it could go pear-shaped very quickly. Whenever I saw Rachel she seemed to be just about managing.

After dinner (Damian ate well) Paula helped him with his schoolwork and then I took him upstairs for his bath and bed. I always ran his bath and then waited on the landing while he washed himself and dressed in his pyjamas, then I went in as he brushed his teeth. He was still talking about Troy as I saw him into bed – all very positive things and I would include them in my log notes. If Troy was going to be a permanent member of their family it was important Damian and his siblings formed a meaningful bond with him, and he with them. I thought perhaps Troy had learnt from the mistakes of the previous weekend and was trying very hard, perhaps too hard. Children don't need brand-new bikes but stability, love, care and attention.

The following morning Damian woke up talking about his new mountain bike.

'I've got to wait a whole week before I can ride it again,' he moaned as I opened his bedroom curtains.

'You could ride one of the ones I have here,' I suggested.

He pulled a face. I had a good selection of bikes, scooters and outdoor play equipment in my shed. There was something for all ages, but they were well used and not the brand-new mountain bike that awaited Damian at home.

'It's light in the evenings now so you could practise riding a bike after school, then you'll be even better next weekend,' I said.

'Maybe,' he replied, unimpressed.

Over breakfast Damian said, 'You don't have to write in that food book any more.'

He knew I kept a food diary as the paediatrician had suggested, although I didn't make an issue of it. I had it in a drawer in the kitchen and added to it as necessary. It was rarely mentioned in my house, so I wondered if his mother had said something.

'Why don't I have to keep it any more?' I asked casually.

'Troy says. He also said I don't have to stay here and can go home any time I like.'

Hmm, I thought. 'That's only partly true,' I said. 'It's for your mother and your social worker to decide when the time is right for you to live at home again. You remember when you first came here, we had a long talk about it being hard work looking after a baby and how your mum needed some extra help?'

He looked at me cautiously and then said, 'We have Troy now.'

'Yes, love, but it will still need to be decided by your mother and social worker.'

'So I can't just go?'

'It's better not to,' I said.

Clearly there had been a conversation about Damian going home and I wasn't sure it was helpful. He was still settling in with me and it could be some months before he returned home.

I saw Damian into school and then texted Lara to see how she was and whether I could visit her that week. I'd just arrived home when Korin, Damian's social worker, telephoned. She said she was going to visit Rachel the following day and wanted an update, including how the weekend contact was going. I told her about Damian's routine, his behaviour – which had been an issue for his mother – how he was at school, what he liked doing in his spare time and the improvements in his eating. I said weekend contact was going well, although there was always a period of readjustment, before and after. I told her about the new bike and what Damian had said about Troy, although it was all in my log notes.

'Does Troy work?' Korin asked.

'I don't know. I've never met him. I'm just repeating what Damian has told me.'

'Rachel phoned me yesterday and said she wants Damian home to live with her.'

'I see.'

'She's also saying she doesn't need Wera any more.'

'Oh.'

'She says she feels stronger now and better able to manage three children. Wera feels Rachel still needs a lot of support.'

'That's my impression,' I said. 'Perhaps it's changed because Troy is there?'

'I've read your reports, thank you, but Rachel says Troy isn't there very often.'

I was surprised. 'I don't know about during the week, but he seems to be there for most of the weekends now, according to Damian.'

'All right, I'll get some more details from Rachel when I see her tomorrow. Also, I'm due to see Damian again. How about Thursday, say four-thirty, after school? It will be online.'

'Yes, we'll be home from school by then.'

Social workers visit the children they are responsible for at least every six weeks; more often if necessary. Since the start of the pandemic most of these visits had been virtual.

Lara replied to my text and said I could see her that afternoon, and if I was going shopping could I bring some washing-up liquid. I wasn't going shopping, but I texted her to say I would see her around 1 p.m. and bring the washing-up liquid. I had a spare bottle, which I took from the cupboard ready to take.

I did a little work at my computer, had a toasted cheese sandwich for lunch that Paula made, then it was time for me to leave to go to Lara's, the bottle of washing-up liquid tucked into my bag. As soon as I pressed their doorbell I could hear Arthur excitedly running to see who was at the door. He was such a sociable little chap. As Lara opened the door he cried, 'Caffy!' and wrapped his arms tightly around my legs in a big hug. I picked him up and cuddled him, then followed Lara into the living room.

'I know what you're going to say,' she said as my gaze fell to the mattress on the floor. 'But Claudette said it's OK.' Claudette was Lara and Arthur's social worker.

'She's seen it?' I asked in dismay.

'She was here yesterday in an unannounced visit. I didn't know she was coming so I didn't have time to clear up.' Which was the point of an unannounced visit – to give the social worker a chance to see the child and their parents/carers on a typical day without any pre-planning.

'Claudette said it was acceptable,' Lara continued, 'as long as I was looking after Arthur, which I am. And there was food in the cupboards – she saw. She said he was thriving and that's what mattered. She's spoken to the manager at the nursery where he goes and they said he was doing well and my timekeeping had improved.'

'Excellent. But why not get Frazer to help you put the mattress away before he leaves on Monday?' I asked. It took up most of the living room.

'Frazer stayed over last night too so it wasn't worth it,' Lara replied.

'All right, love. You're an adult, and as long as Claudette is satisfied, that's what matters. Here's the washing-up liquid.' I put Arthur down and gave her the plastic bottle. 'Make sure you put it in a child-proof cupboard,' I reminded her.

'I will. Do you want tea?'

'Just a drink of water, please.'

Arthur was now bouncing on the mattress, and I inched my way along the edge of it so I could sit on the sofa near him. Lara brought me a glass of water, then, as Arthur bounced, tried to stand on his head and generally played, Lara and I talked. She told me that she'd spoken to Joel's mother, who'd said he had been released from police custody, but that she didn't know where he was now and she didn't care.

'I don't think his mother is a nice person,' Lara said, pulling a face. 'She blames him for being the way he is, like she has no responsibility for him. She keeps slagging him off and tells him he's just like his father, who's in prison. I think she should praise Joel more and support him now he's in trouble.'

'Yes,' I agreed.

'I mean, if one of your kids was in trouble, you would stand by them, wouldn't you?'

'Yes, but perhaps she's come to the end of her tether. It can't have been easy.'

'Frazer and I were talking about it and how she's always putting Joel down. He seemed nice when we talked to him, just a bit lost. We will stand by Arthur whatever he does.'

'I know you will, love. You're good parents.' Frazer, like Lara, should have received more support when he'd left care. It had taken them both some time and quite a few wrong turns before they'd got their lives on track. 'How is Frazer?' I asked.

'Good. Working hard.'

We talked for a while longer, then I played with Arthur and read him some stories until it was time for me to leave to collect Damian from school.

It rained that afternoon after school so Damian didn't have the chance to play outside and practise his bike-riding as I'd suggested.

'I hope it doesn't rain on Friday,' he said pessimistically. 'I don't want my new bike getting wet.'

It was raining the following morning and the showers continued on and off for most of the next day. It was the first thing he told his social worker at her online visit that afternoon.

'I've got a new bike, but I don't want it getting wet.'

'I saw your new bike when I visited your mother yesterday,' Korin told him. 'It's very smart.'

'Troy bought it for me,' Damian said proudly.

'Yes, I know. That was a nice present. Do you see him at weekends?'

'Sometimes.'

'How is it going at home?'

'All right.'

'How are your brothers?' Korin asked. 'Do you still help your mother?'

'Sometimes.'

Korin then asked him what he liked doing at the weekends.

'Riding my bike,' Damian said, fidgeting and wanting to do something else. One of the problems with virtual visits is trying to keep a young child's attention. It was much easier for the social worker to engage with them when they visited in person.

Korin asked Damian about school and his friends, but he wasn't very responsive.

'Can I watch television now?'

'Yes,' Korin replied with a smile. 'Cathy has told me how well you're doing. Thank you for talking to me.'

'You're welcome,' Damian replied in his cute, cheeky way.

I took him to Paula so she could look after him while I returned to the front room and picked up my tablet.

'We had a good chat about Damian earlier this week,' Korin said. 'Is there anything you want to add?'

'Not really. It's all in my log notes.'

'I'll just have a look around your house and then leave you to it.' The child's social worker usually looked around the foster carer's home at each visit, just as the carer's supervising social worker did.

But before I had a chance to begin the tour, Korin said, 'When I visited Rachel yesterday there was no sign of Troy in the home. She said he's a friend who just pops in from time to time. There were none of his clothes in the wardrobe, and just her and the children's belongings in the bathroom.'

'That's not the impression Damian has given me,' I said. 'Unless he's got it all wrong.'

'Possibly. He's only young. But Rachel and I have agreed that Damian will remain with you for the time being and we will review the situation again at my next visit. Can you explain that to him, please, if he asks? He wasn't really in the mood when I spoke to him just now.'

'Yes, of course.'

I showed Korin around the house, then took my tablet into the living room again so she could say goodbye to Damian. He was watching television and called, 'Bye!' without taking his eyes from the screen.

Korin thanked me for all I was doing and we said goodbye.

Damian was so looking forward to going home at the weekend to ride his new bike that his first question when I woke him on Friday morning was, 'Is it raining?'

'No, it's stopped, love.'

'Yippee!' he cried, and jumped out of bed.

I've never seen him wash and dress so quickly. Even breakfast wasn't the ordeal it sometimes was as the thought of riding his bike dominated everything else. It seemed the bike was proving therapeutic. In the car going to school he asked me, 'Am I staying at Mum's?'

'For the weekend.'

'Not all the time?'

'No, you will be living with me during the week as usual.'

'Does Troy know?' he asked.

'I honestly don't know,' I replied, as I concentrated on the road ahead.

'He wants me to live at home.'

'I understand, but it's for your mother and your social worker to decide what's best.'

'Can I bring my bike back with me so I can ride it after school?' he asked.

'If your mum agrees. We'd have to work out how I would collect and return it.'

'I'll ask Troy,' he said, and his little face lit up.

But I thought of Korin's comments that Troy appeared to be only a casual visitor, in which case, why did he have so much authority in Damian's home? One of us must have misread the situation, and when I took Damian home that afternoon it seemed it was me who had got it wrong.

CHAPTER NINE

AN EMERGENCY PLACEMENT

Rachel answered the door with baby Liam in her arms and three-year-old Nathan at her side. As well as being underweight, she was small in stature, which made her look much younger than twenty-four. At a glance you could have thought she was about twelve or thirteen.

'Hello,' she said in her small, self-effacing way. 'Come in.'

'Can I ride my bike now?' Damian asked, rushing in.

'Once you've changed out of your school uniform, like you do at Cathy's,' Rachel replied.

It was true that Damian changed from his school uniform into casual clothes if he was playing in the garden, but I'd never mentioned it. I thought it must have come from Korin's visit, perhaps when they'd discussed Damian's routine with me.

'Shall I put his bag in his room?' I asked Rachel.

'Yes, please.'

Slightly surprised that I was being invited in, I went into the bedroom the boys shared, where I found Damian rummaging in the drawers searching for something to wear. 'Do you want your clothes from your bag?' I asked him.

'No, I've got my own now.'

I left the bag in his room and went to find Rachel in the living room. A new mountain bike was propped against one wall.

'So that's the bike I've heard so much about,' I said, with a smile. 'Very nice.'

'It was expensive, so we have to keep it in here. If we left it on the landing or in the lock-up outside, it would be stolen.' The flats had access to communal lockable storage units on the ground floor, but the padlocks were often prised open and the contents pilfered.

I admired the bike and noticed there was no sign of Troy. I made coochy-coo noises at baby Liam as Damian reappeared in new casual clothes and went to his bike.

'Have you got everything you need for the weekend?' I asked Rachel.

'Yes, I think so.'

'Any plans?'

She shook her head, then said, 'Damian can spend time riding his bike.'

'Can I go out now?' Damian asked eagerly.

Rachel looked at me as if I should answer, then said, 'Korin says you should play at the back, not on the road.'

There was a grass area at the back of the flats, although most children and young people seemed to congregate at the front, such as the small group of teenagers near the main entrance I'd seen before.

'Do I have to?' Damian moaned. 'It's better out front.'

Both he and Rachel looked at me.

'You need to do as your mother says,' I told him.

He pulled a face and then, going to his bike, began struggling to move it from between the back of the sofa and the wall. I went to help him. We lifted it out and then together carried it from the living room, where he pushed it down the hall.

'Use the lift!' Rachel called.

'I'll see him down,' I said. Saying goodbye, I followed Damian out of the flat, closing the door behind us.

I still wasn't comfortable with Damian playing outside without adult supervision, but it was Rachel's decision and Korin was aware.

As we waited for the lift Damian said, 'I bumped it down all the stairs last time and some woman told me off for making a noise.'

I could picture Damian, too impatient to wait for the lift, clattering down the stairs. 'It could damage your bike,' I said.

The lift arrived and we descended to the ground floor. The doors opened and Damian turned right to go out the front.

'You're to play at the back,' I reminded him.

He sighed but turned the bike around and rode unsteadily to the grass at the rear. I went after him. A young woman with a toddler was there so I felt a bit easier about leaving him unattended.

'Once you've had a bike ride, go back up to your flat,' I told him.

But he was too busy riding his bike. I watched him for a while; he wobbled a little until he got the hang of it again after a week's break.

'Well done,' I called.

'You can go now!' he shouted.

I watched him for a while longer and said again, 'When you've had enough go in.'

'Yes!'

Reluctantly, I called goodbye and began to walk away. I paused every so often to look back and check on him. I continued through the concrete passageway that led from the back to the front of the building. As I took my final glance before he disappeared from view one of the teenage girls in the group near the main entrance saw me.

'I'll keep an eye on him,' she said helpfully. 'My brother will be down soon – I have to watch him too.'

'Thank you so much,' I said. 'That is kind of you.'

I guessed most of those in the flats with children faced the same problem of trying to keep them safe while they played outside.

When I arrived home Paula was on a conference call in her bedroom. The door was closed but I could hear other voices, including what sounded like her manager. I assumed it was another update on where the company was in respect of orders and re-employing its staff. I hoped it was good news.

Ten minutes or so later Paula came downstairs. I was in the kitchen making a mug of tea. She looked exhilarated and a little flushed.

'I'm getting my job back,' she announced. 'I start the week after next.'

'That's fantastic,' I said. 'Well done. Tea?'

'Yes, please. I'll be working from home to begin with as the government advice is that people should work from home where possible. Then, when the advice changes and the remaining restrictions are lifted, they're letting staff choose if they want to still work remotely or go into the office. My manager showed us pictures of the changes they'd made in the offices to keep us safe. The workstations are much further apart and they all have plastic screens at the sides and in front, and there's hand-sanitizer at each one.' I knew that many offices were doing similar to help reduce the spread of coronavirus.

'Great,' I enthused. I was delighted for Paula as I knew how much she liked her job.

'You'll be all right with the fostering, won't you?' she asked. 'I mean, I'll be here, but I won't be able to help you as I'll be working in my bedroom.'

'Yes, of course, love. I've appreciated your help, but I'll be fine. I'll pretend you're not here. There's just Damian and he's in a better routine now. I'll have to keep him quiet while you're working. It'll be fine. How about we celebrate with a takeaway tonight?'

'Yes,' Paula agreed. 'My treat.'

I passed her a mug of tea and we took it into the living room where we continued talking. She texted Lucy and Adrian her good news. They were pleased. Adrian was still working from home and enjoying it.

'You'll have to practise getting up on time,' I joked.

'I know. I'll need to start going to sleep earlier,' she replied honestly.

Not having had to rise early to leave for work, she'd got into the habit of watching films on Netflix and other online platforms late into the night – long after I was asleep – then waking mid-morning. This would have to stop now, but it had got her through the lockdowns, and overall, she, like the rest of my family, had coped well with the pandemic and the restrictions imposed. But I was always mindful we had incomes and the support of each other, which not everyone had.

That weekend passed without any drama. I did some gardening and also spent time at my computer. I didn't hear from Rachel, so I assumed the weekend was going well, although I did worry about Damian being out on his bike for long periods, and I wondered if Troy was there helping.

On Monday afternoon Paula came with me to collect Damian from school as this week would be her last opportunity before she returned to work the following week. She waited outside the school gates while I put on my mask and went into the playground to collect him. He came out looking annoyed.

'A mixed day,' Mrs Halas told me, handing me his weekend bag. 'It didn't start well. He was dropped off at the school gates very late, after ten o'clock, and left to come in by himself.'

'I didn't mind,' Damian said defensively.

But that wasn't the point. The school policy was that if a child was late then the parent or carer had to take them into the building where they were signed in. Damian had often been late before coming into care, as well as missing whole days off school.

'He ate a good lunch,' Mrs Halas continued. 'And this afternoon he completed some literary work. But his weekend homework hasn't been done so it's in his school-bag.'

'I didn't have time to do it,' Damian said with attitude, as if that made it all right. 'I was out on my bike.'

Mrs Halas threw me a knowing look.

'We'll do it tonight,' I said.

Damian groaned.

I thanked Mrs Halas, and Damian and I began to walk across the playground.

'Who brought you to school this morning?' I asked.

'Troy. He's got a car.'

'Did you have a nice weekend?'

'It was all right,' he said, scowling.

'Paula's waiting outside,' I said, but that didn't help.

'Oh dear, what's the matter?' Paula asked, seeing Damian's grumpy face.

'I had to leave my bike at Mum's,' he moaned. 'And my phone.'

'Your phone?' I queried, thinking I must have misheard.

'Troy says my phone and bike have to stay at Mum's, because he doesn't want them being nicked.'

'Are we talking about a proper mobile phone?' Paula asked as we walked to the car. 'Not a toy?'

'A proper one!' Damian exclaimed indignantly. 'Troy gave it to me.'

'Why?' I asked as I opened the car doors.

'I don't know.' Damian shrugged. 'He's always buying us things.'

I waited on the pavement while Damian got into the car. I checked he'd fastened his seatbelt, then Paula and I got into the front seats. I started the car and pulled away. In my view a child of seven was too young to be given a mobile phone, although I'm aware that a minority of children his age do have them. Some parents of children in care give them a phone in the hope they can speak to them outside the arranged and permitted contact times.

Had this been so with Damian, I would have called his social worker to discuss the matter. It was very likely she would say he was too young and either return the phone to his mother or tell me to put it away until he was older or went home for good, when it would be his mother's decision. Had Rachel given Damian a phone with the intention of having more contact then it would have made some sense, but that wasn't the case, as the phone had to be kept at home.

'Did you use the phone while you were at your mum's?' I asked as I drove.

'Yes,' Damian replied.

'To play with?' Paula asked.

'I guess,' he said.

I glanced at him in the rear-view mirror; he was gazing out of his side window.

'Did you speak to someone on the phone?' I asked. I wasn't being nosey; I was worried for his safety.

'It was a recorded message,' he said.

'I think it was a toy,' Paula said quietly to me. 'They can be very realistic.'

I nodded. It seemed the mostly likely explanation. Some of the toy mobiles are exact replicas of the real thing, with music for incoming calls and recorded messages when numbers are pressed as though there is someone there.

'Or a Walkie-Talkie,' Paula suggested. 'Do you remember ours, Mum?'

I smiled. 'Yes, they were great fun.'

'We could talk to each other from anywhere in the house and from the bottom of the garden.'

'I know.'

I wasn't going to embarrass Damian by insisting he admit the phone was a toy, and it was possible he hadn't realized that, but I was certain it was. I changed the subject.

'Did you ride your bike?' I asked him.

'Yes, loads,' he said. 'But I wanted to bring it with me.'

'I know, but you'll be able to ride it next weekend. During the week you can use one of mine,' I reminded him. 'Was Troy there?'

'Sometimes, but he had to work.'

'What does he do?'

'Buys and sells cars. He does it on his phone and then goes out to deliver them.'

Once home, I gave Damian a drink and a snack and then Paula helped him with his schoolwork while I made dinner. After we'd eaten the three of us played some board games, and by bedtime Damian's disappointment at not being allowed to bring his bike or phone to my house had disappeared. He was soon fast asleep and when I wrote up my log notes that evening I included what he'd said about the weekend, and that it appeared to have gone well.

Mid-morning on Tuesday, Joy, my supervising social worker, telephoned with a referral. Requests to foster carers to take a child either come through their supervising social worker or the child's social worker. Although I had a spare bedroom and was approved to foster up to three children, I'd previously told Joy I would prefer having just one child but would take more in an emergency.

'It's a newborn,' she said, and my heart sank. 'The mother gave birth last night, before her due date. That's all I know. They want her moved from hospital as soon as possible because of Covid so they need a carer to take the baby today.'

'I don't know, Joy,' I said hesitantly. 'It would be very disruptive for Damian, and a newborn is hard work.'

'You've got Paula there to help you,' Joy said.

'Only for this week. She starts work again next week from home. I honestly don't know if I can successfully manage a newborn baby and Damian,' I admitted.

'You don't have him at weekends, though,' Joy said, which niggled me.

I appreciated the foster care service was stretched to the limit with so many children coming into care, but I needed to be certain I could give each child the level of care and attention they needed and deserved. It wasn't just about providing a bed, regular meals and clothes. There was so much more to it. Also, there was the emotional drain of looking after and loving a child and then having to say goodbye. After nearly thirty years of fostering, I was finding that, far from it becoming easier, it was getting more painful. Perhaps it was age. I seemed to be feeling things more deeply and worrying more about others.

'Shall I get some more details?' Joy suggested, hearing my silence.

'Yes, please.'

'I'll try to speak to the baby's social worker now and call you back. But can I say that if it's an emergency you'll take the baby?'

'Yes.'

CHAPTER TEN

WORRYING MORE

'Lucy is trying to get through to you on your phone, Mum,' Paula said as Joy's call ended. Paula had come to find me in the living room and now handed me her phone. Unable to reach me on my phone, Lucy had called Paula.

'Hello, love – sorry, it was Joy, my SSW,' I said to Lucy. 'Is everything all right? Shouldn't you be at work?' I asked, concerned.

'I wasn't well over the weekend and did a lateral flow test, but it was negative. Then I was sick this morning, so I stayed off work. Mum, I've just done a pregnancy test and I'm expecting.'

'Oh, love, that's wonderful news. Isn't it?' I checked as an afterthought. Lucy's first pregnancy, resulting in my gorgeous granddaughter, Emma, had been a pleasant surprise for us all.

'Yes. We wanted another child, and the time is right with Emma nearly three and being at nursery part-time.'

'Congratulations. I'm so pleased, love.'

'So are we. I just wish I didn't feel so sick.'

'You had morning sickness before and it passed,' I reminded her. 'When is your due date?'

'Around the second week in January, I think.'

'Fantastic.' Clearly Lucy had already told Paula as she was standing watching me and smiling broadly. 'Is there anything I can do?' I asked.

'Stop me from being sick?'

'Oh, love. Try to eat little and often. I think dry crackers helped before. Do you need any shopping?'

'No, Darren's picking up some stuff on his way back from work with Emma.' She and Darren arranged their hours around Emma, and I and Darren's parents helped with child-care as and when necessary.

'OK, tell me if you need any help.'

'I will, Mum.'

We talked for a while longer and then Lucy ended the call in a rush as she needed to be sick again. I felt for her; morning sickness is debilitating and can last all day. It usually wears off by around fourteen weeks' gestation, although it can continue for much longer.

Needless to say, I was delighted at Lucy's news. I texted Darren to congratulate him, and then spent the rest of the day texting Lucy to make sure she was all right. My second grandchild, a little brother or sister for Emma, would be with us early next year. After all the gloom and doom of Covid, this was just what we needed; it had come like a breath of fresh air.

I was still feeling elated at 2.30 when Joy phoned again. I was at my computer, keeping an eye on the time, as I'd have to leave shortly to collect Damian from school.

'I've spoken to the baby's social worker,' Joy began. 'And you won't be needed after all. It seems the messages got confused and there is already a foster carer waiting for the baby.'

'That was quick.'

'The couple were identified some time ago as part of the Fostering for Adoption scheme.'

'I see.'

'Thanks for offering to help. I'll be in touch.'

'Joy, I've just heard from Lucy and she's expecting again.'

'Congratulations.'

'I'll be helping her as much as I can, so unless it's an absolute emergency I'll just foster Damian.'

'Understood.'

We said goodbye.

I wasn't sure she *had* fully understood what I'd said. My first priority had to be my family and the child I was fostering – Damian, who was part of my family while he was with me. The elation I'd previously felt at Lucy's good news had been dinted by what Joy had just told me. Not because the baby was no longer coming to me – this happens in fostering: a carer is put on standby and then no longer needed. This could be because the judge doesn't grant the care order or a suitable relative – usually considered the next best option – comes forward to look after the child. No, my heart was now heavy because of the nature of the fostering placement: Fostering for Adoption.

I'll explain.

Usually when a child comes into care it is hoped that the parents will resolve their problems so the child can eventually return home. But with a Fostering for Adoption placement (which is being trialled in some areas) the baby is placed with foster carers who are also approved to adopt, with a view to them adopting the baby. These placements are used when there is little chance the birth parent(s) will be able to look after their child. It is intended to stop multiple moves for the infant and to give them the stability of a permanent family right from the start. It also means bonding between the child and adoptive parents can begin straight away. The match still has to be approved by the court and I don't know how many aren't. It played on my mind. That poor mother had just given birth and there was little hope of her ever having her baby back. I didn't know the circumstances, but was there really no level of support that could be put in to at least give her a chance of parenting her child? It made me sad thinking about her, and the carers who could bond with the child and then have them taken away. But as I said, I found I was worrying more than ever these days about those less fortunate than me.

On Wednesday, having checked on Lucy, who was going to work, I visited Lara and Arthur in the afternoon, taking with me the groceries from a list Lara had texted. That damn mattress was still on the living-room floor! I didn't immediately comment as I handed Lara the bag of groceries, which she put in the kitchenette. The mattress seemed to have become a feature, the focus of the room, with the detritus of day-to-day living displayed on it. There were empty cereal bowls, plates with the remnants of sandwiches and other snacks on them, crisp packets, biscuit wrappers, a hairbrush, an empty water bottle, Arthur's sippy cup, his toys and some of their clothes, including Lara and Arthur's pyjamas.

'You don't really need any other furniture with the mattress,' I quipped as Lara returned from the kitchenette.

She understood my sense of humour and laughed. 'We're going to put it back,' she said. 'Frazer didn't have time when he left for work. Arthur doesn't like being alone in the bedroom and has been sleeping in here with us.' Which rather defeated the object, as the mattress had been moved to allow them all to sleep better and give them some privacy.

'Shall I give you a hand to move it?' I asked.

Lara's face dropped as she surveyed the mess that needed to be cleared up first. 'It needs a clean duvet cover,' she said.

She was right. It was stained and grubby.

'It won't take us long,' I encouraged. 'Arthur can help.'

'OK, let's do it,' she said decisively.

'You can help by putting your toys in the toy box,' I told Arthur, and showed him what to do.

If a child is included in a task, they are more likely to cooperate and not just get in the way. So while Arthur put his toys away, Lara and I set about clearing the rest of the mattress. We put the rubbish in the bin in the kitchenette, the crockery in the sink with the other washing up, the dirty clothes in the laundry bag, and then we took off the duvet cover and pillowcases. Once the mattress was clear, we persuaded Arthur to stop jumping on it, then lifted it onto its side and dragged, pulled and pushed it out of the living room and into the bedroom, where we dropped it onto the bed.

'Bed,' Arthur said, immediately trying to jump on it again.

'No, this is where you sleep,' Lara told him. She lifted him off the bed and put him into his cot.

He didn't like that and shouted, 'Out! Out!'

She took him out of the cot and we kept him occupied by getting him to 'help' us put the clean sheet on the mattress, then the pillowcases and duvet cover. Returning to the living room, I had a glass of water, and then spent some time playing with Arthur as well as chatting to Lara until it was time for me to leave to collect Damian.

Mrs Halas said Damian had had a good day. That evening passed pleasantly too. I spoke to Lucy on the phone and Adrian called.

'I hear I'm going to be an uncle again,' he said.

He was pleased for Lucy and Darren, and although we didn't mention that he and Kirsty were hoping to start a family soon, I thought I detected a yearning in his voice, suggesting he was hoping he would be able to make a similar announcement before long.

On Thursday Korin phoned and said that Rachel had asked for Damian to spend a few extra days at home with her the following week. Monday was a bank holiday and most schools had the week off for half-term. Korin had agreed in principle but wanted to know what I thought.

'I don't see why not,' I said. 'Rachel can call me if she needs me to collect Damian early. Which days?'

'Thursday and Friday and then he'll stay the weekend as usual.'

'All right.'

'I've suggested you collect him on the Sunday evening at the end of the week and prepare him ready for school on Monday.'

'That's fine with me.'

'He'll go this weekend as normal, but you'll need to collect him on Sunday as there is no school on Monday.'

'Yes,' I said, and made a note of the new arrangements.

That afternoon when I collected Damian from school I explained what was happening over half-term. He was a bit confused, so I went over it again in the car as I drove.

'Tomorrow I collect you from school as normal and take you home for the weekend. I will collect you on Sunday evening as there is no school next week. You will spend Monday, Tuesday and Wednesday with me. I will take you home on Thursday and you will stay with your Mum until Sunday. Don't worry, I'll explain it as we go.'

'You'll enjoy spending more time with your family,' Paula said positively.

'And I can ride my bike loads!' he cried with glee.

Did I have any concerns about Damian spending that extra time at home? Only that Rachel might find parenting three of them too much, in which case she'd call me and I'd collect him early. Korin had approved the arrangement and we were working towards Damian being able to return home permanently, so this seemed like a step in the right direction.

On Friday when I collected Damian from school, his weekend bag in my car, I wished Mrs Halas a happy half-term holiday and she did the same to us. Damian had told her he was spending some of it with his mother and she was pleased for them. She knew Rachel from when Damian had lived at home and she'd brought him to school. Mrs Halas felt as I did, that Rachel was kind, sweet and 'wouldn't harm a fly', but was easily taken advantage of, and was struggling to bring up three children alone.

Rachel answered the door looking stressed, which wasn't a good start. I could hear baby Liam crying in the background.

'Sorry, I can't stop and talk,' she said, reaching for Damian's bag. Damian shot past her to go to his bike.

'Is there anything I can do?' I asked.

'No, thanks.'

'Shall I see Damian down in the lift with his bike if he's going straight out?'

'There's no need. Troy's here; he'll see to him.'

'OK. I'll come back to collect him on Sunday. What time?'

'I don't know. Six?'

'Fine, but call me if you want me to collect him earlier.'

She nodded and closed the door.

When I returned home Paula was involved in another conference call on her laptop in her bedroom. When she'd finished she explained it was in preparation for starting work on Tuesday. The company had introduced new software that should make it easier for their office staff to work remotely. She spent some of the evening familiarizing herself with what was involved and then we watched a film together.

On Saturday Paula and I took Emma to the park for the afternoon to give Lucy and Darren a break, and Lucy the chance to rest. She was still being sick but was managing to eat a little. On Sunday Paula and I went for a walk with Adrian and Kirsty. I said I was looking forward to being able to make Sunday dinner for us all again as soon as the remaining restrictions were lifted on socializing indoors.

At 5.45 I set off to collect Damian from his mother's. As I pulled up opposite the block of flats I saw him with three older lads on the grass verge a little way from the main entrance. He was standing astride his bike, at ease and chatting to the older lads, apparently oblivious to the fact it was time to leave. It was still light and clearly he knew the lads, but even so I felt a stab of concern. There were no other children his age out. I cut the engine, went over and said a general hello. One of the lads just turned away from me while the other two muttered hellos from under their hoodies.

'It's time to put away your bike,' I told Damian.

'I'm not going with you,' he said, his face setting in anger. 'I'm staying here.'

'No, love. Your mother and I have agreed that you're to come with me, then I'll bring you back on Thursday,' I reminded him. I don't think he'd forgotten, he was just exerting his will, as children can do. I could see the attraction for him to be out with these older lads rather than with Paula and me. 'We need to put away your bike,' I said.

'I'm not,' he replied, gripping the handlebars more tightly.

One of the lads who'd said hello looked at me suspiciously, so I thought I'd better explain. 'I'm a foster carer who's helping the family.'

'I'm not coming with you,' Damian said, his body stiffening in confrontation.

'Yes, love, it's time to go,' I replied calmly.

I was now envisaging a prolonged period of negotiation, which would probably involve fetching his mother before he came with me. But then the lad I'd just spoken to said, 'Damian, you need to do as you're told. Troy wouldn't be pleased if he knew you were making a fuss. You know what he said.'

I had no idea what Troy had said, but it worked. Damian raised the right pedal on his bike and rode to the main entrance.

'Thank you,' I said to the lad. But the boys were already sauntering off in the opposite direction.

I caught up with Damian and we went into the building and then the lift. We rose in silence. I could tell he wasn't happy with me, but at least he'd done as he was supposed to.

'Nice weekend?' I asked.

He didn't reply.

The lift doors opened and Damian pushed his bike out ahead of me and to his front door, then pressed the bell for much longer than necessary.

'Don't do that,' I said. 'You could wake Liam.'

'Can if I want to,' he retorted.

Rachel opened the door looking flustered.

'Oh, is that the time?' she asked.

Damian, still annoyed, wheeled his bike roughly past her, catching her as he went.

'Be careful,' I told him, when Rachel didn't.

She threw me a weak smile. 'I'll get his bag.'

I wasn't invited in, so I waited by the open door. Damian had disappeared down the hall and into the living room where his bike was kept. Nathan came towards me, a fish finger in each hand and a bib around his neck.

'Hello, love,' I said, and took his arm to stop him from leaving the flat.

It was a few moments before Rachel reappeared carrying Damian's bag. 'Oh, there you are,' she said to Nathan. She gave me the bag and picked up Nathan. He struggled to be put down and then ran into the living room.

'Damian,' she called, 'you have to go now.'

There was no reply and Damian didn't appear. Then I heard a man's voice in the living room. I couldn't hear what he said but Damian came down the hall.

'Have you got your jacket?' I asked him.

'No,' he said moodily, and made no attempt to find it.

Rachel went to get it, while Damian stood looking at me angrily. I assumed the man's voice had been Troy's, and I wondered if he would come to the door and say hello, but he didn't.

Rachel reappeared with Damian's jacket.

'Thank you,' I said. 'What time do you want me to bring him on Thursday?'

'I don't mind.'

'Morning or afternoon?'

'Morning,' Damian said.

I looked at Rachel. 'Shall we say around ten-thirty to eleven?' I suggested.

'Yes,' she said in her small, unassuming way.

I told Damian to say goodbye to his mother, which he wouldn't have done otherwise, and we left. I felt, as I often did when leaving Rachel, that she was at the mercy of life. With little routine or order, she seemed to bounce around, buffeted by whatever came along. I wondered how many hours Wera was there for and if they should be increased, but that was really for Korin to discuss with Rachel and Wera.

'I'm hungry,' Damian said as we got into my car.

'I'll get you something as soon as we're home. When did you last eat?'

'Don't know,' he replied moodily. 'I've been out on my bike all afternoon.' So I guessed it could have been lunch-time.

Later, once he'd eaten, he was in a better mood, especially when I told him of some of the activities I was planning for the following week. Like so many children who come into care, he wasn't used to days out during the school holidays.

It was when I was reading him a story before bed that something crossed my mind.

'Those boys you were with, do they all know Troy?' I asked.

'I guess. Lots of people know Troy.'

'What was it that Troy told you?'

'He tells me loads of things,' Damian replied.

'When I collected you today one of the boys you were with said that you needed to do as you were told, because Troy wouldn't be pleased if he knew you were making a fuss.'

'Oh, that,' Damian said. 'Troy says I mustn't draw attention to myself when I'm out on my bike.'

'Why?'

'Don't know.' He shrugged and told me to finish reading the story, which I did.

CHAPTER ELEVEN

UNSAFE

On Bank Holiday Monday Paula and I took Damian to the zoo. He'd never been before and was enthralled. I'd had to pre-book a time slot for entry as numbers were being limited to allow for social distancing. Some of the indoor attractions were closed due to the enclosure being too small to social distance, but that didn't stop our enjoyment. I took lots of photographs of Damian and the animals. We had a picnic lunch outside, although Damian was too excited to sit still for long and eat. Until that day he'd only ever seen most of the animals in books or on the television. He said he wanted to work in a zoo when he was older.

Tuesday was Paula's first day at work. She was showered and dressed by 8.30, ready to start at 9 a.m. in her bedroom. I'd tried to explain to Damian that although she was home, she would be working so we mustn't disturb her. I'd arranged it so we wouldn't be in the house for long. Shortly after breakfast I took him to a museum, returning at 4 p.m. On Wednesday morning I took him shopping to buy him some new shoes. We had lunch out and then in the afternoon I took him to the cinema where a children's film was showing during the half-term holiday. This was another new experience for him and he loved the popcorn. I had to wear a face mask getting to and from my seat, but there was hardly anyone there. Pre-pandemic, it would have been packed during a school holiday.

Paula spent time with Damian both evenings, playing games or reading to him. He loved being read to. His mother never had the time and struggled with reading due to her learning difficulties, but she wanted Damian to do well at school. I felt the week was going well. Paula had been able to work without interruption and Damian and I had enjoyed a few days out. Tomorrow I was taking him home for the rest of the week and then collecting him on Sunday evening. School began again on Monday, so my concerns about Paula being constantly interrupted while trying to work had been unwarranted.

On Thursday morning I packed Damian's bag. Last time some of the clothes had been used, so I put in enough to last him the rest of the week. Before we left we knocked on Paula's bedroom door to say goodbye.

'Come in,' she called.

He rushed in and gave her a big hug.

'That's nice,' she said, hugging him back. 'You have a great time and I'll see you on Sunday.'

'Don't work too hard,' he said as we came away, which he'd heard me say.

It was 10.45 when Damian and I arrived at his mother's and I rang the doorbell. Rachel took some time to answer and was still in her dressing gown. Liam and Nathan were also in their nightwear. I thought Rachel looked paler than usual and there was a dark mark on her cheek, which could have been a bruise.

'Are you all right?' I asked, concerned. Damian shot in.

'I'm a bit behind – I didn't realize the time.'

The poor girl never realized the time.

'Is there anything I can do?' I asked.

'No, Troy will be back soon.' But it was said in a flat voice, as if she wasn't expecting a lot of help.

'When does Wera come?' I asked.

'She doesn't any more.'

'Really?' I was surprised.

'I told the social worker.'

'And what did she say?'

'That we needed to discuss it. I think she's phoning me next week.'

'I thought you appreciated Wera's help,' I said.

Rachel looked confused. 'Troy says I don't need her now.'

'And what do you think?'

'I'm not sure.'

It wasn't for me to tell Rachel she needed all the help she could get. I asked her again if there was anything I could do, and when she shook her head I said to call me if she wanted me to collect Damian before Sunday, and then I left.

I did a big grocery shop on the way home and then Paula broke for lunch. She said she was still getting used to the new software and there'd been a few glitches, which weren't her fault, but generally it was going well. I was pleased.

It was strange not having Damian in the house, but I put the time to good use. I cleaned and tidied, especially Damian's room, and then spent some time at my computer. I also baked a cake. When Paula finished for the day we had dinner together, then she said that, as she'd been sitting all day, she needed some exercise and did I want to go for a walk? I agreed. It was a reasonably mild evening, so shortly after seven we put on light jackets and set off up the road at a brisk walk. The park gate was still open, so we walked through the park, past the play area and the duck pond, and out of the gate at the far end. We'd been walking for about twenty minutes and were on our way back when my mobile rang. I hadn't bothered with a bag but had tucked my phone and keys into my jacket pocket. I slowed my pace to answer. Paula slowed too. It was a private number calling and I was half expecting a scam call.

'Yes?' I asked guardedly.

'Is that Cathy Glass?' a female asked.

'Who's calling?'

'I'm Detective Constable Morgan Baycote.'

I immediately assumed something dreadful had happened to one of my family. My stomach clenched and my pulse soared. I stopped dead in my tracks as all the worst-case scenarios flashed through my mind. Paula looked at me anxiously.

'I believe you're the foster carer for Damian Webb?' the police officer checked.

'Yes. What's happened to him?' I asked as fear gripped me. Straight away I thought of his bike. He must have been knocked off his bike while riding it on the road.

'Damian's not hurt,' Detective Constable Baycote said. 'The duty officer at the social services gave me your number and said you would be able to collect Damian. He's at ***** police station.'

'He's at a police station?' I asked incredulously.

'Don't worry, Damian's not in a cell. A colleague is with him, but he does need to be collected as soon as possible. There's been an incident and he can't return home with his mother.'

'What sort of incident?' I asked. Paula was looking at me, also very worried.

'I can explain more when you arrive. How long do you think you'll be? We're very short-staffed tonight.'

'Half an hour,' I said. 'I'm on my way home, as I need to collect my car.' I began walking hurriedly, Paula at my side. 'I'll be there as soon as I can. And Damian's not hurt?'

'No. Just a bit upset. A colleague is with him.'

'Tell him I'm on my way.'

As the call ended I quickened my pace even more and told Paula what I knew.

'Why's he at the police station?' she asked, sharing my incredulity.

'I don't know. All the officer said was that there'd been an incident and Damian couldn't go home.'

'Perhaps he's been caught stealing?' Paula suggested. Which had happened to a few children we'd fostered. One boy had been Damian's age. His mother had taught him how to steal, aware that he couldn't be prosecuted. The age of criminal responsibility in England is ten, which means that children under ten can't be charged with a crime. There are other ways of dealing with children who break the law, and in that boy's case he was brought into care, where I'd had to teach him right from wrong.

As far as I knew there'd been no suggestion Rachel had taught Damian to steal. I doubted she had the cunning or guile to do so. She loved her children and wanted what was best for them. She just couldn't cope.

Five minutes later Paula and I arrived home, out of breath and hot from running most of the way. I grabbed a bottle of water and we jumped into my car. I knew roughly where the police station was, about a fifteen-minute journey away. Paula found the exact location on her phone.

A few minutes into the journey my mobile rang from my bag and Paula answered it.

'She's driving,' she told the caller. 'I'll put you on speaker.' Then to me, she said, 'It's the duty social worker.'

'Hello,' I called out as I concentrated on driving.

'Damian Webb is at ***** police station; our records show you are his foster carer.'

'Yes, I'm on my way there now. DC Baycote phoned me a short while ago. What's happened?'

'Damian was caught trying to sell drugs.'

'What!' I exclaimed. 'There must be a mistake. He's only seven.' I glanced at Paula, who looked as horrified and confused as I did.

'They found class-A drugs on him,' the duty officer said. 'The police have spoken to Damian and now we need to get him home to you. How long will you be?'

'No more than ten minutes. Who gave him the drugs?' I asked. Class-A drugs are considered the most harmful and include heroin and cocaine.

'His mother's boyfriend.'

'Troy?'

'I don't have his name. Why? Do you know him?'

'No, but Damian has talked about Troy.'

'I'll make a note. Please phone once you have collected Damian.'

'I will.'

As a foster carer you get used to dealing with all sorts of situations you hadn't anticipated, but this was a first for me. A seven-year-old in my care had been caught dealing drugs. Only, of course, it wasn't Damian doing the dealing but Troy. Damian must have simply followed his instructions and may not have even known he was doing wrong. My thoughts went to Rachel. Was she involved? I had no idea, but she was easily led. Surely, she must have at least known what was going on? Troy had been spending a lot of time there, even though Rachel had told Korin he didn't. Either way, she'd failed to protect her son. Damian was in care at present under a voluntary agreement, a Section 20, with a view to him returning home. I hoped this didn't change that.

The map on Paula's phone took us to the front of the police station where there was no parking, so I turned left and parked down a side road.

'Have you got a mask with you?' I checked with Paula as we got out.

She took one from her jacket pocket. Like me, she kept one tucked in the pockets of all her outdoor wear. I also took my foster carer's identity badge from my bag.

All manner of thoughts flashed through my mind as we hurried to the main door of the police station, but my priority was supporting Damian through this dreadful ordeal. I pressed the buzzer beside the security-locked door and it was a few moments before it clicked open. Two people were in the waiting area, sitting on socially distanced benches, but only one was wearing a mask. Some people were exempt due to health conditions.

We crossed to the reception desk where the duty officer was enclosed behind a Perspex screen and spoke through an intercom. 'Good evening,' he said as we approached.

'Hello, I'm Cathy Glass, foster carer for Damian Webb, and this is my daughter.' I showed him my ID. 'I had a phone call from DC Baycote to collect Damian.'

He nodded. 'Just a minute.' He pressed the keypad on his handset. 'The foster carer for Damian is here,' we heard him say. 'Yes, thank you.' Then to me he said, 'Damian is being brought now. Take a seat.'

'Thank you.'

We sat on one of the benches and a few minutes later a door to the right of the reception desk opened and Damian appeared with a plain-clothes officer. He looked relieved to see us and ran over and hugged Paula, while I went to the officer.

'Thank you for coming so quickly,' she said. 'I'm Detective Constable Morgan Baycote. Please check your details are correct and sign to say that you've collected Damian. I've filled in the time.' She passed me the tablet.

'What happened?' I asked as I checked the information.

'We'll be sending a full report to his social worker, but Damian was caught delivering drugs to a third party and collecting money from them.'

I looked up, shocked.

'We've been watching the dealer for some time,' she said. 'He's in police custody.'

'Is that Troy, Damian's mother's boyfriend?' I asked as I handed back the tablet.

'Yes. We've suspected him of dealing on the estate for a while, using young people to deliver the drugs, but now he's been caught red-handed. I understand he bought Damian a new bike?'

'That's correct.'

'It's here, together with the phone Troy bought him.'

'So it was a real phone?' I asked.

She looked puzzled.

'When Damian told us Troy had bought him a phone we thought it might be a toy one.'

'Oh, no, it's real enough. Troy had a number of burner phones that he gave to the kids on the estate for dealing. Some of the older lads are still here being questioned, so I need to go. You'll be able to collect Damian's bike once forensics have finished with it. We'll contact you. Did Damian ever come back with money?'

'Not that I'm aware of, but Troy bought him that bike.'

'Yes. All the lads seem to have been given a bike or money. Again, thanks for coming in so quickly.'

She was clearly in a hurry, but I said, 'Just one thing – what about Rachel? Damian's mother. How is she? She has special needs.'

'We're aware of that. She's at home; an officer is with her now and waiting for an appropriate adult before she's interviewed.' An appropriate adult is assigned to a minor or vulnerable adult when they are questioned by the police to safeguard their interests and rights and make sure they are fairly treated.

'I see. Was Rachel involved?'

'We don't know yet.'

I thanked her and we left the building.

* * *

Damian was very quiet in the car going home, clearly shocked by his ordeal. However, once in the safe and familiar surroundings of our home he began to perk up a little and talk about what had happened.

'There were loads of police cars full of police officers. They jumped out and put handcuffs on Troy. We had to get into the back of the police cars. I thought they were going to lock me in a cell, but I had to sit in a room with a police lady. She got me a drink and asked if I wanted something to eat, but I didn't because I felt sick.'

'I expect that's because you were feeling very anxious,' Paula said.

'No, I wasn't,' Damian replied indignantly, his confidence growing.

We were in the living room and Damian was stroking Sammy.

'Did you know what you were doing was wrong?' I asked him.

'No. I told the police. I just did what Troy or one of the older boys told me to.'

'Which was? What did they tell you to do?'

'To go on my bike and give a package to someone and bring the money back. Troy bought me the bike and phone, so I thought he was nice.'

'Who were the older boys?'

Damian shrugged. 'I don't know. We just did what we were told without making a fuss.'

I made a connection. When I'd collected Damian from his mother's on Sunday and he hadn't wanted to come with me, one of the older lads he was with had said, 'Troy wouldn't be pleased if he knew you were making a fuss.' Then later, when I'd asked Damian what he'd meant, he'd said Troy had told him not to draw attention to himself when he was on his bike. Of course he mustn't make a fuss and draw attention to himself if he was delivering drugs.

'Had you been doing that on Sunday when I collected you?' I asked.

He nodded.

I'd read news articles about children being used by drug dealers; it was sometimes referred to as 'county lines'. Now it had happened to a child I was fostering, and I was outraged. I'd had concerns about Damian being unsupervised on his bike for long periods, but that was to do with keeping him safe, especially near the road. I'd never imagined anything like this: that an adult had befriended a vulnerable single parent and then taken advantage of her son.

'Did Troy ever give you money?' I asked.

'No. I had to get the money and take it to Troy. He always counted it and said if there was any missing I'd be dead meat.'

'What was the phone for?' I asked, half guessing.

'Troy and some of the other boys phoned me to tell me where to go on my bike. When will I get my bike back?'

'I don't know. The police will contact us. Where was your mother while you were out doing this for Troy?' I asked.

'In the flat.'

'Did she know what you were doing?'

'The police asked me that, but I don't know.'

'All right, love. I understand. It's late now and you've had a traumatic day, so let's get you up to bed.' It was after nine o'clock, past his usual bedtime, and he was starting to look very tired.

As we went upstairs Damian asked, 'Is my mum in trouble?'

'I don't know, but try not to worry; she's being looked after,' I replied.

Damian didn't have a bath that night – he was too tired – so he had a good wash instead and brushed his teeth. I saw him into bed and once I was sure he was going to settle for the night I went downstairs and, with a mug of tea to hand, typed up my log notes while the events of the day were still fresh in my mind. I assumed most of what Damian had told me he'd already told the police, but I included it just in case it was needed in future by the social services or the police. I also emailed Korin. Damian was supposed to have been staying with his mother for the rest of the week and I assumed that Korin would contact me the following day.

She did, and Damian's story took another tragic turn.

CHAPTER TWELVE

TOO TRUSTING

D amian slept in late the following morning, but as soon as he was awake he began talking about what had happened to him the day before, reliving the drama step by step. After a good night's sleep, the last of his worry and anxiety had vanished, and it sounded as though he'd starred in a cops-and-robbers television police drama. I had to tell him more than once that what he'd been involved in was very wrong and that Troy would probably go to prison for a long time. I said some of the older boys might too, and that drugs ruined lives. I appreciated Damian was only seven, but he needed to know how wrong Troy's actions were. I knew that his mother must have been affected by all of this, but it wasn't until the afternoon when Korin phoned that I found out the extent.

'We're going to court on Monday for a care order,' she said, 'to bring Liam and Nathan into care.'

'Oh, no,' I blurted. 'Is that really necessary?'

'We think so,' she said, rather sharply.

I knew I'd overstepped the mark. Foster carers are expected to do as they're told, not question the actions of the local authority. It had been an emotive response, for clearly I didn't know all the circumstances.

'Damian will remain in care and we'll need to show the judge we have somewhere to take Liam and Nathan. Can I tell the court you'll take them?'

'I'm sorry, no, I can't manage three young children. I'm a single parent,' I reminded her.

'Your supervising social worker said you were willing to take extra children in an emergency. We don't have any other carers with the space to take a sibling group of three.'

It was true I had a spare bedroom, but that wasn't the issue, as I'd told Joy. It was about meeting the needs of a six-month-old baby, a three-year-old and Damian, not just providing somewhere for them to sleep. If something went wrong, I would be held accountable. I also knew that if the judge granted the care order the children were likely to be with me for most of the year while all the assessments were made and the reports completed.

'I know my limitations and I'm sorry but I can't manage all three,' I said.

'That's very disappointing,' Korin replied curtly.

'I'm sorry.'

'Hmm. If we can't find carers to take all three by Monday, could they come to you for a few days until we do?'

I hesitated.

'It will be better for Nathan and Liam to be with their brother,' she added. Which I appreciated. It was going to be devastating for them to be taken from their mother, and it would be made a little easier if they were with their older brother. Sibling groups who come into care are kept together whenever possible.

'All right, but just for a few days if you can't find another carer.' It was Friday afternoon so the chances of them finding carers who could take all three by Monday were very slim. There is always a shortage of foster carers and the pandemic had made the situation worse. 'Is Damian seeing his mother this weekend?' I asked.

'No, but he can have phone contact.'

'Any particular day or time?'

'Make it tomorrow afternoon. I'll tell Rachel. But you need to put the phone on speaker and supervise the call.'

'I will.' I didn't like supervising phone contact – it seemed intrusive – but sometimes the social worker felt it was necessary. 'How is Rachel?' I asked.

'Bewildered and upset, as you'd expect,' Korin replied. 'I can't believe this was all going on under my nose. That she'd allowed him to take over her flat and deal drugs.'

I thought Korin had sounded brusque and now I realized why. There'd been social services' involvement in Rachel's family for a long time, with regular social worker visits, so it wasn't wonderful that Troy had managed to infiltrate the family and deal drugs from her flat.

'It was kept well hidden,' she added. 'Did you have any suspicion?'

'No. Not that Troy was dealing drugs from her flat.'

'I'll need to speak to Wera. We're in court first thing on Monday so I'll phone you once we're out.'

'All right. If Nathan and Liam are coming to me [which I assumed they would be], can you find out if they have any health issues or allergies, and also what formula Liam has?'

'Will do.'

I felt desperately sorry for Rachel. She now had all weekend to fret and worry, although there was the chance the judge might not grant the order to remove Liam and Nathan. I was hoping that would be the outcome, but I thought it was unlikely. Rachel had been struggling to raise her children for some time, and now she'd failed to protect them, putting them at risk by allowing a drug dealer into their home. There had been no suggestion she was taking drugs, and as far as I knew she hadn't in the past. She wasn't abusive towards her children and didn't wilfully neglect them. She was vulnerable and naive and struggled to cope with a young family. Had she received more support she might not be in this position, but on Troy's instructions she'd cancelled Wera's visits. I thought Rachel must have seemed the perfect victim for Troy: guileless, susceptible and all alone. My heart went out to her as my anger flared towards Troy.

I'd left Damian in the living room playing a game on my tablet while I'd taken the call from Korin. Paula was upstairs working in her bedroom. I'd had to stop Damian from disturbing her a few times during the morning, and I now suggested to him we went to the park.

'You could bring a bike from the shed,' I said.

'I want my own,' he said, pulling a face. 'Is Paula coming?'

'No, love, she's working until five-thirty. But she has the weekend off. If you don't want to bring the bike, you could take the skateboard.' He'd been practising skate-boarding on the garden path.

He liked this idea better, so we fetched the skateboard from the shed, then put on our shoes and jackets and walked to the park. I didn't interrupt Paula to tell her we were going out so I texted from the park to say where we were and that we'd be back in a couple of hours, in case she wondered.

As I sat on the park bench watching Damian skateboard I made a list on my phone of what I needed to do over the weekend to prepare for Nathan and Liam's arrival. If the care order was granted on Monday morning, they were likely to be with me in the afternoon. It didn't matter that it was short term, just for a few days – there was still a lot to do, especially in connection with baby Liam. I needed to make up the spare bed and the cot, buy nappies, wipes, new feeding bottles and formula – once Korin let me know what he was used to. Clothes? Hopefully they would come with some; if not, I should have some that would fit him in my spares. The two car seats and the stroller I needed were in the loft, so those would have to come down. There was a highchair up there too, if needed. Was Liam using one at home? I wondered. I'd only ever seen him in his mother's arms.

When you think of all the months of preparation expectant parents have for the arrival of their baby, it seems extraordinary that foster carers often have just a few days, sometimes only hours. It was a daunting prospect, and I knew Nathan and Liam would be upset at having to leave their mother and the only home they'd known. True, their home wasn't perfect, but it was still home. And, as well as looking after them, I would need to keep them reasonably quiet so Paula could work. I had yet to tell her they might be coming.

A boy about Damian's age came over and enviously watched him skateboarding for a few minutes, then asked if he could have a go.

'Good boy,' I told Damian as he passed him the skate-board.

They took turns. The boy's mother was a little way off, pushing a younger child on a swing. She kept glancing over to check on her son, so I waved to say he was all right and I was keeping an eye on him. When her daughter finished on the play equipment they came over and she thanked me.

'Say thank you for sharing the skateboard,' she told her son, which he did.

'You're welcome,' Damian replied. 'Any time.'

It was nearly 4.30 when we returned home. I made Damian a drink and a snack. He wanted to watch television, so I settled him in the living room with a children's programme while I went upstairs to start getting the spare bedroom ready. I gathered together some bedding, made up the single bed that Nathan would be using and added a few soft toys. His room was next to Damian's. Over the weekend, with Paula's help, I would set up the cot in my bedroom for Liam. I had the bedding ready.

Satisfied that I'd at least made a start, I returned downstairs and checked on Damian, who was still engrossed in the television.

'I'll be in the kitchen making dinner if you need me,' I told him.

He nodded without taking his eyes from the screen.

Once dinner was in the oven, I checked my emails. There was nothing from Korin. A little after five-thirty Paula came down, having finished work for the week. I told her of Korin's phone call and what I'd agreed to.

'Don't worry, I'll keep the little ones quiet so you can work, and Damian will be at school,' I added.

'It's a lot for you,' she said, concerned.

'It's only for a few days while they find a carer who can take all three of them.'

'So that means Damian will be leaving us?' she said regretfully.

'He was always going to leave us at some point, love,' I reminded her. 'The care plan was for him to return home.'

'I know, and that would have seemed right. But he won't be going home. He'll be going to another carer he doesn't know.'

'It can't be helped,' I said, with a stab of guilt. 'I can't offer to have all three of them indefinitely. It's not certain yet that they will come, so don't say anything to Damian yet.'

'I won't.'

Damian appeared in the kitchen, having heard Paula's voice.

'Are you finished up there?' he asked her.

'Yes. Let's have dinner and then we can play.'

'I'll show you how good I am on the skateboard,' he said proudly.

Damian was hungry after all the exercise of the afternoon in the park. As I watched him eat I thought how far he'd come. Being in care had helped him towards a better relationship with food, as well as in other areas. I'd given him a routine so he knew what was expected of him, put in place boundaries, supported him in his learning, and praised and encouraged him. All of which I had hoped he'd take home with him to his mother.

It was a mild evening and Damian wanted to demonstrate his skateboarding skills to Paula, so after dinner they went into the garden while I cleared away the dishes. I checked my emails again and there was still nothing from Korin so I sent an email that she would probably pick up on Monday morning, reminding her to let me know if Liam and Nathan had any allergies or medical needs, and what formula milk Liam was used to. If they were definitely coming to me then I would receive their Essential Information Forms, which should tell me more, but for now I just needed the basics. I already had Damian's from when he'd first arrived, which included his mother's contact details.

I joined Paula and Damian in the garden until it was time for his bath. Once he was settled in bed, Paula helped me set up the cot in my bedroom. I was still secretly hoping it wouldn't be needed and the boys could stay with their mother. Later, Paula spent some time in her room relaxing while I phoned Lucy to see how she was. She'd been to work but had been sick a number of times during the day and was now having something to eat. She'd made an appointment with her doctor to start the antenatal care. I didn't tell her about Liam and Nathan. She had enough on her mind. I would do so if they arrived. I also texted Tash: *Thinking of you. Any news? Phone if you want to talk.*

She texted back: *Nothing. LADO is involved but that's all we know. Impossible to get on with our lives with this hanging over us!*

LADO is short for Local Authority Designated Officer. They are appointed when there are concerns about an adult working with children or young people. They liaise with police and other agencies and monitor the progress of cases to ensure that they are dealt with as quickly and fairly as possible. I had no idea of the time scale as, thankfully, I'd never been in Tash's position, but it seemed to be going on for a long time.

On Saturday morning I took Damian shopping with me, leaving Paula to have a lie-in.

'Are you expecting a baby?' he asked when he saw me buying nappies and bottles.

I couldn't lie. 'There's a chance we may be looking after Liam and Nathan for a few days next week,' I said.

'Why?'

'Because Korin may want us to.' Which he accepted.

'When am I phoning Mum?' he asked a short while later.

'This afternoon.'

Paula was up when we returned home and we all had lunch together. A little after one o'clock I decided to make the call to Rachel. Korin hadn't specified a time for the phone contact, just Saturday afternoon, and I assumed Rachel would be waiting to hear from Damian.

When I have to initiate phone contact for a young child I usually make the call away from them so they aren't disappointed if their parent doesn't answer. If they don't pick up, I try again later when hopefully they will, or I leave a message to say I've called and will try again in half an hour, or similar.

Damian was in the living room playing with toy cars and play people on the floor. It was now June and the patio doors were open on another mild day. Paula was sitting on the bench on the patio reading a book on her Kindle. I slipped from the living room to make the call. I was feeling slightly anxious, wondering how Rachel was coping. I was phoning a mother who faced the prospect of losing all her children. She took a while to answer, then said a tentative, 'Hello?' in her characteristically small voice.

'Rachel, it's Cathy, Damian's carer.'

'Yes?'

'Korin asked me to call you this afternoon so you could speak to Damian.'

'That was nice of her. I was hoping to see him this weekend.'

My stomach tightened. 'Didn't Korin explain Damian wouldn't be coming?'

'Oh, yes, she did. Sorry. I didn't sleep well. I've been up all night with the baby, worried about what's going to happen to him. Has Korin told you what Troy did? About the drugs?'

'Yes, she did. I am sorry. How are you?'

'If I'm honest, Cathy, not good really. I had to talk to the police for a long time. I told them everything I know about Troy. I said he was nice to us and I trusted him and thought he was my friend. But he wasn't, was he? I could have my children taken away because of him.' Her voice trembled and I could have wept.

'Is there anything I can do?' I asked.

'Korin said Nathan and Liam may have to come to you if the judge says it's better for them. I will be able to see them every day, won't I?'

Undoubtedly Rachel would have contact, but it was likely to be supervised, and I wasn't sure it would be every day. Family Centres where supervised contact was held had only recently reopened. During lockdown, most contact had been online.

'If the judge makes a care order, he is likely to include the contact arrangements,' I said.

'I think Korin said that too,' Rachel replied, seemingly lost in the complexity of it all.

'Have you got someone there to help you?' I asked.

'My neighbours have been nice since the police have been here. They keep popping in.'

'Good.'

It would have made sense for me to have taken the opportunity to ask Rachel if Liam and Nathan had any medical conditions or allergies, which formula milk Liam was used to, about the boys' routines, and so on, but I didn't have the heart. Rachel sounded so fragile, and I clung to the hope that the court order wouldn't be granted to bring the boys into care and that an alternative could be found.

'Is Damian behaving himself?' Rachel asked.

'Yes, he's fine.'

'You've been very good for him,' she said self-effacingly. 'I know he's done well with you. Korin said how much better he was doing now he was living with you.'

I didn't know the context in which this had been said – possibly it wasn't as insensitive as it now sounded.

'I only have Damian to look after, and I have a lot of experience raising children, as well as having the benefit of foster-carer training,' I said. 'You're the boys' mother and they love you.'

'Thank you. That is kind.' Her voice faltered. 'Korin said I shouldn't have stopped Wera coming because she was helping me. I can see that now. I needed her help. I told Korin she can help me again if they let me keep my children. It was wrong of me not to let her in, but Troy said she was nosey and interfering, and she and Korin were against me, and to send her away.'

'It suited him not to have anyone going into your home, in case they suspected what he was doing. You used to invite me in, but that stopped when he was there.'

'I am sorry. I've made a lot of mistakes, Cathy. I trust people. I believe what they say. I'll try not to believe them in the future.'

I thought what a sad indictment of our society it was that we had to be cautious and distrustful of others to protect ourselves, but some wariness of those we don't know is necessary.

'I think it depends on the situation and who the other person is,' I said. But how did you teach someone as uncomplicated as Rachel to spot a snake in the grass?

'Shall I put Damian on the phone now?' I asked.

'Yes, please.'

'You know it will be on speaker so I will hear what you say?'

'Korin told me. I guess she doesn't trust me. But I trust you, Cathy.'

I swallowed my emotion. 'Good. I'll put him on.'

Damian and his mother spoke for about ten minutes. Their conversation was awkward, as it often is when a young child uses the phone. Rachel asked Damian what he'd been doing and I prompted him when he couldn't remember. He asked her if he would be going home next weekend and she said she didn't know. Neither of them mentioned Troy, but Damian asked when he would have his bike back and Rachel said to ask me.

'I'm waiting to be told,' I said, so they both heard.

Presently, we heard baby Liam crying in the background. 'You need to go,' Damian told his mother, and then said goodbye. He handed me the phone.

'Bye, Rachel,' I said. 'Good luck on Monday. I shall be thinking of you.'

'Thank you, Cathy. I'm going to need all the luck I can get.'

CHAPTER THIRTEEN

THE COURT DECIDES

On Sunday, while I was out with Damian, I popped into the chemist and bought baby formula in case Korin didn't let me know which brand Liam was used to. After lunch I spent some time checking the house was ready for a baby and three-year-old while still hoping it wouldn't be needed. Damian had school the next day so before he went to bed I took his uniform from the wardrobe and set it out ready. I put his PE bag containing his freshly laundered games kit with his schoolbag in the hall for the following morning.

The news on the television that evening warned that we could be in the early stages of a third wave of coronavirus. That I didn't want to hear! There was some discussion about postponing the lifting of the final restrictions that were supposed to happen later in the month, although it was felt this was unlikely to be necessary. Most of those falling ill hadn't been vaccinated and we were again urged to 'get jabbed'. There was always a close-up of someone receiving a jab and as usual I looked away. I couldn't watch the needle going into my own arm and it wasn't any different with someone else, although it never hurt. Like many millions of others, I was immensely grateful to the doctors and nurses in our wonderful health service for all they were doing. Many had worked extra shifts since the start of the pandemic and were exhausted, yet they, like other front-line workers, carried on for the good of us all. It was very humbling.

Damian had no idea his mother was in court on Monday morning, so he happily went to school, pleased to see his friends and Mrs Halas again. She was pleased to see him and asked him if he'd had a nice half-term holiday. I looked at him wondering what he would say.

'Yes, thank you, Mrs Halas,' he replied.

'So you're ready to work hard again?'

'Not sure about that,' he said, in his cheeky way.

She laughed. I wished him a good day and came away. If he told Mrs Halas about Troy and the drugs, and being taken to the police station, which I thought he might, I'd have to explain.

I was assuming that the social services were applying for an Interim Care Order (ICO) or an Emergency Protection Order (EPC). These hearings don't usually take long, unlike the final court hearing, which can last a week or longer, at the end of which the judge makes a decision on where the child or children will live permanently. If the judge granted the social services a care order today it would be so the children could be removed to a place of safety – namely into care. It gave the Local Authority parental rights and had to be renewed every few weeks.

I felt I was as prepared as I could be for Liam and Nathan's arrival, but as I waited for news I couldn't settle to anything. Paula was in her bedroom working while I roamed the house and garden, moving from one displacement activity to another, my mobile always close at hand. I checked my emails regularly. There'd been nothing from Korin or Joy.

Paula broke for lunch at 12.30 and we had a sandwich together. She knew I was waiting for news. She took her usual half-an-hour break and then returned to her bedroom. An hour later my phone rang and it was Korin.

'We've just come out of court,' she said hurriedly. 'We've been granted the care order.' My heart fell. 'We're going to collect Liam and Nathan now,' she continued. 'They're with a neighbour of Rachel's. She'll pack a bag for them, then we'll bring them straight to you.'

'You know I'm out between three and four o'clock collecting Damian from school?' I checked.

'Noted. I'll email the Essential Information Forms as soon as I can.' Korin sounded as though she was walking as she spoke.

'Do you want me to tell Damian his brothers are coming when I collect him from school?'

'Probably best, as I won't have a chance to talk to him beforehand. I'll answer his questions when I arrive.'

'OK. Was Rachel in court?'

'Yes.'

'How was she?'

'Distressed, but she had a neighbour with her.'

Thank goodness she had the support of her neighbours, I thought. They seemed to have really rallied round.

'I'll see you later then,' Korin said, in a rush. 'The judge was pleased the boys weren't being separated.'

'You know this arrangement is only temporary?' I reminded her, with another stab of guilt.

'Yes, fine. See you later.' She said a quick goodbye.

I sat on the sofa, my phone in my hand, and stared glumly across the room to the sunny day outside. Usually when a new child or children are on their way the adrenalin kicks in. I'm not excited – that's the wrong word; a mother has lost her child – but I'm animated and ready to meet the new challenge. I go through a mental checklist, making sure I have everything to hand to meet their needs. I hope the child will like me and I want them to feel safe and cherished as I help them towards a better future, whatever that might be.

Now all I felt was abject disappointment and despair.

Rachel, who I'd got to know, was about to lose her children. She'd put Damian in care voluntarily with the aim of him returning when she could manage all three boys. Now there was a court order to remove the other two. Of course her children needed to be kept safe, but was it really necessary to remove them? Was there no acceptable alternative? Clearly the judge had thought not or they wouldn't have made the care order, and they had far more information than I did. Poor Rachel. My heart clenched. Would she ever get her children back? It was impossible to know at this stage, but I thought the odds were stacked against her, given her past.

Eventually I forced myself out of my gloom and concentrated on the task ahead of me. It would be after 4 p.m. when little Nathan and Liam arrived and the social workers were likely to stay with me for about an hour, so I'd prepare dinner now, then reheat it after they'd left. I went into the kitchen and put together a pasta bake. Most children like pasta and it's a favourite of Damian's. I then went upstairs to check Nathan's bedroom and the cot in my bedroom. I had all the nappy-changing equipment in there too.

I knocked on Paula's bedroom door and waited for her to call 'Come in' before I opened it.

'I'm leaving now to collect Damian from school,' I said. 'Korin phoned. They have the court order, so they'll bring Nathan and Liam here after four o'clock.'

Paula looked at me, concerned. 'Shall I see if I can take some time off work so I can help?'

'No, love. You've only just returned to work. I just thought you should know. I'll see you at dinner.'

'All right,' she said, and returned her attention to the laptop screen. I quietly closed her bedroom door.

Thoughts of Rachel ran through my head as I drove to Damian's school. I could picture her in court, confused by the complexities of the legal process, intimidated by the grandness of the courtroom and lost in the formality of the proceedings. I could see her breaking down in tears when she was told of the decision, then being led from the courtroom and comforted by her neighbour. Was she at home now packing a bag of the boys' belongings? It's always best for a child going into care if they can have some of their own clothes and toys. The familiarity is comforting and helps them settle into their foster home, but not all parents can do this. Some are too angry to cooperate, and some find it too painful, which I fully understand. There is a finality in packing, which forces an acknowledgement that the child has gone. How was Rachel coping?

I parked in the side road by Damian's school and

reined in my thoughts. Shortly I would need to tell him what was happening.

I put on my face mask and entered the playground where I stood in my usual place. At the end of school Mrs Halas came out with Damian at her side. I went over.

'Hi, Cathy. It took him a while to settle into work after the half-term break. Some of the other children were the same. Hopefully he'll be better tomorrow.' I could read the subtext – Damian had been playing up.

'Oh dear,' I said, looking pointedly at him.

'I've got a lot on my mind,' he said, scratching his head.

'Is it true he was taken to the police station?' Mrs Halas asked me.

I nodded.

'There! I told you,' Damian exclaimed.

'Don't be rude,' I said to him.

'Well, I did tell her!' he replied, with attitude. 'And I said Troy was arrested because he made me and other kids sell drugs.'

'That's about it,' I said to Mrs Halas.

She looked shocked. Perhaps she'd thought Damian had made it up or exaggerated and embellished the story, which he had been known to do sometimes. But I didn't have time to discuss it then. Korin was arriving.

'I'm sorry. We need to go,' I said to her. 'I've got his social worker coming soon.'

'Yes, of course. I won't keep you. I've changed his reading book, and he has some numeracy homework in his schoolbag. Have a good evening.'

'Thank you.'

'You have a good evening!' Damian shouted as we left, which sounded cheeky, but I let it go. I had more pressing matters on my mind. I needed to tell him what was happening.

'Damian,' I began as we crossed the playground.

'That's my name!' he interjected before I could get any further. I could tell he was in one of those moods, but again I ignored it.

'When we get home Korin will be coming,' I continued. 'I'm not sure what time but –'

'I know; you told Mrs Halas,' he interrupted again.

'Damian, will you just listen, please? This is important. Korin will be bringing Liam and Nathan with her.'

'My brothers?'

'Yes. Do you remember I said they may be coming to live with us for a while?'

'Is Mum coming too?'

'No, love. I shall be looking after them as I do you – as your foster carer.'

'Why?' he asked as we left the playground.

'Korin will explain more but she felt it was best to keep them safe. A judge agreed.'

'Does Mum know?'

'Yes.' I opened the car door and we got in. I turned in my seat to face him. 'You'll see your mother again before long. Korin will give us the details.'

'When will we go home?'

'I don't know, love. But I'm sure your brothers will be very pleased to see you. You can help me look after them if you wish,' I added, as I thought it might help if he was involved.

'I'm not changing any more nappies. Yuck,' he replied, pulling a face. 'You can do that.'

'I will, and I wouldn't ask you to change nappies. I was thinking more that you could cuddle them and do as I ask you first time. That would be a big help. It's a lot, looking after three children.'

'That's what Mum used to say.' His voice dropped. 'I think I should have helped her more.'

'You did plenty, Damian, more than most children your age do. Let's go home so we're ready for when they arrive.'

Damian fell silent as I drove. When I glanced at him in the rear-view mirror he always looked deep in thought – processing what I'd told him, I guessed.

I parked on the drive and then let us into the house, reminding Damian that Paula was upstairs working and shouldn't be disturbed. I made him a drink and a snack to see him through to dinnertime, then he wanted to watch some television, which he sometimes did after school. We found a programme he liked, and I was about to check my emails when my phone rang. I stepped outside the living room to take the call. It was Joy.

'Has Korin phoned you?' she asked. 'They've been in court today.'

'Yes, I know. I'm expecting her soon with Liam and Nathan.'

'OK. I've had one of those days. I'm only just catching up. Have you got everything you need?'

I was about to say 'I think so' when the doorbell rang, so I changed it to, 'I hope so. It sounds as though they're here.'

'Good luck – although you're so experienced, I don't suppose you need luck.'

We said goodbye and I went to answer the door feeling a little piqued by the assumption that I'd manage no matter what.

I took a face mask from where I kept some on the hall stand and put it on before opening the door. Korin and a colleague stood there, both wearing disposable face masks. Korin was holding Nathan's hand; he was looking sad and confused. Her colleague was carrying Liam. Already close to tears, he took one look at me and wailed.

'He can't be hungry, he's just been fed,' Korin's colleague said as they came in.

Damian heard his brother and, leaving the television, ran down the hall.

'Liam! Nathan!' he cried excitedly, rushing towards them. He hugged Nathan so enthusiastically it made Nathan stagger and nearly fall.

'Be careful, love,' I said. 'He's much smaller than you.'

'Do you want to watch television?' Damian asked him enthusiastically. Then, grabbing his arm, he began dragging him down the hall towards the living room. I quickly intervened.

'Careful, love,' I said again, stopping him. Nathan looked at me, bewildered and a little frightened. He'd had so many changes that day.

The social workers followed me into the living room where I picked up the remote control to turn off the television.

'No!' Damian shouted over the noise of Liam crying. 'Nathan and me are going to watch it.'

'It might be easier to leave it on low,' Korin said.

I lowered the volume as the social workers sat on the sofa where Damian had been sitting. 'Me and Nathan are sitting there,' he told them rudely. They were about to move.

'You can sit here,' I said to Damian and Nathan, and put the two children's stools in front of the television. They sat on them.

'I'm Olga,' Korin's colleague said. 'And this is Liam.'

'Yes, I used to see Damian's brothers when I took him home for the weekend.'

Liam was now sucking on a dummy that Olga must have brought with them.

'We've got a bag of their belongings in the car,' Korin told me. 'Don't let us leave without giving it to you. I've emailed the Placement Forms and Joy is completing the Initial Placement Agreement. Can you print out the last page, sign it and scan it back, please?'

I nodded.

They kept their masks on as they spoke, although I was sitting on the opposite side of the room. I kept mine on too. I'd left the patio doors open a little so there was plenty of fresh air.

'Rachel said to tell you none of the boys has a medical condition or allergy as far as she knows. She's sent the formula milk that Liam uses. It's in my car.'

'That was good of her,' I said.

'I'm not sure how much is there, but it should see you through tonight. There's a couple of nappies too, but Rachel said she's run out of baby wipes and nappy bags.'

'I've got plenty of those. How is Rachel?'

'A neighbour is with her,' Korin replied.

Liam was sitting on Olga's lap sucking the dummy and looking at me warily. I smiled, but of course he couldn't see it under my mask. I would take it off once the social workers had left. Damian was holding Nathan's hand as they sat side by side watching the television, apparently oblivious to what we were saying.

'I'll set up supervised contact at the Family Centre for tomorrow,' Korin said. 'I'll try to make it after school if possible. You can take and collect them?'

'Yes.' It was usual for the foster carer to do this.

'Any questions?' she asked me.

'Is Liam used to the dummy?' I asked. I hadn't seen it before and it was useful to know.

'I assume so,' Olga said. 'Rachel gave it to us.'

'And his feeding routine? Do you know about that?'

They looked at each other. 'I'm not sure he has one,' Korin replied. 'I'll ask Rachel.' She took a notepad and pen from her bag and wrote. 'Anything else?'

'Has Rachel started to wean Liam?'

'I'll check.' She made another note and looked at me. 'Anything else?'

'The boys' likes and dislikes and anything else Rachel can tell me that might help them settle in would be good. I usually try to follow the parent's routine when a child first comes into care.'

Korin nodded and wrote again, then said, 'You told Damian his brothers are staying?'

'Yes, briefly.'

'Damian,' Korin said, to get his attention. He turned from the television to look at her. 'Do you understand why your brothers are here?'

'Yes,' he said, eager to continue watching the programme.

'Do you have any questions you want to ask me?'

He shook his head and returned to the programme.

Korin took a laptop from her bag and went through a few formalities that were usual when placing a child. She told me where I could find a copy of the care plan online – most of the forms in fostering were digital now and accessed through the council's online portal.

'I'll have a look around the house and then we'll leave you to it,' Korin said, putting away her laptop. She stood and I stood too.

'I'm just going to show Korin around the house,' I told Damian and Nathan, in case they wondered where I'd gone.

Damian nodded without taking his eyes from the screen and Nathan glanced at me, slightly puzzled. I smiled. 'I'll see you in a moment, love.'

Leaving Olga in the living room with the boys, I showed Korin the kitchen-diner, then the front room. Upstairs I showed her all the rooms except for Paula's.

'I won't disturb my daughter; she's working in there,' I said.

'Good luck with that, with all this going on,' Korin said. 'I tried it during lockdown with mine and it was near impossible.' Which didn't really bolster my confidence at all.

As we went downstairs we heard Liam start to cry from the living room. 'I'll get their bags and then we can be off!' she called down the hall to Olga. I felt like telling her to be quiet as Paula was working.

I went outside with Korin to help with the bags, but it wasn't really necessary. There was one dustbin liner containing the boys' clothes and a carrier bag with the formula milk and some bottles. I peered inside the carrier bag as I brought it into the hall and was relieved to see it was the same brand of formula I'd bought. Liam was crying more loudly now and Olga came down the hall with him in her arms.

'All yours,' she said, passing him to me.

Startled by the change, Liam briefly paused from crying to look at me, then continued even more loudly, his little cheeks red and tears springing from his eyes.

'It's all right, love,' I soothed, and gently rocked him.

'I can't hear the television!' Damian shouted from the living room.

Olga rolled her eyes.

'They'll settle once we've gone,' Korin said, and opened the front door. 'I'll phone you about the questions you had for Rachel and the time of contact tomorrow. Also, I'll need to arrange a review before the end of the month – it will probably still be virtual.'

As they disappeared down the front path I knew the temporary nature of me fostering all three boys was disappearing. They were safe now they were in care and Korin would have other, more pressing matters to address. Perhaps I could successfully manage all three, I thought, and closed the front door.

CHAPTER FOURTEEN

THANKS TO PAULA

With Liam still wailing in my arms and refusing to be comforted, I quickly checked on Nathan and Damian in the living room.

'Good boys,' I said. 'I'll be in the kitchen.' Although that would be obvious from the noise Liam was making.

He was sucking ferociously on his dummy so I thought he might be hungry. I sat him in the bouncing cradle so he could see me as I quickly made up a bottle of milk, using the formula and bottles I'd bought. I'd go through the bags Rachel had sent later when I had the chance. Right now I just needed to get Liam more comfortable.

Once the bottle was ready, I gently lifted him from the bouncing cradle and carried him to a chair at the table where I laid him in the crook of my arm. He latched onto the teat immediately and sucked ravenously. He was definitely hungry. He paused for a breath two-thirds of the way through. I rubbed his back and then he finished the rest. As he spat out the teat of the empty bottle he looked at me with a mixture of relief and bewilderment. How to explain to a six-month-old baby that I was his foster carer who would be looking after him instead of his mother? You can't. But by meeting his needs, answering his cries, and making him feel warm and secure, I could gradually help him be less anxious as his confidence in me grew.

Now Liam was no longer hungry, he allowed me to settle him into the bouncing cradle without crying so that I could put the pasta bake I'd previously made into the oven. I then picked him up again and, holding him close so he could feel the warmth of my body, I went into the living room.

'I'm going upstairs to change Liam's nappy,' I told the boys. 'Nathan, do you need the toilet?'

He didn't reply.

'Nathan, love, do you need to do a wee?'

'He's still in nappies,' Damian said, which I'd forgotten.

I hoped I had some nappies Nathan's size; I usually kept a few of most sizes in case a child arrived as an emergency. I began a mental list of items I needed to buy the next day.

'Nathan, come upstairs with me, love, and I'll see if you need a clean nappy.'

He looked at me, frowned, then shook his head.

'Come on, love. Then you can watch some more television.'

'I can't hear the television,' Damian moaned. 'You keep talking.'

'Now, love, please,' I said to Nathan.

'Go on,' Damian told him.

Nathan stood and came over. I thought Damian was going to be a big help.

'Good boy. It won't take us long,' I told Nathan, and we went down the hall. I opened the safety gate I'd put at the foot of the stairs and we went up.

All I knew of Nathan was his age, what I'd seen of him at his mother's and that it had been suggested he was showing signs of developmental delay – that he wasn't reaching the milestones the average child his age would be expected to. I had no idea what assessment, if any, had been done; hopefully there would be more information in the forms Korin sent. A child of three usually uses about two hundred words and many can form short sentences of three or four words. I didn't think Nathan had said anything since he'd arrived, but that could have been due to all the upheaval of being removed from home. Delayed development can also affect a child's fine and gross motor skills; for example, their ability to throw a ball, jump, hop, ride a tricycle, hold a crayon, wash their hands or even walk up and down stairs. Nathan needed help getting up the stairs, but then he wasn't used to stairs as he lived in a flat.

I took the boys into my bedroom, where I kept spares, and found half a packet of nappies that would fit Nathan – enough to get us through the night. I placed Liam in the middle of my bed while I changed Nathan's nappy. It was sopping.

'Good boy,' I said as I finished, and helped him off the bed. 'Just wait there while I change Liam's nappy.'

Nathan took no notice; he ran out of my bedroom and around the landing. Although there was a safety gate at the top of the stairs, it wasn't wise to leave him unattended and I didn't want him disturbing Paula. Taking Liam with me, I found Nathan in Damian's bedroom and brought him back. I closed my bedroom door and gave him a bag of soft toys to look through (also from my spares), telling him he could choose one if he wished.

This allowed me enough time to change Liam's nappy. I put both the soiled nappies and the wipes into a bag, ready to take downstairs and put in the dustbin. Before I left my bedroom my mobile, which was tucked into my pocket, rang. It was Olga. I closed my bedroom door again. Nathan had finished with the soft toys and was now exploring my room; I kept an eye on him as I held Liam and listened to what Olga was telling me.

'We've spoken to Rachel and she says Liam has his dummy if he cries. She hasn't started to wean him, and he has a bottle about every three to four hours, day and night. I asked her about the boys' routine. She doesn't have one so do what you feel is right. Nathan eats anything but will play up and copy Damian, who can be very fussy.'

'Yes, although his eating has improved. Does Nathan have any likes or dislikes?'

'I don't think so. Rachel didn't say. Contact is at the Family Centre tomorrow, four o'clock to five-thirty. Can you tell the boys?'

'Yes.'

'Rachel said Nathan's security blanket is in the bag. He has it at night.'

'Thank you.' That was useful. Security blankets or a favourite toy can be invaluable in settling a child into a new home.

Olga wished me a nice evening, and I took the boys downstairs. Opening and closing the safety gates with Liam in my arms and Nathan holding onto my leg was a bit of an exercise, but necessary. Nathan was fast but not that steady on his feet, and at his age wouldn't spot danger. I saw him into the living room where he sat beside Damian to watch television, and I returned down the hall to the dustbin liner Rachel had sent. I rummaged through it until I found the security blanket – although it was not so much a blanket, more a grubby piece of blue muslin cloth frayed at the edges from sucking. With Liam still in my arms, I went upstairs and into Nathan's room where I placed the cloth on his bed ready for later. As I came out Paula's bedroom door opened.

'Sorry, love. I've disturbed you.'

'No, you haven't,' she said. 'It's after five-thirty. I've finished for today.'

'Oh, I didn't realize the time.'

'You must be Liam,' Paula said and stretched out her arms to take him. But she was another new face and his bottom lip trembled as he clung to me, close to tears. 'What can I do to help, Mum?' she asked instead.

To say that Paula was a big help that evening is an understatement. I doubt I could have managed without her. The first few days after a new child arrives are always a bit of a challenge for everyone. Then, by the end of the week we're in a routine, the children know me and I know them, the house is familiar and they are much happier and more relaxed. But on that first night everything is strange for them.

Any thoughts I'd entertained of Damian being a 'big help' with Nathan quickly vanished. No longer the only child in the house, he began vying for attention and his behaviour regressed to when he'd first arrived. He took every opportunity to play up, wouldn't stop when I told him not to do something and tormented the cat. I told him off as Sammy fled for cover.

Added to this, Liam cried if I put him down and Nathan began to sob, 'I want Mummy.'

Damian refused to let Nathan sit next to him again to watch television and at one point even pushed him off the stool. I took Damian aside and told him he needed to stop it or there would be no more television.

'Don't care,' he retorted.

I'm not sure how, but eventually Paula and I managed to get dinner on the table. I sat with Liam on my lap and gave him a bottle while trying to feed myself. Paula helped Nathan, who was struggling to use a spoon. Damian played with his food, and then started eating the pasta bake with his fingers.

'You know how to use a fork,' I reminded him lightly.

'No, I don't,' he replied.

After we'd finished eating we left the clearing up for later and went into the living room where Paula tried to get Nathan interested in the toys, and I sat with Liam on my lap.

'I want the television on,' Damian demanded.

'You can watch some more when you've done your schoolwork,' I said. He'd been watching it more or less non-stop since we'd arrived home. Usually we had his homework done by now.

'I'm not doing it!' he shouted.

'I want Mummy,' Nathan began to sob again.

He was rubbing his eyes and I thought he must be worn out after the day he'd had.

'If you could help Damian with his schoolwork, I'll take Liam and Nathan up for a bath and then get them into bed,' I said to Paula.

'I'm not doing my schoolwork,' Damian retaliated.

'Then there won't be any more television,' I reminded him.

'Come on,' Paula encouraged. 'Show me. I wonder if I know how to do it.'

I fetched Damian's schoolbag from where he'd left it in the hall and took it into the living room. He folded his arms crossly, but then, as Paula opened the bag, he went to sit beside her.

'Thanks, love,' I said to her, and left the room with Liam and Nathan while the going was good.

I stopped at the bag Rachel had sent to see if there was any sleepwear in it for the boys. There were no pyjamas for Nathan, but I found a sleep suit that I assumed Rachel used for Liam.

With Liam in my arms and Nathan holding onto my leg, I opened the safety gate and we went upstairs and into my bedroom. I found pyjamas in my spares that would fit Nathan, then gathered towels and so forth and took the boys into the bathroom, where I ran a bath. I undressed Nathan first and sat him in the warm water with some toys, then did the same with Liam, steadying him with my hand as I washed him. The boys weren't in the mood to enjoy their bath as they hopefully would in the days to come, so once I'd washed them both I took Liam out first, dried him, and put him in a clean nappy and the sleep suit. I then helped Nathan out and got him dressed.

'Damian?' he asked.

'He's downstairs, love.'

It was quiet downstairs, so I hoped Damian was cooperating with Paula. I'd found before that sometimes a child related to Paula better, regarding her as an older sister, rather than to me, the carer who had usurped their parent's position.

I'd already set out a toothbrush for Nathan and I brushed his teeth. He yawned and rubbed his eyes.

'Mummy?' he asked hopefully.

'You'll see her tomorrow,' I reassured him with a smile.

He looked very tired and close to tears again. I thought he'd feel a bit better after a good night's sleep. Leaving the bathroom with Liam in my arms, I showed Nathan where I slept, and then Damian's room, before I took him to his bedroom. As soon as he saw the security cloth he picked it up and pressed it to his face. The smell, texture and taste would be a comforting reminder of home.

I helped Nathan climb into bed and then sat on the edge, gently rocking Liam.

'Call me if you need me in the night,' I told Nathan. 'I'll leave your bedroom door open a little and the landing light stays on.'

His little brow furrowed.

'It's OK, love. I'm going to look after you and you'll see Mummy tomorrow.'

Exhausted, he turned onto his side and began sucking the cloth. Very quickly his eyes closed and he was asleep.

I quietly left the room with Liam asleep in my arms. I had no idea what time Rachel put Liam to bed, so I decided to try him now. I'd give him a bottle when he woke later, for it was unlikely he'd sleep through the night. I took him into my room, gently laid him in the cot and then quietly closed the curtains. His eyes flickered open for a second, but he went back to sleep. Relieved, I crept out. It was 7.30. Damian's bedtime. Indeed, he usually had his bath around 7 p.m.

Downstairs, I was pleased to find that, with Paula's help, Damian had completed his schoolwork. She was now reading him a bedtime story.

'Well done,' I said to them both. I sat in an armchair and waited until she'd finished reading. 'It's time for your bath now, love,' I told Damian. 'And we need to be quiet so we don't wake Nathan or Liam.'

He gave Paula a big kiss on the cheek, which was nice, and then ran down the hall. Before I could stop him, he was over the safety gate and upstairs into Nathan's bedroom, where he startled him awake.

'That was naughty,' I told him as I arrived. 'I asked you to be quiet. You've lost ten minutes from your television time tomorrow.'

'Don't care,' he answered back.

Paula appeared and took Damian to run his bath while I settled Nathan. Fortunately, he was still very tired and returned to sleep quite quickly. I then took over from Paula in the bathroom and she went downstairs. As Damian sat in the bath I washed his back and he did the rest.

'Good boy,' I told him as he clambered out.

'Have I earnt back my television time?' he asked.

'We'll see how nicely you get into bed,' I replied with a smile.

Damian had been with me long enough to know how losing 'screen time' worked. I find that if a sanction is necessary then losing ten minutes of an activity at a time is more effective than stopping it in one go. Also, if a child is being particularly challenging, you can quickly run out of sanctions. Allowing the child to earn back the lost time makes for better behaviour.

Damian dried himself, then put on his pyjamas and brushed his teeth.

'Well done, you've earnt your television back,' I told him.

He grinned at me in his cheeky but endearing way. His angry outbursts never lasted long.

Once Damian was settled in bed, I went downstairs. I was feeling positive. With Paula's help all three children were in bed and it was only 8.30. There was still time for her to relax after a day of working, and I needed to read the information Korin had sent, then write up my log notes to include Nathan and Liam's arrival.

As I walked into the kitchen I found that Paula had cleared up the dishes from dinner. She now passed me a mug of tea. I was grateful.

'I'm going to my room to chill,' she said.

'Thanks again, love, for all your help.'

But at that moment we both heard Liam cry.

'Could you make him a bottle while I settle him?' I asked Paula. 'I don't want his cries waking Nathan or Damian.'

'Sure.'

I went upstairs and found that Liam had a dirty nappy. By the time I'd finished changing it, Paula had arrived with his bottle.

'Thank you so much.'

'I'll be in my room if you need me,' she said.

As I fed Liam I could see him looking around at his surroundings, which were clearly not what he was used to. Although he couldn't talk, he would intuit that a lot had changed in his life; this wasn't the room he usually slept in and I wasn't the person who usually fed him. He finished the bottle but wouldn't settle and go back to sleep. If I put him in his cot, he cried. I'd never advocate leaving an infant to cry; I think it creates insecurity. I always answer their cries. I kept resettling him, lying him down, stroking his forehand and talking to him in a low, soothing voice. It was an hour before he was finally asleep, by which time Paula was in the shower getting ready for bed. I went downstairs, made myself a tea and took it to the front room. I began checking my emails and was about to open the one from Korin when I heard Nathan shout, 'Mummy! Mummy!' then his footsteps running around the landing and into my bedroom, waking Liam.

I rushed upstairs, resettled Liam and took Nathan back to his room, before returning to resettle Liam again. Current guidelines suggested that at six months old Liam should sleep in the carer's room. I'd put Nathan in his own room so he wouldn't wake Damian if he woke, but perhaps he'd like to share, I wondered. I'd see how these arrangements worked and then review them if necessary. For now, I kept taking Nathan back to bed, then resettling Liam. When Paula finished in the bathroom she sat with Nathan while I saw to Liam. It was nearly 11 p.m. before both children were asleep. Thankfully they hadn't woken Damian.

'I'll be in a better routine tomorrow,' I reassured Paula. 'If they do wake in the night, I'll see to them. You have work tomorrow.'

I kissed her goodnight, thanked her again for all her help and went downstairs. Although I was tired, I needed to go quickly through the forms Korin had sent. There wasn't much I didn't already know apart from the fact that a referral for an assessment for Nathan had been made but then cancelled due to the pandemic. I completed my log for all three boys, shut down the computer, checked the doors were locked and went to bed. It was midnight.

Liam woke shortly after 1 a.m. I tried his dummy, but he wasn't interested, so I made up a bottle. As I returned to my room Paula came out of hers to check if I needed any help. I thanked her and told her to go back to bed as she was working in the morning. The same happened at 3.30, and again at 6.30, when I showered and dressed after feeding Liam. I was shattered and I knew Paula would be too. She'd been awake as often as I had. But my thoughts went to Rachel and how she, a single parent the same as me, had coped. Only, of course, without enough help, she hadn't.

CHAPTER FIFTEEN

THE RIGHT DECISION?

Paula, bless her, got up when she heard me moving around getting Damian and Nathan ready so I could take Damian to school. Liam, having been up most of the night, was now fast asleep. My morning routine, established when Damian had arrived, was no longer. And with my attention now shared between Nathan and Damian, he messed around in his bedroom instead of getting dressed. I kept going in to chivvy him along as well as seeing to Nathan. Paula was in the bathroom having a shower – earlier than she needed to – so she could help me.

Finally, both boys were dressed and, leaving Liam asleep in his cot with the baby monitor on, I took them downstairs.

Part of our morning routine was that Damian gave Sammy his breakfast while I made ours, but today Nathan wanted to help. Although he didn't say much, he could make himself understood in other ways. He tried to snatch the scoop of dry cat food away from Damian, who resisted, resulting in the contents flying all over the kitchen. Sammy began eating some of the stray pellets as Damian shouted at Nathan, who then accidently tripped over the cat's water bowl, adding to the mess.

I spent some time clearing up the floor as Sammy looked on, unimpressed. I then told each boy to fill the scoop once. Cat fed, I told the boys to sit at the table while I made them breakfast.

'Come on,' Damian said, taking Nathan's arm. 'Better do as she says – she's in a bad mood.'

'I'm not in a bad mood, love, I'm just tired,' I said.

'Like my mum,' Damian replied.

As the boys began eating their breakfast – Nathan with my help – Liam woke.

'I'll see to him,' Paula called from upstairs.

'Thanks, love.'

I heard her go into my room; the crying stopped, and a few moments later Paula appeared with Liam in her arms and joined us at the table.

Both boys stopped eating. 'Hello, baby brother,' Damian said. Leaving his chair, he went round and kissed Liam rather forcefully on the forehead, which startled him.

Not wanting to be left out, Nathan got off his chair and, joining Damian, kissed and hugged Liam. There was a lot of love in their family, I thought. Children who are given affection tend to show it to others.

'Tea or coffee?' I asked Paula, going into the kitchen.

'It'd better be coffee today.' She looked as tired as I felt.

'Toast?' I asked her.

'I'll get some later.'

I made a coffee for Paula and a bottle for Liam. I returned to the table and fed Liam as Paula helped Nathan with his cereal. He finished before Damian.

'Mummy?' he asked me.

'You'll see her later, love.'

I now took the opportunity to explain the arrangements to Damian. 'When I collect you after school I'll be taking you to see your mother.'

'At home?' he asked.

'No, at the Family Centre.'

He looked puzzled.

'It's nice. Lots of children I've looked after have seen their family there,' I reassured him. 'It's like a house with living rooms. You'll see your mother in one of the rooms. It will have a sofa, table and chairs, and lots of games and toys. Other children will be seeing their families in the other rooms too. You may be able to play outside. A contact supervisor will be in the room to make sure you're all right. It's likely Korin will be there too.' The social worker usually attended at least part of the first supervised contact, and then every so often until the final court hearing.

'Will you be there?' Damian asked.

'No, I'll take and collect you. It's for you and your brothers to see your mother.'

'Will Troy be there?'

'No.'

Once Damian had finished breakfast, I left Liam with Paula and took the boys upstairs for them to brush their teeth. I was running late. I'd usually left the house by now to take Damian to school. I returned downstairs as Paula came into the hall. Liam had finished his bottle.

'Are you coming straight back after you've taken Damian to school?' Paula asked.

'Yes.'

'Shall I look after Liam here while you go?' she offered.

'But you have to start work at nine and I won't be back until nine-fifteen at the earliest.'

'I'll still start work at nine. If he's not asleep I'll keep him amused while I work. My first video call isn't until nine-thirty.'

'If you're sure, love, that would be a big help.'

'Sure.'

Paula was one of my two nominated support babysitters. Lucy was the other. Most carers have someone they can ask. Approved by the Local Authority, they are allowed to look after the children for short periods.

I helped Nathan into his shoes and jacket as Damian put on his, taking much longer than usual. Eventually we were ready to leave the house.

'Say goodbye to Liam,' I told Damian and Nathan.

Paula bent down so they could kiss him goodbye. Then, each taking one of Nathan's hands, we left the house, only five minutes late, thanks to Paula.

I helped Nathan into the car seat and fastened the buckles on the belt. Then I checked Damian's seatbelt.

'Mummy?' Nathan asked again, hopefully.

'You'll see her later, love. We're taking Damian to school.' At his age, even if he was developmentally delayed, Nathan would understand a lot more than he could say.

As I drove I put on some children's music and glanced at the boys in the rear-view mirror. Damian was holding Nathan's hand protectively. He could be so kind and caring to his young brothers, but like many siblings he could also vie with them for attention.

Because I was later than usual arriving at school, I had to park further down the side road. I helped Nathan out and then held his hand as Damian walked beside me into the playground. Mrs Halas was there looking out for us. I saw her surprised look when she saw us.

'Nathan and Liam are living with me!' Damian cried, rushing to her.

'They arrived yesterday evening,' I told her.

'Really, and Rachel?' she asked, concerned.

'They're seeing her after school.'

Mrs Halas would clearly have liked a fuller explanation, but I didn't have time now. I had to return home to relieve Paula of Liam so she could work. The school would be informed that Damian's brothers were now in care, so at some point Mrs Halas would be told.

'Was it to do with what happened last week?' she asked.

I nodded.

She looked sad as she took Damian into school. I think everyone who knew Rachel had been rooting for her, hoping that eventually she would be able to successfully parent her children.

It was 9.20 when I arrived home. Paula brought Liam downstairs and immediately returned to her bedroom to work. She had a video call in ten minutes. I gave Nathan a drink and a snack, Liam a bottle, then changed both their nappies before leaving the house again to walk to the local shops. Liam was in the stroller and Nathan walked beside me, holding the handle of the stroller. The bag containing all I needed for Liam was tucked in the compartment beneath the stroller. Every so often Nathan looked at me and asked, 'Mummy?'

'You'll see her later,' I reassured him, with a smile. 'After we collect Damian from school.' Which he

accepted for a while and then asked again: 'Mummy?'
But at least he wasn't upset as he had been yesterday.

In the High Street I bought nappies and the other
items on my list and then headed home. I stopped off in
the park. Liam had fallen asleep in the stroller so I
thought it would be nice for Nathan to play in the children's activity area. He was a bit reluctant to begin with,
but with some encouragement and help from me he tried
the swings, roundabout and rocking horse. We were
there for about twenty minutes and then walked home.

Paula broke from work at 12.30 and amused the boys
while I made us lunch. She returned to her bedroom at 1
p.m. I played with both boys for a while and then I sat on
the sofa with Liam on my lap and Nathan beside me and
showed them a picture book. Liam fell asleep and I laid
him on the sofa next to me. It wasn't long before Nathan,
tired from a broken night and the walk to the High
Street, leant his head against me and began to doze. I
could have nodded off too.

Suddenly, my mobile rang. I quickly grabbed it from
the coffee table so it didn't wake the boys. It was from a
private number.

'Hello?' I asked tentatively.

'Cathy Glass?' a female voice asked.

'Speaking.'

'I'm the Guardian ad Litem for Damian, Nathan and
Liam. I understand you are their foster carer?'

'Yes, I am, hello.'

The Guardian ad Litem is appointed by the court in
care proceedings for the duration of the case. They work
within the organization known as CAFCASS (Children
and Family Court Advisory and Support Service) and are

qualified social workers but independent of the social services. They have access to all the files and see all parties involved in care proceedings, including the children, their parents, the foster carer and social services. They report to the judge on what is in the best interests of the child, and usually the judge is guided by their view, which may uphold the social services' care plan, but not always. The Guardian hadn't been involved in Rachel's case until now, as Damian had previously been in care voluntarily.

'I wanted to make contact with you and introduce myself,' she said, 'although I understand this is a temporary arrangement and the children may be moved.'

'Yes, possibly. I'm not sure. Damian's been with me for two months. Liam and Nathan arrived yesterday.'

'And you don't know if or when they will be moved?'

'No, I'm sorry.'

'Why are they thinking of moving the boys? It wasn't clear yesterday in court.'

'I'm a single carer and I had doubts I could successfully manage all three.'

'Fair enough. I'll need to see the boys, but I'd better clarify the arrangements with their social worker first. I don't want to arrive at your house and find they've gone.'

'No.'

'I'll speak to their social worker and get back to you,' she said.

I had no idea what had been said in court; foster carers are rarely told the details, just the outcome. But clearly something had been said about the temporary nature of me fostering all three boys. I now had mixed feelings. While my head told me I'd been right to say I'd only look after the children until a more suitable carer could be found, my heart told me something different. As I looked at Nathan and Liam asleep on the sofa beside me I felt a surge of love and protection. Perhaps they wouldn't be able to find alternative carers, in which case the decision would be made, and all three boys would stay with me.

Liam woke first with a cry that woke Nathan. I gave Liam a bottle, Nathan a drink in a cup, and then kept both boys amused in the living room with the door closed so Paula wouldn't be disturbed while she was working.

I began preparations to leave the house to collect Damian from school half an hour before I needed to go. Everything takes so much longer with very young children. Once I'd collected Damian, I was going straight to the Family Centre, so I needed to pack the baby bag with enough supplies for Liam until we returned after contact, around 6 p.m. The foster carer is usually responsible for providing what a baby or young child needs during contact, although the mother usually feeds and changes them. I fed Liam before we left and also changed his and Nathan's nappy. As we left the house I told Nathan again what we were doing and I wondered how Rachel was.

It was likely she had been asked to arrive early at the Family Centre for a meeting with Korin and the centre's manager. That's what usually happened when a parent first started using the centre. She would be shown around the building and asked to sign a contract, which set out the rules for using the centre – for example, arriving on time, not bringing alcohol or drugs into the centre and not arriving under their influence, and leaving the room clean and tidy. I could picture Rachel being overwhelmed by all of this. She wasn't a rule-breaker. She did as she was told, which had made her vulnerable in the past and got her into trouble now.

I arrived at the school in good time, parked and got Liam out first. Once he was in the stroller, I helped Nathan out. 'Keep hold of the stroller,' I reminded him.

I slipped on my mask before entering the playground.

'Mummy?' Nathan asked again, looking around.

'She's not here, love. We'll see her soon.' I thought he probably remembered being with his mother when they'd collected Damian from school.

When Mrs Halas came out she made a point of saying hello to Nathan. Then she said to me, 'We've had a few issues with behaviour. Damian has been unsettled for most of the day and didn't eat much lunch. Not surprising with all the changes.'

'I am sorry. I'll speak to him,' I said.

'The Head told us what happened,' she said, raising her eyebrows.

I nodded and knew she would like to talk, so I said, 'I need to get going. We have contact at four.'

'Give Rachel my best wishes and tell her I hope to see her here again before too long,' she said a little stiffly.

'We need to go,' Damian said, tugging on my arm, eager to see his mother.

I said goodbye to Mrs Halas and we left. As we crossed the playground Damian said, 'Mrs Halas is annoyed. She said it wasn't right.'

'What wasn't right?' I asked him.

'That we have to live with you. She said we should be allowed to go home.'

'It was wrong of Mrs Halas to say that. She doesn't have all the facts like the judge did. They made the decision that you and your brothers need to be in foster care for now to keep you all safe.'

I appreciated Mrs Halas wasn't happy with the decisions being made, but she shouldn't have expressed her concerns to Damian. She didn't know all the facts, and even if she did, Damian was a child who was having to adjust to a lot of changes in his life. He needed to hear positive comments about being in care, not negative ones. I hoped in future she would keep her thoughts to herself. If she didn't and it happened again, I'd have to speak to her or the Headteacher.

I left Liam in the stroller on the pavement as I helped Nathan into his car seat and fastened the harness. Before I knew it, behind me Damian had taken Liam out of the stroller and was about to step into the road to access the door on the other side of the car, thinking he was helping.

'No, love!' I said, stopping him and taking Liam.

It was a timely reminder of how quickly accidents can happen. With three children I needed eyes in the back of my head, and again my thoughts went to Rachel.

As I drove to the Family Centre I told the boys again what to expect.

'Is Mummy there now?' Damian asked.

'Yes, she should be.'

'Mummy?' Nathan asked.

'Yes, soon, love.'

We arrived at the Family Centre with five minutes to spare. I parked in a bay at the side of the building and put on my mask before getting out. I could hear a child's voice coming from the play area at the rear of the centre, which was enclosed by high wire-net fencing. I didn't bother with the stroller but carried Liam the short distance to the main entrance, with the baby bag looped over my shoulder. Nathan was walking on one side of me, holding onto my trouser leg. Damian was on the other side. He'd gone very quiet.

'OK, love?' I asked.

He nodded.

We went up the path to the security-locked main door where I pressed the buzzer. The closed-circuit television camera above us was monitored in the office. A few moments later the door clicked open and we went in. I paused to use the hand-sanitizer pump and then spoke to the receptionist, who was seated at a computer behind a large Perspex screen.

'Damian, Nathan and Liam to see their mother, Rachel,' I said.

'She's here with the social worker. I'll sign you in.'

Prior to the pandemic there'd been a Visitors' Book in reception that we all had to sign in and out of. I guessed the move to the receptionist doing it digitally was to prevent cross-contamination. She went through a short checklist.

'The boys are all well?' she asked.

'Yes.'

'None of you has a temperature?'

'No.'

'You're not having to self-isolate or waiting for a Covid test result?'

'No.'

'You haven't been in contact with anyone who is?'

'No, not as far as I'm aware.'

These had become standard questions before many appointments.

She typed and then, looking up, said, 'All done. You can take the children through now. They are in Blue Room. Do you know where it is?'

'Yes, thank you.'

I'd been bringing children to the Family Centre to see their parents for years, so it was nearly as familiar to me as my own home. Each room is named after the colour it is decorated. I went down the corridor towards Blue Room. The door was open. We went in. Rachel was sitting on the sofa beside Korin. She looked so small and frail. Korin had her hand on her arm as though she had been comforting her. They were both wearing masks.

'Mummy!' Nathan cried and ran over.

Damian followed more slowly.

As I carried Liam to Rachel I saw the tears in her eyes.

'Oh, thank you so much,' she said gratefully as I passed Liam to her. 'You are kind. It seems ages since I saw them all together.'

She had an arm around Liam on her lap and the other around Nathan. Damian had virtually ignored her and gone straight to a toy box; his face was set.

'It's your fault we're all in care,' he said angrily. 'I hate you.'

CHAPTER SIXTEEN

COPING?

I saw the hurt in Rachel's eyes caused by Damian's remark and a tear slipped down her cheek. Korin went to Damian and, drawing up a child's chair, began talking to him in a gentle, reassuring way.

'Are you all right?' I asked Rachel, going to her.

She nodded and wiped her eyes.

There wasn't much I could do. I was here to bring and collect the children, and her social worker was on hand. If the parents have any questions or want feedback from the foster carer, it's usually done at the end of contact. I gave Rachel the baby bag, explaining what it contained, then I said goodbye and left. My heart ached for what she was going through.

Liam and Nathan were too young to make value judgements, but Damian had worked out that at least some of what had happened was a result of his mother making bad choices, despite me trying to put it in general terms and stay positive for him. No foster carer should ever demonize a parent, apportion blame or make negative comments to the child about their parents. Neither should a social worker. There are ways of age-appropriately explaining to children why they are in care. How to handle this is usually explored during foster-carer training. Korin was now talking to Damian, and if he made any similar comments to me I'd talk to him too. Of course, eventually, when a child is much older, they make their own judgements.

I had just enough time to go home and prepare dinner for later before I had to return to the Family Centre to collect the boys. Korin hadn't yet told me when the next and following contacts would be. When children first come into care it's often three times a week, sometimes every day with a baby. Saying goodbye at the end of contact is very difficult to begin with, until they get into a routine.

I parked outside the centre. It was quiet in the play area. The centre closed at 5.30 so those still using it would be getting ready to leave. Going in, again I used the hand-sanitizer pump and the receptionist signed me in on her computer, though without the previous health-check questions. I was a few minutes early so I waited outside the door to Blue Room. This was the family's time, and every second counts when a family are separated and they only see each other at supervised contact. It was just gone 5.30 when the contact supervisor opened the door.

'Come in,' she said. 'Korin had to leave but she asked me to tell you there is another contact here tomorrow, same time. Then every afternoon this week. She said she'd email you with the details for next week.'

'Thank you,' I said.

Damian appeared to have recovered from his earlier anger and was now chasing Nathan around the room, making him squeal excitedly. Rachel was sitting on the sofa with Liam on her lap, watching them, not upset but bemused. Neither Damian nor Nathan had their shoes and socks on and both seemed far from ready to leave. Usually the room had to be vacated at the time stated, and it was the parent's responsibility to get the children ready and say their goodbyes. The contact supervisor had packed away her laptop and was ready to leave.

'Everything all right?' I asked Rachel.

'Yes.'

'Damian's been fine since Korin spoke to him,' the contact supervisor added.

'Good.'

I waited. It wasn't really for me to tell the boys to put on their socks and shoes because it was time to leave, but I could see that Rachel didn't really know where to begin, so I took the initiative.

'Shall I tell them to get ready?' I asked her.

'Yes, please,' she said meekly. 'You're better at it than me.'

'Only because I've had more practice.'

The boys were running wild now, really hyped up. I could see there was going to be an accident before long.

'Let's channel some of their energy into a bit of healthy competition,' I said to Rachel, with a smile. Then to the boys, 'Damian, Nathan. I wonder who can put their socks and shoes on first.'

Damian stopped in his tracks, spotted his socks and, rushing to them, began pulling them on. I picked up Nathan's and helped him – I was dressing him at home too. Damian then found one shoe and began hunting for the other.

'Can I ask you something?' Rachel said to me in a small voice.

'Yes, of course.'

'What do I have to do to get my children back?'

The contact supervisor looked over but didn't say anything.

It was a big question, and I wasn't comfortable discussing it in front of the boys, especially Damian, who was already paying us attention.

'Has Korin talked to you about it?' I asked.

'A bit, but I didn't really understand. I mean, I put Damian in care voluntarily like she said, and I made sure there was food in the cupboard, and I started a bedtime routine for Nathan. But now they're all in care and I have to get a lawyer for the next court hearing.'

'That is important,' I said. But I could see how confusing it might be. 'I don't think we should discuss it now, but you can phone me this evening if you like.'

'Yes, I will. Thank you.'

'You still have my number?'

'Yes.'

The boys now had their shoes on, and a knock sounded on the door. It opened and the centre's manager came in.

'Are we ready to go?' she asked firmly but kindly. 'It's five forty-five.'

'Sorry, it's my fault,' Rachel said in her self-deprecating manner, and stood.

The contact supervisor helped me pack away the toys, then I picked up the baby bag and looped it over my shoulder.

'I changed both their nappies,' Rachel said to me. 'And gave Liam a bottle.'

'Excellent. He'll be OK until I'm home then.'

Now came the most difficult part. Rachel had to give Liam to me and watch me leave with her children. Some parents can put on a brave face, some are hysterical, and some are angry and threatening – blaming the foster carer. But Rachel, placid and cooperative as ever, just passed Liam to me. Then she kissed Nathan and Damian goodbye.

'See you tomorrow,' she said quietly.

I felt so sorry for her.

The manager was still standing by the door, waiting for us to leave.

'How are you getting home?' I asked Rachel.

'They're going to get me a cab,' she said.

'It's here,' the manager said.

Usually the parents stay in the contact room while the foster carer leaves with the children. This is to avoid prolonged and upsetting goodbyes taking place on the street. But Rachel left with us, holding Nathan's hand, which was fine with me. She was so compliant, she wouldn't make a scene outside.

The receptionist signed us all out, then the manager opened the door for us to leave, pointing out Rachel's cab parked on the street. It seemed we were the last to go. The car park was nearly empty. The contact supervisor said goodbye and headed to her car.

The cab driver was standing on the pavement and, seeing us approaching, opened the rear door for Rachel to get in. I took Nathan's hand and Damian stood beside me.

'I'll see you all tomorrow,' Rachel said to the boys. 'Be good.' She kissed them again and got in. 'Love you.'

'Love you,' Damian said. 'I promise I won't be horrible tomorrow. I didn't mean it.'

'I know.' And tears filled her eyes again.

Damian and Nathan were quiet on the way home and Liam fell asleep. It was after six o'clock when I arrived home with the boys and Paula had cooked the dinner I'd prepared earlier, which was a great help. We washed our hands, Liam woke and then we sat down to eat. I also fed Liam. Once we'd finished, Paula helped me bath the children and put them to bed. It was 8.30 before I checked my phone again and saw a missed call from Rachel.

I texted: *I'm free now if you want to talk. Cathy*

I didn't have a problem talking to Rachel, explaining the process and offering advice if that's what she wanted. As a foster carer I'm expected to remain neutral in care proceedings, otherwise any input could be seen as biased. But when Damian had first come to me it was with the intention of working with Rachel so that he could return home. Although the legal situation had changed, I saw no reason not to support Rachel now as I had before.

Five minutes later she phoned my mobile. I was in the kitchen tidying up. I stopped what I was doing and sat on one of the dining chairs to take the call.

'Are you all right, love?' I asked.

'I'm very lonely without my boys, and Troy gone.'

The mention of Troy set alarm bells ringing for me.

'You're not still seeing him, are you?'

'No, I'm just saying. He was here a lot and now I'm all alone.'

'It must be difficult, but you know if you were to start a relationship with him again it would jeopardize your chance of ever having your children back?'

'Yes, one of my neighbours said that. I won't. But the trouble is, I don't know how to tell if someone is telling the truth or lying to me. It's happened before.'

'It isn't always easy,' I agreed. 'I think it takes a long time to really get to know someone.' And even then, you might not truly know them, I thought, mindful of my ex-husband, who'd had an affair with someone at work before leaving us.

'Wera phoned to see if I was OK,' Rachel said.

'That was nice of her.'

'I told her I was sorry. She's going to come and see me tomorrow.'

'Good.'

'She said she feels bad the boys have been taken into care and wants to help. I can trust her, can't I?'

'Yes.'

'And I can trust you.'

'Yes, absolutely. You asked me at contact what you should do to get your children back,' I reminded her.

'You've been fostering a long time; have other children gone home?'

'Plenty. But it can take many months. Has Korin explained the process?' I asked.

'Sort of, and the lawyer will know.'

'Do you have a lawyer?'

'I've got the name and phone number of one to call.'

'Make sure you do. It's important. Write down any questions you have and don't be afraid to ask. Also, keep a note of all your phone calls with the lawyer and the social services. Attend all meetings you are invited to, and contact of course. And, Rachel, I know you will, but work with the social services. Don't blame them for what has happened. If they suggest you enrol for a parenting course, do it.'

'I'll try to remember,' she said. 'What does a Guardian do? She phoned me and said she needs to visit.'

'That's correct.'

I explained the role of the Guardian ad Litem; how she would speak to all parties, including the boys, and write a report for the judge based on what was in the best interests of the children.

'And then I get them back?' Rachel asked.

I swallowed hard. 'That will depend on the judge's decision.'

'Thank you for explaining,' she said, in the same humble tone. 'Are the boys asleep now?'

'They are.'

'Even Liam?'

'Yes. I'll give him another bottle before I go to bed and then when he wakes in the night. I always answer his cries straight away like you did, so don't worry.'

'He wakes a lot. It was very quiet here last night.'

'I can imagine. How are you in yourself?' I asked, concerned for her wellbeing.

'Sad. I don't feel like eating. My neighbours are good; they keep calling in and bringing me some of their food. They said if I need them, to phone.'

'That's nice of them. You must eat, Rachel. You can't afford to lose any more weight.'

'I know. I'll speak to someone at the clinic if they're open again.'

'Do you have any more questions about the boys or the court process?' I asked.

'I don't think so. Can I phone you if I think of anything?'

'Yes, of course, love. I'll see you at contact tomorrow at the Family Centre. You know it's the same time?'

'Yes, it's in my phone. Goodnight, Cathy. Thank you for talking to me and looking after my children.'

'You're welcome.' And again, my heart ached for her.

That night was a repetition of the previous one. I was up for much of it, either giving Liam a bottle or settling him and Nathan. Damian got up to use the toilet in the night but went back to sleep, and Paula was only woken once. I think she was still exhausted from the previous night followed by a day of working and then helping me for most of the evening when she should have been relaxing. I hoped that by the end of the week the boys would be more settled and in a better routine.

I gave Liam a bottle around 2.30 a.m. and then again at 5.30 a.m. Once he'd finished, I changed his nappy and settled him in his cot. I staggered downstairs in my dressing gown for a coffee so I would be up before the boys. Sammy looked surprised to see me but didn't object to having an early breakfast. I then returned upstairs where I had enough time to shower and dress before Nathan woke, shouting, 'Mummy!'

I went to see to him and then Paula showered and dressed early and helped me get all three boys dressed and eating breakfast. She offered to look after Liam again while I took Damian to school and I gratefully accepted.

'I couldn't manage without you,' I said truthfully.

But even with Paula's help that morning I found I was stretched to the limit all day. There wasn't a minute spare. The washing machine churned, and if I wasn't hanging laundry on the line to dry or bringing it in, I was preparing food or a bottle, changing two lots of nappies, clearing up and trying to find time to play with them. I felt that Nathan was receiving the least attention. Damian was at school so had the stimulation and social interaction there and Liam got the attention that babies demand, but little Nathan, the middle child, just had to fit in. From what I'd seen at his mother's it was similar there and could explain some of his developmental delay. Children of all ages need stimulation.

On Thursday I drove home from taking Damian to school determined to spend some quality time with Nathan. I had plenty of early-years learning toys and activities, so once we'd had a drink and a snack I got some out and took them into the living room.

'What would you like to do first?' I asked Nathan.

He pointed to the crayons and colouring book.

'Let's do some crayoning then,' I said brightly, and opened the colouring book to the outline of a parrot.

I'd just shown him how to hold the crayon when my mobile rang. It was Joy. I also had Liam on my lap, so I put my phone on hands-free.

'How are you all?' she asked. 'Coping?'

'Just about,' I replied. 'Liam and Nathan are here and Damian is at school.'

'How's contact going?'

'Reasonably well. Rachel does her best to stay positive.'

'Has Korin spoken to you about moving the boys?' she asked.

I immediately took my phone off speaker and put it to my ear so Nathan couldn't hear. He was watching me carefully, waiting for me to help him crayon.

'No. I saw Korin briefly at the start of contact on Tuesday. She's going to let me know the contact arrangements for next week.'

'That won't be necessary,' Joy said. 'They have identified carers who can take a sibling group of three, long term if necessary.'

'Oh, I see.'

CHAPTER SEVENTEEN

LIKE A DAD?

'They live out of county,' Joy continued. 'But they have agreed that Damian will stay at the same school, for now at least. They are a married couple in their forties, with previous experience of fostering sibling groups. I understand they can take the boys from Saturday, but Korin will be in touch with the details.'

'Does Rachel know?' I asked, with a massive stab of guilt.

'Korin is telling her today,' Joy replied. 'If you could put together a short résumé of the boys' routines, what they like to do in their spare time and so on, for the new carers, that would be useful. Although I appreciate they haven't been with you long.'

'I will,' I said, my voice flat.

'I thought you'd be relieved,' Joy said.

'I have mixed feelings,' I admitted. Damian was doing very well here, he'd made good progress, but three young children is so different, especially if it's long term.

'You wonder how grandparents manage when they suddenly have their grandchildren to live with them.'

I knew what she meant. There were more grandparents now than ever acting as kinship carers and bringing up their grandchildren when the child's own parents couldn't.

'I was going to arrange to visit you this week,' Joy continued. 'But it's not necessary if the boys are going on Saturday, so I'll phone you next week. We might have another referral by then. We're very busy. Let me know if Korin doesn't get in touch today or tomorrow and I'll give her a reminder.'

'All right, thank you.'

We said goodbye and I returned my phone to the coffee table. Liam was still on my lap and I now laid him on his front on the floor for some 'tummy time'. This is recommended to help babies strengthen their neck and shoulder muscles and improve their motor skills. I put some toys within his reach.

'Come on, love,' I said to Nathan. 'Let's colour in this parrot.'

I sat beside him and showed him again how to hold the crayon and colour in.

So the boys were leaving on Saturday, I thought, and already Joy was talking about another referral. Another child or children to look after with their own heartbreaking story. I knew the number of children coming into care was still rising and that foster carers were in short supply, but …

My phone sounded with a text message. I picked it up as Nathan crayoned. The message was from Lara asking me if I was going to see her this afternoon, and if so, could I bring some eggs? Another pang of guilt as I texted back: *Sorry, love. I'm so busy fostering three little boys I won't be able to make it this week. I'll see you next week. Are you OK?*

Three! she replied with a shocked emoji expression. *We're OK. See you next week. L x*

I now realized I hadn't spoken to Lucy or Adrian all week either. I tended to phone or see Adrian at weekends, but I was usually in touch with Lucy most days – either by phone or text, especially since she'd been suffering from morning sickness.

I felt bad as I texted Lucy a well-overdue message: *How are you, love? Sorry I haven't been in touch. I'll phone this evening. I've been looking after three young boys. They're leaving on Saturday.*

Lucy replied: *Paula told me you had the boys. Speak later. Still throwing up.*

Let me know if there is anything I can do, I texted. *I'll be able to help after Saturday.* For, realistically, I was of no help with three children in tow. It was taking up all my time to look after them.

Liam grew tired of being on his front and I sat him in the bouncing cradle, which allowed me to play with Nathan. He'd had enough of colouring in the parrot and was now stabbing a red crayon at a picture of a dolphin. 'Like this,' I said, showing him again how to use a crayon. But he'd grown bored of crayoning, so I put away that activity and he chose another from the selection.

When it was time for lunch, not wanting to leave the boys unattended in the living room, I took them with me into the kitchen-dinner. I put them the other side of the safety gate with some toys while I made us something to eat. They could see me and I could see them from where I worked. When lunch was ready I called upstairs to Paula. She came down but said she would eat in her room as she needed to finish something for work. She was clearly preoccupied so I didn't tell her the boys were leaving. I'd do so this evening.

Nathan and Liam had a sleep after lunch, which gave me a chance to check my emails. One had arrived from Korin, confirming the boys were going to live with Maurice and Anne Knight, full-time carers, and they would collect them on Saturday. She asked me to phone them to arrange the time and gave a mobile number. The email continued to say that she'd told Rachel the boys were going and asked me to tell Damian when I collected him from school, as she wouldn't have the opportunity. She didn't say how Rachel had taken the news and guilt crept up on me again. I replied, confirming that I would tell Damian and phone the new carers this evening, but as I clicked on send I felt I had let everyone down. If only Nathan and Liam hadn't had to come into care, then Damian could have stayed with me. Now all three were having to move again, and I had to tell Damian and face Rachel. Would she blame me? I felt she had a right to, although I doubted she would. The only person Rachel ever blamed was herself. She never apportioned blame to others even when she had a right to, which made me feel a whole lot worse.

It wasn't long before I was setting off to collect Damian from school. As I drove I made a mental note to buy Mrs Halas a thank-you gift for all she'd done. Although Damian would still be seeing her, tomorrow would be my last day at the school.

As I waited in the playground with my mask on, Liam in the stroller and Nathan standing beside me, my thoughts drifted back to the many different school playgrounds I'd stood in, taking and collecting my own children and those I'd fostered. In normal circumstances I got talking to other mothers and carers as I waited, but not this time. Social distancing and mask wearing had made striking up new friendships very difficult.

Damian's class came out and Mrs Halas brought Damian to me. She didn't mention the move, so I guessed she hadn't been told yet. Korin would notify the school, presumably by Monday. As well as informing them of the new carers' contact details, it was important they were told about what was happening as a change in a child's circumstances or living arrangements can impact on their behaviour and learning.

'I won't keep you,' Mrs Halas said. 'I know you're going straight to see their mother.'

'That's right, yes, thank you.'

As we crossed the playground I asked Damian if he'd had a good day.

'It was all right,' he replied.

I waited until we were in the car before I told him what I had to say.

'You're seeing your mother shortly, but I need to tell you something first.' I turned in my seat so I could see him and Nathan. 'It's nothing for you to worry about, but it is a bit sad. So, the three of you can stay together, but on Saturday you are going to live with new foster carers, Maurice and Anne. Your mother knows. She might mention it when you see her. Anne and Maurice are very nice and will look after you all well. They'll bring you to school and take you to see your mother as I have been doing.'

'Who's Maurice?' Damian asked.

'Anne's husband.'

'Does he live there?'

'Yes.'

'Like a dad?'

'Yes, a foster dad.' We weren't supposed to call ourselves foster mum and dad, although many children do.

'I think I'm going to like having a dad,' Damian replied, which took me by surprise.

I realized then that the boys had never had the experience of a father or a decent male role model, and as a single carer I hadn't been able to provide that either. My spirits rose a little. This move wasn't just about me not being able to successfully foster three young children long term; it had the advantage of showing them what a two-parent family was like.

Rachel was waiting in the contact room with the supervisor when I arrived. I passed Liam to her and placed the baby bag on the floor out of the way.

'Korin said the boys are going to move,' she said. The contact supervisor glanced across at me.

'Yes, I'm sorry. Did Korin explain why?'

Rachel nodded. 'I know the boys are hard work, but I'll miss you. I'm meeting the new carers online tomorrow. They are going to video-call me. What are their names? Korin told me but I've forgotten.'

'Maurice and Anne Knight,' I said. 'I'm sure they're lovely people and they are experienced foster carers.'

'They're going to give me a virtual tour of their home. And they'll bring the boys to contact like you do, and take Damian to school,' Rachel said.

'Yes, that's right. I shall phone them this evening so the move goes as smoothly as possible.'

'I'll miss you,' Rachel said again.

'I'll miss you too, love, and the boys, especially Damian. I've got to know him well. But the new carers will look after them, and as there's two of them full-time they'll have more time to spend doing fun stuff with the boys.'

'There's three of them,' Rachel said. 'They have a grown-up daughter who helps too.'

'Excellent.'

My spirits rose again. With one-to-one attention the boys would get the help they needed and deserved to reach their full potential.

I said goodbye and left the Family Centre feeling less guilty and more positive.

I had just enough time to go to the shops, where I bought Mrs Halas a bath-oil gift set and a box of chocolates and leaving presents for the boys. A skateboard for Damian, an early-years construction kit for Nathan and a soft-toy rabbit for Liam. I also bought a very large leaving card. Returning to the Family Centre, I hid the gifts in the boot of my car before going in. I would wrap them later when the boys were in bed and give them to them when they left on Saturday. I usually gave the children I fostered a leaving party, but current restrictions didn't allow that.

Nathan and Damian were arguing over a toy when I went into the room. The contact supervisor had put away her laptop and was waiting for them to stop squabbling and put on their shoes so they could all go. Rachel met my gaze. She was sitting on the sofa with Liam in her arms. Suddenly she stood and said in a small voice, 'I wonder who can put on their shoes first.' Bless her.

They didn't hear her as they were making too much noise, so she repeated it, more loudly this time. Damian heard, let go of the toy and went to put on his shoes. Left without anyone to squabble with, Nathan dropped the toy and went to his shoes. I returned the toys to the boxes and then helped Nathan with his shoes. I could see that Rachel was pleased with herself and I smiled at her.

We all left the room together.

'I phoned the lawyer,' Rachel told me on the way out.

'How did it go?'

'She was nice. She explained how she's going to get reports from the school and health visitor and my doctor and the paediatrician for Nathan. That will take a while. I asked her if she could get my boys back for me and she said she couldn't make any promises, but she'd try her best.' It would be standard procedure, but Rachel seemed satisfied.

'I've thought of other things I want to ask her,' she said as we left the building. 'So I've started a list for the next time we talk.'

'Good idea.'

'I'll see you tomorrow, won't I?' she asked.

'Yes. It will be my last day at contact.'

'It's sad.'

'I know,' I said, and swallowed hard.

She kissed the boys goodbye and we waited on the pavement as she got into the cab. I took the boys to my car. 'Mummy?' Nathan asked as he got in.

'You'll see her tomorrow, love,' I said.

Once home, I juggled looking after the three of them while I made dinner. When Paula finished work she came downstairs to help, and I took the opportunity to tell her they were leaving on Saturday. She already knew; Lucy had told her.

'We think it's for the best,' Paula said, mashing the potatoes. 'They're lovely children, but three so young is just too much long term with me working full-time.'

'I know,' I quietly admitted.

'Also, Mum,' Paula said seriously, pausing from what she was doing, 'Lucy is also hoping that when their baby is born you'll be able to help out, like you did with Emma.'

'Yes, of course I will. I've said so. I'm going to phone her later. I also need to speak to the new carers.'

I served dinner while Paula brought Nathan and Damian to the table. Liam was already in the bouncing cradle as I'd just given him a bottle. Damian ate half of his meal, saying he was full, but possibly he was feeling unsettled by the forthcoming move. Nathan ate his with my help. Once we'd finished, Paula helped Damian with his schoolwork while I played with Nathan and Liam and then took them up for a bath and put them to bed. When they were settled I brought Damian up, ran his bath and then, when he was washed and in his pyjamas, saw him into bed. It was nearly 8.30 before I was able to phone the new carers.

Maurice answered. I introduced myself, and he said, 'Just a second, Cathy, I'll put you on speaker so Anne and Sophie can hear.'

There was a short silence and then a friendly female voice said a bright, 'Hi, Cathy. Anne here.'

'Nice to meet you,' I said.

'And I'm Sophie,' another voice said. 'I'm their daughter and help with fostering.'

'Lovely to meet you.'

'Sophie is studying childcare at college, so she practises on the children we foster,' Maurice joked.

I smiled. 'Sounds good. Korin asked me to put together something on the boys' routines, like and dislikes, and so forth, which I'll do later. I'll make sure you have it by Saturday. I know Damian better than I do Nathan and Liam as I've been fostering him for much longer. I can tell you a bit about their background, their personalities and how they've adjusted to being in care.'

'Yes, please,' Maurice said. 'Korin suggested we Skype tomorrow when the boys are home so they can meet us, virtually at least.'

'That would be good.' Pre-pandemic, when a move was planned in advance as this was, the children usually visited their carers briefly, to meet them and see their new home. But those introductory visits hadn't begun again yet.

'What time is best to Skype, Cathy?' Anne asked.

'Around six-thirty would be good. They will have had dinner by then.'

'That's fine with us. When we've finished on the phone today I'll text you our Skype details. So, what can you tell us about the boys that would help us?'

'They're lovely children,' I began. 'Damian's eating has improved since he's been in care, but it might take a dip with having to move. It was thought he was copying his mother. I expect you know she's in treatment for an eating disorder?'

'Yes.'

They would have been sent the Essential Information Forms as I had been, so I was now supplementing them with details that might help. 'I'll send you the paediatrician's reports,' I said. 'Nathan has been referred for further assessment, but I haven't been given a date yet.'

'We'll chase it up,' Anne said.

'Damian has responded well to clear and consistent boundaries both at home and at school,' I continued. 'He has TA support from Mrs Halas. She'll give you feedback at the end of each day on his work, behaviour in the class-room and eating. She's aware of what's been going on and knows Rachel. She's been a great help to Damian, but she did tell him she thought it was wrong they were in care, so if it's mentioned again you might have to say some-thing.'

'Good to know,' Maurice said.

It was information like this that wasn't included in the Essential Information Forms but could be useful. I then talked about Rachel and how I'd worked with her in line with the original care plan, when it was thought that Damian would be returning home. Maurice asked about Troy and I told him what I knew. I then went on to the existing contact arrangements. 'Rachel is a lovely person,' I said. 'She won't give you any trouble. She just wants what's best for her children, but she is vulnerable. She struggles to protect herself and her children. I feel bad the boys are going to have another move, but she's not blaming me at all.'

'I should think not,' Anne said. 'When will the social services learn that a sibling group of three is too much for one carer! Most of our children come from other carers, or relatives of the children who offered them a home but found they couldn't cope. We had a sibling group of four last time. There's three of us and we were on the go all day. Often we didn't sit down until ten o'clock at night. It's not just looking after the children – foster carers have all the additional stuff: contact and school runs miles away, form-filling, meetings, training, assessments, report writing, appointments, visits from social workers, supervising social workers and other professionals. Don't get me wrong, we love what we do. But don't feel bad. Korin said you'd built up a good working relationship with Rachel and hopefully we can do the same.'

'That is kind of you,' I said, and I felt quite emotional. 'In some ways I worry more about Rachel than I do about the boys.'

'I can understand that,' Anne said. 'We'll look out for her just as you have.'

I heard Sophie say, 'You need to ask about fur allergies.'

'Oh, yes,' Maurice said. 'I just wanted to check that none of the boys have allergies to animal fur. Korin said she didn't think they had.'

'Not as far as I know. We have a cat and they've been fine with him. None of them has asthma either.' If a child has asthma, it can be triggered or made worse by animal fur and bird feathers, among other things.

'Good, because we have dog – a Labrador, Gracie. The children usually love her.'

'I am sure the boys will,' I said. 'Rachel bought a puppy some time ago but had to have it rehomed. Damian has wanted another pet. He's very good with our cat, Sammy, most of the time. He likes to feed and pet him.'

'He'll be able to help with Gracie,' Sophie said. 'She loves her walks and being petted.'

'Fantastic.'

I continued by telling them that Damian's bike was still at the police station and I'd let them know when it could be collected. I said I'd begun Damian's Life Story

Book but hadn't had a chance to start one for Nathan and Liam. I also said I'd give them the details of the savings account I'd opened online for Damian. Foster carers are expected to put aside a set amount each week for the children they foster, which they take with them when they leave.

We finished by arranging the time they would collect the children on Saturday morning. I felt better for having spoken to them. I immediately then tried to phone Lucy. It was 9.30 p.m. She didn't answer her mobile, so I tried Darren's.

'Lucy wasn't feeling good, so she's gone to bed,' he said.

'Not Covid?' I asked anxiously.

'No, morning sickness that lasted all day. I'll tell her you phoned.'

'Thank you, and please tell her I'm sorry I didn't call earlier.'

'It's OK, she knows how busy you are.'

Which made me feel worse. I shouldn't be too busy to speak to my daughter.

CHAPTER EIGHTEEN

SAYING GOODBYE

Still feeling bad, I sent Lucy a text message to read when she woke: *Sorry I didn't get a chance to phone. I'll speak to you tomorrow. I love you so much xx*

Of course Lucy knew I loved her, but it didn't hurt to say it. I often told my family how much I loved them, and they told me.

Paula had cleared away the dinner dishes and was now in her bedroom. I went to my computer. Tired, and with a heavy heart, I spent the next hour putting together a résumé of the boys' routines, likes, dislikes and so forth, for the new carers. After which I spent another half an hour completing their log notes for the day. I checked my emails, shut down the computer, gave Liam a bottle and climbed into bed, too exhausted to sleep.

I was still beating myself up for not finding the time to phone Lucy. Tomorrow wasn't going to be much easier either. First thing in the morning we'd both be fully occupied getting our children ready, then she'd be at work and later I had contact, dinner and the Skype call so the boys could meet their new carers virtually. I made a mental note to phone Lucy after the call and before I began taking the boys upstairs for their baths. The weekend should be very different. Once I'd said goodbye to the boys, I could make calls without any interruption and hopefully see Lucy and family, and Adrian and Kirsty. I was looking forward to that. The occasions when we'd been together as a family had been severely limited this year due to the pandemic, as they had for most families. Now the restrictions were being lifted and, for this weekend at least, I wouldn't be looking after another child, unless an emergency placement arrived. And to be honest, I didn't feel ready for that.

As I lay awake, too tired to sleep, I found my thoughts wandering in a direction they hadn't before. In order to have more time with my family, should I consider retiring from fostering? There! I'd said it. After thirty years of fostering, and now a grandparent with another grandchild on the way, was this the point where my life should enter a new phase? I didn't want to miss out on spending time with my own family by being too busy looking after other people's children. My family had always been very supportive of fostering, and perhaps now I needed to be able to offer more support to them. But if I retired, wouldn't I miss fostering? It had become a way of life. However, I could still offer occasional respite fostering, I reasoned. Or outreach work – supporting families and young people in the community. I already did that with Lara and others I'd fostered. The role could be extended if I wanted. I also had my writing, which had developed from being a hobby to me becoming a bestselling author. I knew how lucky I was. I'd been blessed with wonderful parents and fantastic children of my own, and had been allowed to foster many, many more. Perhaps it *was* time to take stock. I shouldn't outstay my welcome, so to speak. I'd found I was becoming increasingly intolerant of the flaws in our childcare system and cynical at some of the decisions made. I didn't want to lose sight of that young carer I once was, full of hope and enthusiasm, and with an unstoppable passion for fostering.

Clearly there was a lot to think about and eventually my tired brain gave up and I fell asleep. But not for long. Liam woke at 3 a.m. and then at 6.30, when I stayed up. I checked my phone and read Lucy's text message: *Love you too, Mum. Speak soon. Xx*

Bleary-eyed from lack of sleep and too much thinking, I fell into what had become my weekday routine for the last time. Paula helped me get the boys up, dressed and ready to leave the house, although today she couldn't look after Liam while I took Damian to school. Senior management at her firm had arranged a video-conferencing call at 8.45 to outline their plans for an eventual return to working in the office. So I took Liam as well as Nathan with me, and the thank-you gift and card for Mrs Halas. I'd give it to her this morning as I'd be rushing at the end of the day to take the boys to contact.

'Will Mrs Halas give me a present?' Damian asked, when I explained what it was for.

'No, love, you're not leaving the school.'

I could see he was pondering this and a few moments later he said, 'I'm leaving you. Are you giving me a present?'

'Possibly,' I replied, with a smile.

'What is it?' he asked.

'A surprise. I'll give it to you when you leave.'

'Have you bought Nathan and Liam a present?'

'Yes, love.'

'Good. I don't want them left out.'

'That's kind of you,' I said.

He was kind and caring like his mother.

I wasn't sure if Mrs Halas knew yet that Damian and his brother were moving on Saturday, so I prepared to explain. She did know. She said they'd had a short staff meeting that morning, as they did most mornings, and the Head had told them.

'Thank you for everything,' I said, as I gave her the gift and thank-you card.

'That's nice of you,' she said. 'I'm pleased Damian is still able to attend this school. Will Nathan come to the nursery here in September?'

'I don't know. It will depend on their social worker and the new carers,' I replied.

'Not their mother?'

'She will be consulted too,' I said.

I wished Mrs Halas and Damian a good day and came away. I went straight home, where I spent every available minute, when I wasn't seeing to the boys' needs, packing their belongings. I used large lightweight zip-up bags – I always kept a few spare – for it's unacceptable to use dustbin liners to move a child. Even in the short time Nathan and Liam had been with me they'd acquired extra clothes and toys, in addition to those Rachel had sent. I packed them all. Damian had a lot more as he'd been with me longer. I kept finding stray toys, activity books, action heroes and so forth around the house and under his bed. Everything he owned would go with him, even the clothes he had outgrown, as they were all part of his history. Eventually his permanent family and social worker would decide what to dispose of.

I was so busy that at midday, when I gave Nathan lunch and Liam a bottle, I didn't have time to eat myself. So when Paula came down she helped keep the boys amused as we ate.

'How did the conference call go this morning?' I asked her.

'Good. They're hoping to have everyone back in the office in September,' she said. 'Other businesses are doing the same.'

'That sounds promising,' I said.

'Yes, except I won't be here to help you, other than in the evening and at weekends.'

'And that's fine, love. You have your own life to live. Also, I've been thinking ...' I began but stopped. I needed to give it more thought before I said anything.

'Been thinking you need to cut back like Adrian said?' Paula suggested.

'Yes, possibly, and I need to phone Lucy. I'll do so after the boys have spoken to their new carers this evening. I would appreciate your help then.'

'Of course.'

'By the way, does Adrian know I've been looking after the boys?' I asked. 'I haven't spoken to him all week.'

'Yes, and he was worried.'

'Oh dear. I'll phone him at the weekend.'

That afternoon, while Nathan and Liam had a nap, I wrapped their presents and put them with their bags out of the way in my bedroom. When they woke I gave Liam a bottle, then played with them until it was time to leave to collect Damian from school. This would be not only my last school run for him, but also my last trip to the Family Centre with the boys. Fostering is full of endings and last days, and for that reason some people who consider fostering don't go ahead with it. I always try to console myself that I've done my best to help the children and their family during a difficult period and hope they stay in touch. Whether they do largely depends on the parents or new carers, or the young person if they are old enough.

When Mrs Halas came into the playground with Damian she said he'd had a 'reasonable day' but was 'confused' by the move.

'I'll explain to him again what's happening,' I reassured her. I thanked her for all she'd done, wished her well for the future and, with a final goodbye, left.

'I wasn't confused,' Damian grumbled as we crossed the playground. 'She's the one who's confused!'

'I hope you didn't tell her that,' I said. But I could tell from his expression he probably had.

'Damian, I'm sorry you're leaving us, but I hope you'll remember some of the things I've taught you. You've been doing very well. Mrs Halas, your mother and your social worker have all said so. We're all proud of you and I hope that will continue.'

'How?' he asked.

'Well, by not being cheeky to Mrs Halas or your mother, and doing as they ask first time is always good.'

'I'll think about it,' he said, in the same manner.

'Excellent.'

Rachel was in the contact room with the supervisor when we arrived; as usual she was pleased to see her sons, as they were her. She gave me a bunch of flowers. 'Thanks for everything,' she said.

I was really touched. It was completely unexpected.

'That is kind of you, but there was no need,' I said. She didn't have much money and I'd have rather she had spent it on herself or her children. I placed Liam in her arms.

'Anne and Maurice seem friendly,' she said. She'd met them online.

'Yes, they are, and very experienced carers. When Liam has settled you could talk to them about weaning him,' I suggested. 'I think he's ready and it will help him sleep longer at night. Anne will know what to do.'

'OK. I will,' she replied. Had the boys stayed with me, I would have suggested that I began weaning Liam.

I left the baby bag beside the sofa, wished them a nice time and said I'd see them later, and then came away.

I drove home thinking about them all, then put the flowers in water and prepared dinner for later. I was cooking a meal I knew Damian liked – cottage pie – and I'd included it in my notes to the new carers. It had been the only proper meal he'd eaten when he'd first arrived and could be relied upon if he went off his food, probably because it's easy to eat and doesn't require much chewing. Leaving a note to Paula to put the cottage pie in the oven when she finished work, I left the house and returned to the Family Centre.

I knew that saying goodbye to Rachel was going to be difficult, but I hadn't anticipated just how upset she would be. At 5.30 I knocked on the door to the contact room and went in. Rachel was sitting on the sofa, Liam in her arms, crying. The contact supervisor was comforting her, and Damian and Nathan were looking on, very worried. I thought something bad had happened.

'She thinks she won't see you again,' the contact supervisor told me.

'Oh, Rachel, love.' I went over. 'Don't be upset. You can phone me if you want, and the boys will be fine with Anne and Maurice.'

'I know, but you've been such a big help. I felt I could cope knowing you were there. I was doing OK when you had Damian during the week and I had him at weekends, wasn't I?'

'Yes, you did well,' I said, and swallowed the lump rising in my throat.

'That's because I knew if I wasn't managing you would come and collect Damian early. It gave me confidence,' Rachel said.

'But you never needed me to collect him early. You coped.'

'So why haven't I got my children?' she said, fresh tears forming.

We both knew the answer to that and there was little I could say on the matter.

'Rachel, don't lose hope, love.' I touched her arm reassuringly. 'There's a long way to go, but you've got yourself a lawyer who's helping you. Phone me any time if you want to.'

I felt choked up and I could see that Damian and Nathan were looking anxious. This wasn't the way to say goodbye. Nathan ran to this mother and hugged her while Damian, wanting to be helpful, picked up their shoes and brought them over.

'Good boy,' I told him.

The contact supervisor gave Rachel a box of tissues and she wiped her eyes and blew her nose. The supervisor and I still had our masks on, but Rachel always took hers off during contact.

'You go,' Rachel said to me at last. 'I'll wait here while you leave.' She took another tissue from the box.

'Whatever you feel is best,' I said gently.

'You have contact again on Monday,' the supervisor reminded Rachel.

'I know,' she said, but she still looked very miserable. I think it was a build-up of a number of things. She'd had a lot to cope with during the past two weeks: police involvement, discovering Troy had betrayed her trust, and Nathan and Liam being taken into care. I think having to say goodbye to me was the final straw.

I helped Nathan into his shoes and Rachel put on a brave face to kiss and hug her boys goodbye. It was so sad. As we were ready to leave I put the sealed envelope I'd brought with me into her lap. 'A little something to open later,' I said.

'Thank you,' she said.

'You're very welcome. Take care. Look after yourself and phone if you want to.'

I didn't tell her what was in the envelope as I didn't want her thanking me, but rather than buy her a present I'd given her a gift card that she could spend in a number of stores or online.

With Liam in my arms and Nathan and Damian walking beside me, we headed out of the room. 'See you on Monday,' Rachel called to the boys. 'Bye, Cathy.' But her voice broke as she said it and she was in tears again.

I said a final goodbye and continued out of the room, for I knew to return with the children would be even more upsetting and make parting more difficult. I hated to leave Rachel like this, but the contact supervisor was with her and wouldn't let her go until she had recovered. The Family Centre's staff are used to comforting distressed parents.

I said goodbye to the receptionist. Outside, the cab driver was waiting on the pavement. Normally we all left together so I went over and told him that Rachel would be out shortly. He thanked me and said hi to the boys, then I took them to my car.

As I drove home I kept checking on Nathan and Damian in my rear-view mirror. Liam had fallen asleep but the other two were very subdued.

'Mummy will be all right,' I reassured them. 'You'll see her again on Monday.' Then to Damian I added, 'We've got cottage pie for dinner and jelly and ice-cream for pudding,' which I knew he liked. Jelly and ice-cream was all he had been eating at home prior to coming into care.

'I'd rather have McDonald's,' Damian grumbled.

'Really?' I asked, surprised. He'd never shown any interest in that before, even when I'd been trying to tempt him to eat and had suggested it, among other things.

'Yes, *really*,' he said, mimicking me. 'Some of the kids at school have it.'

'If that's what you want, we'll stop off and get you one.'

I made a detour to our nearest drive-through where we held up the cars behind us while Damian chose what he wanted from the menu board outside the car window. He kept changing his mind, but eventually decided on chicken nuggets and French fries with a chocolate milk-shake. Nathan was asleep and he, Paula and I would have the cottage pie that would now be in the oven.

Damian was fascinated by the drive-through process, having never been in one before – the large board displaying colourful pictures of food, the intercom where I gave my order, the payment window where I tapped my card, and the last window where I was handed the paper bag containing his meal. He wanted to hold it, so, turning in my seat, I handed it to him, and he held it protectively.

'Have you ever had a McDonald's before?' I asked him as I drove.

'Don't think so.'

If he'd ever shown any interest, I would have got him one sooner.

He was still clutching the bag when I arrived home and parked on the drive. I let Damian out first, and he went to the door and rang the bell as I woke Nathan.

'I wondered where you'd got to,' Paula said, answering the door. Then, seeing the bag Damian was holding, she added, 'I put dinner in the oven, Mum.'

'Yes, that's fine. We'll have it. Damian wanted a McDonald's.'

Paula helped me get Liam and Nathan out of the car; Nathan was still groggy from sleep. After we'd washed their hands, she dished up dinner and gave Damian a plate for his chicken nuggets and French fries. We were later than I'd anticipated – I'd told Anne and Maurice we'd Skype at 6.30 so I fetched my laptop and set it up on the table ready. I ate my meal quickly and at 6.30, as the others were finishing, I logged in to Skype.

Maurice appeared on screen first.

'Sorry, we're just finishing dinner,' I said. 'We don't mind chatting if you don't.'

'Fine with us,' Maurice said. Anne and Sophie appeared beside him and I angled the laptop so they could see us.

'Mmmm, cottage pie, my favourite,' Anne said, smiling.

'Ours too, but Damian wanted to try a McDonald's,' I explained.

I then introduced them properly to the boys and Paula, and explained to Nathan and Damian that these were their new foster carers – the family I'd talked about.

'It's lovely to meet you all,' Maurice said. 'We'll tell you a bit about ourselves and then show you around our house.'

Damian was more interested in his meal, but as the family talked it soon became clear just how child-centred they all were. They knew what to say to put a child at ease, and before long Damian was answering their questions about what he liked to do while continuing to eat. Even little Liam, seated on my lap, was enthralled by seeing them on screen, and started gurgling and waving his arms.

After about ten minutes, when they'd all spoken, Maurice said, 'We'll show you around our house and garden now, but before we do there is someone else you need to meet.'

Paula looked at me questioningly and I shrugged. As far as I knew there was just the three of them. Maurice then moved the device they were using so the webcam panned across their living room to their Labrador dog, stretched out lazily on the floor.

'Gracie, come here, good girl,' Maurice called to her. 'Say hello.'

She stood and came over, sniffing the air, her tail wagging happily.

'They've got a dog!' Damian cried excitedly, dropping the chip he was holding.

'Yes, Gracie,' I confirmed with a smile.

'Wow. Can I take her for walks?' he asked.

'Yes, you can certainly help,' Anne said.

'Does she run and catch a ball?' Damian asked.

'She does,' Sophie replied.

'Hi, Gracie!' Damian called. 'Gra-cie!'

Hearing her name, she wagged her tail and gave a little bark at the screen.

'She likes you,' Anne said.

'I like her,' Damian said. 'Gra-cie!'

She barked again.

'Dog!' Nathan said, pointing, while Liam giggled.

It was a very positive beginning. We stayed at the table as they showed us around their house. Damian was more interested in Gracie than seeing the playroom, their garden or his bedroom. Nathan kept saying 'dog'.

'Shall we bring Gracie with us tomorrow when we collect you?' Anne asked as they wound up and prepared to say goodbye.

'Yes!' Damian shouted gleefully.

'We will then,' she laughed. 'Now you finish your meal – you've got a busy day tomorrow, so you'll be going to bed soon. Sleep tight and see you in the morning.'

They blew kisses and then, waving goodbye, ended the call.

'What a lovely family,' Paula said.

'Yes, they are,' I agreed.

CHAPTER NINETEEN

THE HOUSE WAS
UNCANNILY QUIET

As soon as the Skype call ended I left Paula to give Nathan and Damian their pudding while I took Liam into the living room so I could phone Lucy. I began by apologizing to her for not being in contact and asked how she was feeling.

'Today's the first day when I haven't been sick for most of it,' she said. 'So hopefully it's starting to wear off.'

'That's good, I am pleased. Is Emma still up?'

'Darren is just giving her a bath.'

'OK, I'll speak to her another time.' I asked Lucy about forthcoming antenatal appointments and if she needed help with Emma, but Liam began to grizzle and rubbed his eyes.

'Sorry, love. He's tired. Can I phone you later when he's in bed?'

'Rather than talk this evening, Mum, let's meet at the weekend,' Lucy suggested.

'Yes, good idea.'

'We're free Sunday.'

'We are too.'

'The weather is supposed to be fine so we could have a picnic. I'll see if Adrian is free.'

'Yes, please, that would be great.'

'I'll text you when we've decided where to go.'

'Thanks, love. I'll look forward to it.'

'Me too.'

Paula helped get the boys ready for bed as she had been doing every night since they'd arrived. Once they were all settled, I put the last of their belongings, including Damian's schoolbag, in the zip-up holdalls and took them downstairs. I left them out of the way in the front room. All that needed to be added tomorrow was their night-wear and toiletries from the bathroom.

'Thank goodness it's the end of the week,' Paula sighed. 'Two days off work.'

'Yes, you can have a lie-in tomorrow. I'll see to the boys. They're not leaving until ten-thirty.'

'I'll see how I feel.'

She helped me clear up the dinner dishes and then went to her room to relax and watch a film on her laptop, while I went to my computer in the front room. Their bags took up most of the floor space; on top were their presents and leaving card. I turned my attention to the computer screen and emailed the reports I had on the boys to Anne and Maurice, and then completed my log notes. I'd include the details of the boys leaving tomorrow after they'd gone, but I didn't foresee any problems. As I checked my emails I saw some from readers that needed a detailed and considered reply. I was too tired to do them justice now so I'd reply over the weekend when I had more time. I felt moved that people I'd never met trusted me enough to confide in me and ask for advice. I took the responsibility very seriously.

Closing down the computer, I decided not to wait up to give Liam a bottle but to get a couple of hours sleep in first. As I was pouring a glass of water to take up to bed Lucy texted.

Adrian & Kirsty can make Sunday. Meeting at 12 with picnics at the main gates of Oak Park. Love L x

Fantastic. Thanks for organizing xx, I replied.

Upstairs, I checked with Paula that she knew of our picnic and she did. I said I was having an early night and I'd see her in the morning.

After the restless night before I was asleep as soon as my head touched the pillow. Liam obliged by not waking for a bottle until 1.30 a.m. and then again at 5.30. After I'd fed and changed him, I put him in his cot while I quickly showered and dressed. Damian woke at 6.30, excited to be seeing Gracie. He came downstairs in his pyjamas and gave Sammy his breakfast for the last time. He stroked Sammy as he ate.

'I won't forget you,' Damian said.

'I won't forget you either,' I said, thinking he was talking to me.

'No, I meant the cat,' he replied.

I smiled. I was pleased he was finding the move comparatively easy. It can be very difficult for children to say goodbye to their carers – especially, as in this case, when they weren't going home and there was uncertainty around their future.

Despite telling Paula not to get up early, she did. She helped me wash and then dress Liam and Nathan in some of the new outfits I'd bought them, while Damian dressed himself in his new clothes. I always liked the children I fostered to look smart and today was no different.

We had breakfast together and I took the opportunity to explain to Nathan again what was going to happen this morning. Damian already understood. It was only 9.15 a.m. by the time we'd finished breakfast and the boys were ready, but the new carers weren't due for an hour. It was a lovely warm June morning with the sun high in a clear blue sky, so I suggested we went into the garden. I sat on the patio with Liam on my lap as Paula played bat and ball with Damian, and Nathan explored the flowerbeds, searching for stones and grubs. It was at moments like this, when I saw the children I was looking after happy and contented, that I knew why I'd fostered for so long. I was still struggling to make a decision about what to do in future, but for now I shelved further thoughts on the subject and made the most of my last hour with the boys.

I'd left the patio door open so I would hear the front doorbell and at 10.20 I heard it; so did Damian.

'Is that them?' he asked, stopping what he was doing.

'It could be,' I said, standing.

'Have they brought Gracie with them?'

'I hope so,' I replied.

With Liam in my arms, I led the way into the house and down the hall, and opened the front door.

'Gracie!' Damian cried.

She wagged her tail excitedly. Anne, Maurice and Sophie were wearing masks, so I took a couple from the hall stand and passed one to Paula.

'Good journey?' I asked, as Damian made a fuss of Gracie.

'Yes, thanks,' Maurice said.

'Are you coming in?' I asked, standing aside to let them pass.

'Just to help with the bags,' Maurice said. 'Our supervising social worker said we shouldn't stay to reduce the risk of spreading Covid.'

'Sure. I'll bring the bags into the hall,' I said, and passed Liam to Anne.

In normal circumstances they would have come in for about an hour so the children saw us all together, when I would gradually transfer Liam to Anne. But that wasn't an option now. Many babies Liam's age cry if suddenly passed to a stranger, but Liam didn't. I suppose he was used to abrupt change, having recently been taken from his mother and given to me and Paula. If he was unhappy, he didn't show it. The resilience of children in care never ceases to amaze me.

Anne remained in the porch holding Liam as Sophie made coochy-coo noises so he chuckled. Damian was on the path petting Gracie, who, having been told to sit by Maurice, was obediently complying. Nathan was watching them warily.

'Don't got out of the front garden until we are all ready,' I told Damian and Nathan.

'I'll keep an eye on them,' Anne said.

Paula and I took the bags from the front room to the door where Maurice loaded them into the back of their car. They had a large seven-seater.

'Do you have car seats for the boys?' I checked with Anne. 'If not, you can borrow mine.'

'They're all in place,' Anne confirmed.

As Maurice took the last bags Paula and I gave the boys their leaving presents and card. Anne held Liam's. 'You can open them in the car or at your new home,' I told Damian and Nathan.

'Say thank you,' Anne prompted.

'Thank you,' Damian said.

'Is that everything?' Maurice asked, returning.

I quickly checked the front room. 'Yes. If I find anything, I'll send it on.'

'We'll give you a ring in a couple of weeks to let you know how they are,' Anne said.

'Earlier if we have any problems and need your input,' Maurice added, with a smile.

'I'm sure you'll be fine, but phone whenever you want,' I said. 'We'll be pleased to hear from you.'

Nathan suddenly lost his wariness of Gracie and, holding his present in one hand, he began tentatively patting her with the other. She was about the same height as him.

'Would you like some drinks to take with you?' I asked Anne. The day was already heating up and they had an hour's journey ahead of them.

'We've got some packed,' Anne said. 'And some snacks, and some boiled water if we need to make up a bottle for Liam.'

They'd clearly thought of everything. So now it was time for them to go.

Maurice picked up Gracie's lead and went down the front path; Nathan and Damian followed. Sophie took Nathan's hand as they went onto the pavement. Damian stood beside them. Anne put Liam into his car seat in the back and Sophie helped Nathan clamber up. Their car was higher off the ground than mine, so it was a big step up for a small child. Damian brushed off Sophie's offer of help, climbed in and fastened his seatbelt.

Gracie was sitting on the pavement, nonchalantly sniffing the air and appearing to know the routine of getting children in and out of the car. Once all three boys were in, Maurice went to the back of the car and called, 'Here, Gracie.'

She immediately stood and, tail wagging, went to him, then jumped into the back of the car. It was divided into two compartments: one for luggage and the other for her.

'She's so well behaved,' Paula said, and I agreed.

'One of the family,' Maurice added.

'We'll text once we're home,' Anne said. 'Then call in a few weeks. Don't worry, we'll look after them just as you have done.'

'I know you will,' I said. 'But having to say goodbye to the children we've fostered is always sad.'

'It is,' Sophie agreed, looking unhappy. I guessed she'd had to say goodbye to many of the children they'd looked after, just as my family had.

'A skateboard!' Damian cried from inside the car, having unwrapped his present. 'Thanks, Cathy.' He then threw the wrapping paper out of the car window.

Anne raised her eyes indulgently as I picked it up.

As the new Covid rules advised, the adults didn't hug goodbye, and we were all still wearing our masks.

'Take care, safe journey,' I said.

Sophie and Maurice got into the front of the car and Anne went in with the boys. They lowered the windows a little to wave.

'We've enjoyed having you,' I called to the boys. 'Bye.'

'Bye,' Paula called.

But Nathan's attention was on his present as he tore off the paper, and Damian was turning in his seat, more interested in Gracie.

We waved until they were out of sight and then, taking off our masks, returned indoors. The house was uncannily quiet. Sammy came into the hall as if looking for the boys.

'They've gone,' Paula told him. He meowed and went upstairs to check. 'I'm going into town shopping this afternoon,' she said to me as we went into the kitchen to make ourselves a drink. 'I'll buy what we need for the picnic tomorrow.'

'Thanks, love. Even though the boys have gone, I've still got plenty to do today.'

But, weirdly, having been so busy since their arrival, now I had time to spare, far from it energizing me to accomplish what I had to, it did the opposite. I spent a while wandering aimlessly around the house, unsure what to do next. Then, as I gazed out of the patio window, I realized it was ideal weather for drying laundry, so I stripped the boys' beds and Liam's cot and loaded the washing machine. Paula helped me dismantle the cot and we stored it in what had been Damian's room.

Paula and I had a sandwich lunch outside and then she left to go shopping while I went to my computer in the front room. Logging into the council's portal, I completed my logs for all three boys, while wondering how they were doing. I then turned my attention to the emails from readers, prioritizing those that appeared urgent. As I worked I kept feeling I was missing something, or rather someone. Paula was out, and having had Nathan and Liam with me constantly it was difficult to shake off the feeling I should be tending to their needs. At one point I even thought I heard Liam cry, but it was a child outside. I hoped they were settling in to their new home.

One of the emails I replied to was from a woman trying to escape an abusive partner. Some years before I'd been a volunteer at a refuge and appreciated the fear and conflicting emotions of being trapped in an abusive relationship. I wrote *Run, Mummy, Run* to highlight the issue of domestic violence. I empathized with the woman, and gave her the contact details of organizations that could help, telling her to call the police if she was in immediate danger. She knew she had to leave; it was a matter of finding the courage and going. Another email was from a young British-Asian girl who'd read my book *The Child Bride* and believed her parents were plotting something similar and planning to marry her off against her will. She was only sixteen. I gave her the details of where to get help – also listed on my website. Another email was from a mother of three who'd contacted me a number of times before. She was at her wits' end trying to get help for her son, who she suspected had autism. From what she'd told me she was doing all she could, but the assessment he required to get him the help he needed had been repeatedly delayed due to Covid. I'd previously suggested some strategies for managing her child's behaviour, which she said had helped. (These strategies are explained in my book *Happy Kids*.) All I could do now was offer words of encouragement and support, and I advised her to keep pushing for the referral, which she was doing. Sometimes just being able to vent your frustration to someone who understands helps. I'm lucky in that I have family and close friends to confide in, but not everyone does. And sometimes it's just easier to tell a stranger.

I stopped at four o'clock when Paula returned and helped her unpack the groceries. I poured us cold drinks, which we took into the garden. It was still very warm, a lovely afternoon, and we sat in the shade of the tree. Birds sang from the shrubs and children's voices floated in from neighbouring gardens. As we sat there sipping our drinks my phone bleeped with a text. It was a WhatsApp message from Anne. *Good journey. Now having a picnic in the garden.* She had attached a photo of them all. I showed Paula. They were seated on a large tartan rug in the shade of a tree not dissimilar to ours. Liam was in a bouncing cradle, a rattle in his hand, and the boys were eating picnic food from brightly coloured plastic plates. Anne and Sophie were beside them. Gracie was sitting watching, clearly hoping for titbits. Maurice was in the foreground and appeared to have taken the photo using a selfie stick. It was a lovely family gathering and I was relieved to see them all so happy. My thoughts turned again to Rachel and how she was coping.

If I'm honest, it's only since I've been writing my fostering memoirs and have heard from parents whose children have been taken into care that I've truly appreciated their heartache. Naturally, as a foster carer, I had compassion for the parents, but my first priority was their child, so I didn't give their situation a lot of thought. There wasn't usually much opportunity to learn about it first-hand either. I was sent the Essential Information Forms, which contained basic details, and sometimes the social worker filled in some background information. But apart from meeting the parents briefly at contact, and sometimes at reviews and other meetings, there wasn't the opportunity to hear their stories, unless I was working with them to have their children returned. And while it's true that some parents can never be allowed to parent again as it's simply not safe for their children, there are others, like Rachel, who I feel could. With the right support, in an atmosphere where their shortcomings and failings are managed rather than seen as another reason for taking their children into care, perhaps they could safely keep their children. I hoped so.

CHAPTER TWENTY

ANNOUNCEMENTS

I was looking forward to our family picnic so much that, despite having the opportunity of a lie-in on Sunday morning, I was up at 7 a.m. Being careful not to wake Paula, I slipped into my dressing gown and went downstairs where Sammy looked slightly surprised to see me without the boys.

'They're at their new home,' I told him. 'I'm feeding you now.' I didn't add that Damian had probably transferred his affection to Gracie.

I made myself a coffee and took it into the garden to drink. The air was still and warm. A perfect June morning. Perfect for a family picnic in the park.

No longer needing to be showered and dressed before the boys, I stayed in my dressing gown to make the picnic, returning the boxes of food to the fridge until it was time to leave. I would also put in drinks and take the ground sheet for us all to sit on. Our ground sheet was almost a family heirloom. Durable and waterproof, it was the same one I'd used since my children had been little. It had accompanied us through all our years of fostering, been taken on outings and spread on the ground in countless parks, grassy fields and beaches, as well as in our back garden. My thoughts drifted to the many children we'd fostered who'd enjoyed our picnics and family outings, often having never experienced them at home. Like most foster carers, I had a treasure trove of wonderful, warm memories and photographs.

Paula appeared in her pyjamas, having managed to sleep in. 'I wonder what the boys are doing today,' she said.

'Yes, I was thinking that. Not having a leisurely morning, that's for sure!' I said with a smile.

'No, but there's three people to look after them now,' she reminded me.

'I know.'

It was nearly 10.30 before Paula and I went upstairs to shower and dress. As I was gathering together the clothes I would wear, Lucy texted to check we were still OK to meet at 12.

Yes, looking forward to it. See you at the main gate of Oak Park, I replied with a smiley emoji.

I left my phone in my bedroom while I showered, and when I returned I found a text message from Tash.

I thought you'd want to know the investigation is finally over. No further action will be taken. We've sent an email resigning from fostering but have heard nothing back. We're going away tonight for two weeks, but it will need more than two weeks to get over this. We're so angry at the way we've been treated. Hope you are all OK. Thanks for listening. I'll phone you when I get back. Tash x

It saddened me. What a dreadful way to end a fostering career, full of bitterness and rejection, rather than looking back with fond memories to all the children you'd helped. I certainly didn't blame Tash for feeling that way. From what she'd told me, they should have received a lot more support. They were good carers and had successfully looked after many young people, some of them with very challenging behaviour. They would have continued to do so for many years had this not happened.

Thanks for letting me know. Have a good holiday xx, I replied.

At 11.45 Paula and I put the cool bags containing the picnic food and the ground sheet into the car and set off for Oak Park. Paula knew Tash and her family and was aware of the allegations made against Ryan, so I told her of the outcome.

'Thank goodness, but what a nightmare for them,' she said, which was how Tash had described it – a living nightmare.

'I know. I'll see Tash when they get back.'

We talked about it for a while and then our spirits lifted as we approached the park gates. Lucy, Darren and Emma were already there, and Adrian and Kirsty had just arrived and were getting out of their car. I parked close and as we got out Emma rushed to greet us, crying, 'Nana! Aunty Paula!'

We all hugged. Hugs seemed even more precious now, having been forbidden during lockdown and the worst of the pandemic.

'How are you, love?' I asked Lucy, giving her an extra hug. She looked a bit pale and was holding a water bottle.

'Not too bad. I've had a little breakfast, which stayed down.'

'Good.'

Although we weren't ready for lunch yet, we decided to take everything we needed, including the cool bags, with us now, rather than having to come back for them later. Oak Park is vast and some of the best picnic spots are about a twenty-minute walk from the entrance. Emma was full of energy and as we set off through the main gate and across the park, she ran and skipped around us, going from one person to another. Adrian fell into step beside me. Kirsty was just ahead of us, talking to Lucy and Darren. Paula then began pretending to be a bear and chased Emma – a game they'd played before. Not that we had bears roaming the UK, but Emma didn't mind and was squealing with delight.

'It's strange not having the boys with me,' I remarked to Adrian as we walked.

'Yes, Mum, I wanted to talk to you about that,' he said, his voice serious.

I glanced at him and knew a lecture was about to follow. Lucy, Paula and Adrian were in regular contact by text, and he would have been told about last week.

'Don't worry, I've learnt my lesson,' I said, pre-empting him. 'Looking after three little ones was too much. I won't do it again.'

'Promise?'

'Yes, love.'

'Good. We worry about you.'

'I know, but there's no need. Anyway, I've been doing a lot of thinking recently and …'

I didn't get any further. Emma came rushing over. 'Save me, Uncle Adrian!' she cried. 'A bear is going to eat me!'

Paula loped towards us, growling softly. Just in time, Adrian lifted Emma effortlessly onto his shoulders. 'Can't get me up here!' she cried.

Adrian is over six feet tall, so Emma must have felt very high. He was holding her firmly and she was clinging to his head, screaming and enjoying every second.

'You can't eat me!' she cried to Paula.

'I could if I got on Nana's shoulders,' Paula said.

Emma's face was a picture. She looked at me for a second as if that might be an option, then laughed.

'No, you can't. Nana isn't tall enough!' she called from her vantage point.

'I would be if I stood on that tree trunk,' I said.

And so our walk continued, light-hearted, joyous and fun. We stopped briefly at the play area so Emma could have a swing and a turn on the roundabout, then we continued to the place where we wanted to picnic. Although there were others in the park, not many came this far. Just one other family were there. We found a spot in partial shade, and I got out the ground mat.

'That brings back memories,' Adrian said. 'Didn't Grandpa buy it for us when we all went to the beach one time?'

'Yes, he did,' I said. 'It's lasted well.'

We shook it out and then sat around the edge of it and arranged our food boxes in the middle. We often shared food on these picnics, and with this in mind I'd prepared plenty. Lucy apologized as she produced a container of her own with just cheese and crackers and a sliced apple in it.

'It's what I fancied,' she said.

'Sure, love, that's fine,' I said.

'I'll eat her share,' Darren joked.

It was certainly a good spread. There was cold chicken, quiche, cherry tomatoes, green-leaf salad, sliced cucumber, mini sausage rolls, slices of pizza and a pasta salad. I'd also bought packets and tins of soft drinks and a flask of tea, which I set out. Still in my cool bag were individual jellies, pots of diced fruit and a sliced cake for dessert – I'd get those out later.

Emma sat on the ground sheet next to Paula to eat and then, like most children her age, grew bored of adult conversation and explored the area close by.

'Have you talked to her about the baby yet?' I asked Lucy.

'Yes, we've started. We've said she's going to have a baby brother or sister. We'll explain more as we go along and I get bigger.'

'You know I'm available to give you whatever help you need? Now and after the baby is born,' I said.

'Thanks, Mum. That's nice. I know how busy you are.'

'No, I'm cutting back,' I said. 'In fact, I've even been thinking that …'

But again, I didn't get any further. All attention had suddenly turned to Adrian. He was handing out plastic wine flutes from one of their bags.

'I want to make an announcement,' he said, and produced a bottle of sparkling juice from their cool bag.

'Non-alcoholic,' he said, with a smile. 'We're all driving, and Lucy and Kirsty aren't drinking.'

I should have realized then what he was about to say, but I wondered if he or Kirsty had been promoted at work. The penny didn't drop until he said, 'It's a double celebration. To Lucy and Darren on their forthcoming second child, and I'm delighted to say that Kirsty and I are expecting.'

'Wonderful!' Lucy cried.

I jumped up and went over and hugged and kissed Kirsty and Adrian. 'Congratulations, I'm so very pleased,' I said, tears welling. 'You'll make wonderful parents, just like Lucy and Darren.'

'Yes, congratulations,' Paula said, hugging them both. 'I'm going to be an aunty three times over!'

'Yes, and Emma will have a cousin to play with,' Kirsty said.

'Another baby in the family,' Darren told Emma, but she was looking a bit bemused by all the fuss.

Adrian popped the cork on the bottle and filled our wine flutes, including some for Emma.

'To our future new arrivals,' Adrian said, and we all took a sip of our drinks.

'How are you feeling?' Lucy asked Kirsty.

'So far so good. No morning sickness.'

'Lucky you. When are you due?' Lucy asked, which I was going to ask.

'Early January.'

'So same as us,' Lucy cried excitedly.

Kirsty smiled. It seemed that, whereas Lucy had shared her news straight away, Adrian and Kirsty, perhaps more cautious as it was their first pregnancy, had waited a few weeks.

'It's wonderful news,' I said, addressing them all. 'Two more grandchildren on the way. I can see I'm going to be very busy. But I, too, have an announcement of sorts to make.'

I paused.

'I have decided to cut back on fostering so I can concentrate on my family. I feel the time is right.'

'Are you sure, Mum? It's not because of what I said?'

'Adrian, love, when have I ever done what you've told me to?'

He smiled. 'Point taken.'

'And as we are all together,' I added, 'I'd like to take this opportunity to thank you all for your support during all the years we've fostered full-time, especially Adrian, Lucy and Paula, who have been with me throughout. I truly couldn't have done it without you, and I am very proud of you all – my wonderful, loving and rapidly expanding family. Thank you.'

'So you are definitely cutting back?' Darren checked.

'Yes. I will make sure the social services know.'

I knew if I didn't give a deadline for me to stop full-time fostering then there'd always be another child, such is the shortage of carers and children needing homes.

'OK, cool,' Darren said. 'We'll put you down for some babysitting and grab a night out when Lucy feels up to it.'

'Yes, absolutely, please do,' I said, smiling.

'Nana, can you play with me now?' Emma asked, having had enough of adults talking and tugging on my arm.

'Yes, love, of course. We'll play, and I'll have plenty of time to play with you in the future, but first a toast.' I raised my wine flute. 'To the next stage in my life, and my fantastic family.'

'To Mum,' Adrian said. 'Loving mother, grandmother and foster carer.'

As they toasted me, I said a silent prayer of thanks for the wonderful life I'd been blessed with and the future that lay ahead.

CHAPTER TWENTY-ONE

NOTHING IS AS IT FIRST APPEARS

We stayed in Oak Park all afternoon, playing with Emma, talking and finishing the picnic. There was plenty to talk about – Kirsty's and Lucy's pregnancies, work, my decision to scale back on fostering and the pandemic, to name but a few topics we covered. We played bat and ball, explored the woods that skirted the park and sometimes we just sat in silence enjoying the countryside and our thoughts. It was one of those perfect occasions that contributes to the wealth of happy memories families have, assuming you have a good family, which sadly not everyone does.

It was after 5 p.m. when we finally packed away and headed out of the park, the sun still high in the sky. I took Emma to Darren and Lucy's car. 'See you soon, love,' I said as she clambered in.

'See you soon, Nana,' she replied sweetly, and gave me a big kiss.

We all parted as we had met, with lots of hugs. Everyone had work tomorrow and Emma was at nursery. I was mindful that I needed to write to the social services this evening, before I was identified to foster another child permanently.

Paula and I waved them off and then got into my car.

'Are you OK?' I asked as I drove.

'Yes, fine.'

'I mean, about my decision to cut back on fostering?'

'Yes, I agree with it.'

Once home, Paula fed Sammy and then we unpacked the picnic bags and washed up the dirty containers. Paula went to her room and I went to my computer to compose the email I needed to send so it would be read first thing on Monday morning. I decided to address it to Joy and Vivian Bond, the director of Children's Social Care (Children in Care), who I'd met a few times at functions for looked-after children prior to the pandemic. I kept the email short and to the point.

Dear Vivian and Joy,

After much thought, I have decided to step back from full-time fostering and to concentrate on short-term and respite. It has been a difficult decision and one I have not made lightly. Fostering has meant a lot to me and my family for many years, but with two more grandchildren on the way I feel the time is right.

As you know, Damian, Nathan and Liam left on Saturday, and I am happy to accept another child on a short placement for the next few months.

All best wishes,

Cathy Glass

I read it through and checked it again, and then, with my heart beating slightly faster than usual, I clicked send. Done! I allowed myself to breathe again. Almost immediately two automated out-of-office replies popped into my inbox telling me the offices were closed and would reopen again at 9 a.m. on Monday morning, and that if it was an emergency to contact the duty social worker.

I spent half an hour on social media replying to those who'd been good enough to leave comments about my books. Many thanked me for taking the time to respond, but I love to hear from my readers and I appreciate that they have read my books, so it's the least I can do.

Closing down the computer, I joined Paula in the living room, where she'd switched on the television. The patio doors were open and the heady scent of flowers on a warm June evening floated in. Sammy was sprawled on the patio just outside, enjoying the peace and watching the world – and the occasional bird – go by.

'No,' I told him. 'Leave the birds alone.' He gave me that haughty, insolent stare that cats have perfected.

Paula pressed the remote for a news channel. Since the start of the pandemic we'd tried to watch the news most days, although not while we'd had the boys. There just hadn't been time. During the afternoon Kirsty had mentioned that the number of new cases of coronavirus was going up. As a teacher, she was concerned that schools could be closed again. The news programme now confirmed that new cases had increased for the second week in a row, and while still low there was talk about delaying the lifting of the last of the restrictions planned for 21 June. The government, the speaker said, was committed to keeping schools open even if meant that other sectors of the community had to limit their interactions, wear face masks in public places and maintain social distancing, which seemed sensible to me. Children had suffered as a result of not being able to go to school, not only educationally, but socially and emotionally too.

Paula and I finished our evening by watching a film together. That night I slept very well. A pleasant afternoon in the park, a decision made and my email sent contributed to my feeling of well-being. The following morning, straight after breakfast, I texted Lara and said I was free to visit whenever it suited her. She replied saying tomorrow afternoon would be good, and if I was going shopping could I get her some coffee and tea bags as she was nearly out. I confirmed I would. I was going grocery shopping that morning, and half an hour later, leaving Paula working in her bedroom, I set off.

Although I was feeling relieved that I'd made the decision to step back from full-time fostering, I was also slightly apprehensive as to the reception my email would get at the fostering services. I suppose I could have told Joy first, but there hadn't really been an opportunity. I knew it wasn't the best time to reduce my availability as there were so many children coming into care, but to be honest there would never be a right time in that sense. I had some friends who were in their seventies – one lady was in her eighties – who were still fostering full-time. Obviously, it was right for them. There is no upper age limit for fostering. As long as the carer is healthy and able to meet the needs of the young people in their care, they can continue. We all have regular medicals and an annual appraisal.

I had my mobile in my bag as I shopped. I checked it a couple of times but there was nothing from Joy or Vivian. That continued to be the case for the rest of the day. As Paula and I settled down in the living room to watch the six o'clock news I knew I wouldn't hear from them now as their offices were closed. Slightly disappointed, I concentrated on what our prime minister was saying at the news conference: that due to the number of new cases of Covid, England's relaxation of restrictions planned for 21 June would be delayed by four weeks. Paula and I agreed that, while it was frustrating, it was necessary.

At 9.30 the following morning Joy phoned. She said she'd been off work on Monday so had only just read my email.

'I'm disappointed,' she said. 'That's two of you gone this week.'

'Two of us?' I asked.

'Natasha and Jamal have handed in their notice.'

'Oh, yes, I see, but I'm available for short-term placements, one child, and respite.'

'It's the same result,' she said a little tersely. 'We are two fostering families short at a time when there is already a shortage.'

'I'm sorry, Joy,' I said, slightly aggrieved by her attitude. 'I hope you understand why I've made the decision to scale back over the coming months.'

'You want to spend more time with your grandchildren.'

'That's part of it.'

'And the other part?'

I really didn't like her tone. 'Fostering is twenty-four-seven, all year round,' I said. 'You don't go home at the end of the day, switch off and relax. It's a huge commitment, not just for the carer, but for their family, extended family and friends. As well as being more available to help my family, I would like some more "me" time to relax and do what I want. I think I've earned it.' Joy's job was nine to five-thirty, so I wasn't sure she fully appreciated the level of commitment required to foster full-time.

'It's a pity you didn't discuss it with me first,' she said.

'Sorry, but it wouldn't have made any difference. I thought about it long and hard.' I took a breath. 'I feel the time is right. The boys have just left, so I'm not letting anyone down by cutting back now.'

'But you're still willing to take a single child for a few months?'

'Yes.'

'I'll be in touch then,' she said, and said goodbye.

I wasn't sure if I was angry or hurt – maybe a bit of both. Clearly my email had caught Joy at a bad time, but I was relieved we'd had the conversation and I'd stood my ground. I didn't feel guilty, just irked by Joy's attitude. I'd fostered to the best of my ability all these years. I had nothing to feel guilty about.

Even so, Joy's brusque manner – which seemed to put me in the wrong – played on my mind that morning. As I went about the housework and then spent time at my computer, her words niggled away in the background. Later that morning I received a phone call from the police to say Damian's bike could be collected. I explained I was no longer his foster carer but said that either the new carers or I would collect the bike. The officer asked that it be as soon as possible as it was taking up space, and that whoever collected the bike needed to bring ID.

I felt it was too soon after the boys had left for me to phone Anne and Maurice. It could have appeared intrusive while the boys were still settling in, as if I was checking up on them, so I texted their mobile number.

*Hope you are all OK. The police just phoned to say Damian's bike can be collected from *****.* I gave the name of the police station. *Do you want me to collect it? They want it gone ASAP. Cathy*

Five minutes later Anne replied: *Thanks, Cathy. Damian's been asking about his bike. One of us can collect it tomorrow after we've taken Damian to school. We met Rachel yesterday. I can see why you worried about her. She said to say hi to you. Boys settling in fine. Hope you are OK.*

All well here, thanks, I typed. *Whoever collects the bike needs to take ID.*

Thanks. Speak soon. Anne

When I visited Lara that afternoon I was pleased to see there was no mattress on the living-room floor and the kitchen was reasonably clean and tidy. I gave her the tea bags and coffee she'd asked for, plus a few extras. I sat on the sofa with Arthur while Lara poured us cold drinks. He wanted to show me some toys he'd been playing with. I admired them and when Lara joined us I told her of my decision to scale back on fostering over the coming months.

'Does that mean you won't come here any more?' she asked.

'No, love, seeing you is separate, although the social services know. Lots of foster carers keep in touch with the young people they've looked after. I'll visit as long as you want me to.'

'Thank God for that!' she said, visibly relieved. 'What did they say when you told them? I bet they weren't pleased.'

'I got a bit of a telling-off,' I admitted, and smiled weakly.

'I hope they thanked you. I wouldn't want to look after me, especially as a teenager.'

I smiled. 'You've done very well,' I said, while thinking that Joy hadn't thanked me. Not that I'd fostered to be thanked.

As we sipped our drinks and I played with Arthur, Lara and I talked – about fostering, Arthur, the pandemic, her partner Frazer and life in general. I was there all afternoon and left at 4.45 with that warm glow that comes from being with young people. I felt Lara was one of my success stories, although what she'd achieved was due to her hard work and determination. She'd turned her life around just as Frazer had, and many of the other young people who'd kept in touch with me.

'I'll see you next week,' Lara said as I left.

'Yes, and you know you can phone any time.'

They waved me off at the door. 'Bye, Caffy!' Arthur called.

'Bye, love.'

As I drove home my mobile rang. I didn't check it until I'd parked on the drive. There was a missed call from Joy and a voicemail message, which I listened to before I got out. 'Cathy, please phone as soon as you get this message. We've had an emergency referral for a ten-year-old girl. It's short term. I'll try your home phone.'

I went indoors. Paula heard the front door and immediately came out of her room. 'Joy's just phoned. She said to call her – it's urgent.'

'Thanks, love. I'm just doing it now.'

Joy answered straight away.

'It's Cathy Glass. I've just been visiting Lara; I was driving when you called.'

'You got my message?'

'Yes, about the ten-year-old girl.'

'You can take her?'

'Yes. When is she coming?'

'Today. As soon as the social worker can get her to you.'

'Oh. I see.'

It's not unusual for a foster carer to have a child placed with them at very short notice, but what Joy said next *was* unusual.

'Esme's social worker will give you the details, but Esme has run away from a cult where she was taken to live by her mother.'

'A cult?' I asked, shocked. 'I didn't know we had them in this country.'

'Apparently we do, although I've never dealt with one before.'

'And it will just be short-term?' I checked.

'Yes, her father is coming to collect her as soon as he can.' Which seemed to suggest it might only be a few days, even a few hours.

I should have realized that very little in fostering is how it first appears …

'Bobbie Freeman is the social worker,' Joy continued. 'The referral says very little. The family haven't come to the attention of the social services before. I'll give Bobbie your contact details and she'll call. I've got to try to place a sibling group of four now!' she added with a sigh. 'I'll phone you tomorrow and see how it's going, although Esme might be gone by then.'

'OK, thank you, Joy.'

I sprang into action. Keeping hold of my mobile, I went upstairs to check the bedroom Esme would be using. I'd already vacuumed and dusted it, and made up the bed in case a child arrived as an emergency. It looked fine to me, so then I went to Paula's bedroom and knocked lightly on her door.

'Come in!' she called.

I poked my head around the door. 'Just to let you know we've got a ten-year-old girl arriving this evening. Not sure what time. She'll be short term.'

'OK, I'll be down as soon as I've finished.'

It was five-fifteen when I went downstairs to the kitchen to prepare dinner for later. The social worker was likely to stay for an hour, so we'd eat after she'd gone. If Esme didn't like the quiche I was putting together or had special dietary requirements, I'd make her something else. I'd just filled the pastry case and put it into the oven when my phone rang. It was from a number not in my contacts list.

'Hello?'

'Cathy Glass?'

'Yes.'

'It's Bobbie Freeman. I understand you're taking Esme Carter.'

'That's correct.'

'I'm driving so I've got you on hands-free. Esme is with us. She's been very brave, but she's had a traumatic day.'

'Hello, Esme,' I said, aware she should be able to hear me.

She didn't reply.

'She's exhausted and not saying much at present,' Bobbie said. 'I'll explain more when we arrive. I've got to drop off my colleague first as she has a child to collect from day-care, then I'll come straight to you. Probably about an hour.'

'All right.'

'I should tell you that Esme hasn't got anything with her. Just what she's wearing.'

'That's not a problem. I've got plenty of spares until we can buy her some new things. Although I understand her father is on his way.'

'Not exactly on his way,' Bobbie said. 'Although he has been informed. Sensibly, Esme kept the piece of paper he gave her with his mobile number on. They've spoken to each other, but it might take him some time to get the paperwork in place, and once here, he'll need to test negative before he can see Esme.'

'He's not in this country then?' I asked.

'No, sorry, didn't I say? I'll tell you what I know when we arrive.'

As I said earlier, very little in fostering is as it first appears.

CHAPTER TWENTY-TWO

MAMA AND PAPA

When Paula finished work she came downstairs and I told her what I knew.

'A cult? Where?' she asked, as surprised as I had been.

'I don't know, but I'm guessing it's in the county somewhere.'

'How strange.'

'It is.'

I was expecting Bobbie to arrive with Esme at around 6.15, but it was 6.45 when the doorbell finally rang. Paula and I headed down the hall, grabbed a mask each from the hall stand and put them on before I opened the front door. Both Bobbie and Esme were wearing disposable masks. Esme's was far too big for her.

'Come in,' I welcomed, and stood aside to let them pass. 'I'm Cathy and this is my daughter, Paula.'

'Hi,' Bobbie said. Then to Esme, 'This is the foster carer I told you about. You'll be staying here until your father arrives.'

Esme looked at us with large, wary eyes, just visible over her mask. She was of average height and build for her age, with long black hair and dark eyes. She was wearing a summer dress with a little cardigan, and flip-flop style sandals.

'Let's go and sit in the living room,' I said. 'Would you like a drink?'

'Not for me, thanks,' Bobbie said. 'We picked up something on the way. What about you, Esme? Do you want another drink?'

She shook her head.

I'd left the patio windows open in the living room to keep it well ventilated.

'Are those of your family?' Bobbie asked as she sat down, referring to the photographs on the wall and mantelpiece.

'Yes, some of them are and others are of children we've fostered.'

'So many.' She took her laptop from her briefcase and opened it.

'Does Esme want to take off her mask?' I asked, feeling she might be more comfortable. She sat on the sofa next to her social worker.

'Once I've gone,' Bobbie said. 'She's just come from living in a commune with at least thirty people, possibly more. So maybe test her. You've got lateral flow tests?'

'Yes. The thirty people — is that the cult that was mentioned?' I asked.

'Yes.'

'Where is it?' I could see Paula was dying to know too.

'A farm just outside ****.' Bobbie named a small village situated in the countryside towards the north of the county. I knew the village but wasn't aware of the farm.

'The cult took it over about five years ago,' she said. 'They're reclusive, keep themselves to themselves and try to live off the land. I've sent you the Essential Information Form.' She tapped her laptop.

'Thank you. I'll look at it later. So is it like a hippy commune?' I asked.

'With some religion thrown in,' Bobbie replied. 'There's a leader who seems to rule them. Some of the locals said that occasionally they saw some of them in the village store, but they never spoke to anyone.'

I nodded.

'Esme's father has custody of Esme,' Bobbie continued, glancing up. 'And as I said on the phone, he'll be here as soon as he can. They live in –' and she named an overseas English-speaking country. 'He's spoken to Esme on the phone and I'll give him your mobile number. He'd like to speak to her this evening, then every day, via video call if possible. He hasn't seen her for eight months.'

'I see. How long has Esme been in this country?' I asked.

'He thinks about seven months. That's when he says she disappeared. She was living in a type of cult over there, but her father saw her regularly. After a lengthy legal battle, he was awarded custody and mother and child disappeared.'

'And ended up here?' I asked incredulously. 'How did they know about the cult?'

'We didn't know about it and we live here,' Paula added.

'These places are often hidden in plain sight,' Bobbie said. 'From what Esme's father has told us, the cult they were living in has connections to the one here, and in some other countries, so that helped Esme and her mother flee.'

'Is it legal to keep a child in a cult or commune?' I asked. I had no idea.

'Grey area,' Bobbie replied. 'But as long as it's not abusive and they are looked after and are receiving an education, the courts usually keep out of it. The mother broke the law when she defied the court that gave Esme's father custody and fled the country with Esme. That's the grounds on which she will be returned. Her father is sending the legal documents to our lawyers now. There is no suggestion so far that Esme has been sexually abused, but it's possible,' she added.

I looked at Esme, who was sitting quietly bedside her social worker, undoubtedly taking it all in but not saying anything.

'Esme's father has asked for Esme to have a medical. I've told him I'll check the availability of appointments and let him know.' Bobbie tapped her laptop again. Usually when a child came into care they had a medical, but as a result of Covid most non-essential health checks had been delayed.

'Does she have any medical conditions or allergies?' I asked.

'No. However, her father has issues with the limited diet she's been eating. Her mother has had her on a strict vegan diet, which he maintains was making her lethargic and tired. She ate meat when she was with him. Most of these communes are vegan.'

'So what shall I do?' I asked. As a foster carer I usually followed the parents' wishes and practices as much as possible when it came to diet, religion, culture and similar matters.

'Do you like meat?' Bobbie asked Esme.

Esme gave a small nod. 'Some.'

'Give her what she wants then,' Bobbie said to me. 'Her father has no objections.'

'And she's not taking any medication?' I checked.

'No. Her father says as far as he knows she's healthy.'

'So how did Esme manage to leave the farm today?' I asked.

It wasn't just curiosity. The more I knew of Esme, the better equipped I was to meet her needs.

'She ran away very early this morning while everyone was still asleep, then walked a mile into the village where she knocked on the door of a retired couple. They took her in. It was just before seven o'clock. They gave her breakfast and called the police, who notified us.'

'It's been a long day then,' I said, glancing again at Esme. 'You must be exhausted.'

'I'm sure she is. I know I am,' Bobbie said, and she checked her wristwatch. 'Is there anything else I need to tell you?'

'School? Is Esme going to school?' I asked. Usually when a school-aged child arrived they continued attending the school where they were already enrolled.

'You haven't been to school here, have you?' Bobbie asked Esme.

'No,' she said quietly.

'Most of these groups believe in home education,' Bobbie explained. 'According to the father, he had to take the mother to court to get her into school there. I'll speak to him, but it hardly seems worthwhile finding Esme a school here. Perhaps you and your daughter could do some schooling with her?'

'Yes, I can,' I replied. 'Paula is working full-time, although it's from home at present.'

Bobbie nodded and checked her laptop again.

'There's just the two of you living here?' she asked.

'Yes, and our cat, Sammy.' Having heard strangers in the house, he was nowhere to be seen. 'He'll be in later.'

'OK. I think that's everything,' Bobbie said. 'The father's contact details and so forth are on the forms. Please sign the placement agreement online. There's no contact being arranged with the mother at present. She's aware that Esme is in care, but she won't be given your address as there is a flight risk.'

'All right. And her father is going to phone her this evening?' I checked. Esme was looking very tired and it was now 7.30 and we had yet to eat.

'I'll call him after I've left here, give him your mobile number and ask him to phone as soon as possible.'

'Thank you.'

'Can I just use your bathroom before I go?' Bobbie asked, standing.

'Yes, of course.'

She put away her laptop. Leaving Paula with Esme in the living room, I went with Bobbie to the foot of the stairs and pointed out where the bathroom was.

'You don't mind if I take a look around while I'm up here,' she said as she began upstairs. 'Then I can reassure the father.'

'Go ahead.' It was usual for the social worker and supervising social worker to look around the carer's home at each visit. 'Esme's room is straight ahead of you and the toilet is to your right.'

'Thank you.'

As Bobbie went upstairs, Sammy shot down, having been hiding up there. I followed him into the living room.

'Your cat,' Esme said, and I saw the first glimmer of a smile from behind her mask.

'Yes, do you like cats?' Paula asked.

'I do, very much,' she said in a polite voice.

'Good, he likes you,' I said.

Sammy was rubbing around her legs, purring softy. Like many animals, he seemed to sense when a child needed a bit of extra care and attention. I could hear Bobbie moving around upstairs, then she came down, went quickly in and out of the front room and then the kitchen-diner. She returned to the living room. Esme was now kneeling beside Sammy and stroking him gently.

'Settling in already, that's good,' Bobbie said. 'I'm going now, Esme. I'll phone your father on my way home. Have a nice evening.'

She said goodbye to Paula and I saw her out. Bobbie must have had a long day, just as Esme had.

I was in two minds about giving Esme the lateral flow test for Covid. She'd had a fraught day, had just arrived at a stranger's house and now I was going to swab her – an unpleasant experience and not exactly welcoming. But Bobbie had said I should, and it made sense to do it straight away. If Esme tested positive, I'd take extra precautions, although clearly she couldn't be expected to keep her mask on the whole time. Since the start of the pandemic foster carers were having to make all sorts of decisions they wouldn't normally.

In the living room Paula and Esme had already taken off their masks. I'd taken mine off too. Esme was still stroking Sammy.

'All right, love?' I asked her.

She nodded. She seemed a really sweet child.

'Your social worker wants you to take a Covid test. Do you know what that is?'

'I know Covid is a virus that can make you very sick, even die. Mama says it's because people on the outside don't treat their bodies right.'

Hmm, I thought, and wondered what else her mother had told her.

'Have you ever had a Covid test?' I asked.

'I don't think so,' Esme replied.

'Come with me into the kitchen and I'll show you what it is. Then we'll do one.'

She looked worried.

'It doesn't hurt, and Paula and I will do one too.'

'Thanks, Mum,' Paula said sarcastically.

But it helped – Esme was reassured and came with us into the kitchen.

I washed my hands and the work surface first and took a box of lateral flow tests from the cupboard. I explained to Esme what was in each packet as I set them out, and the process involved. I washed my hands again and did the first test on myself as Esme watched in amazement.

'Ever seen that done before?' Paula asked her.

Esme shook her head, so I assumed the groups she'd been living in hadn't been using lateral flow tests like most households had. I tested Paula and finally Esme, who didn't mind, having watched us. I put the tests to one side to develop.

'Shall we eat, Mum?' Paula asked. 'I'm hungry.'

'Yes.' I was hungry too.

I showed Esme the quiche I'd prepared, along with new potatoes and peas, and asked her if she'd like it.

'I think so,' she said. 'But is it contaminated?'

'What do mean by contaminated, love?' In all the years I'd been fostering I'd had to deal with plenty of food preferences and issues in connection with food, but this was new.

'Axel says people on the outside eat contaminated food,' Esme replied.

'Who is Axel?' I asked.

'The man in charge of the farm. Mum loves him – so do the other women – but I don't.'

'I see.' I suppose you could say that pesticides and food additives were a form of contamination, but I wasn't going down that path. 'I made this earlier using organic eggs, cheese and milk,' I said, referring to the quiche. 'So it's quite safe.'

Thankfully I was stopped from having to justify the pastry case, which I'd bought ready-made, by my mobile ringing.

'Is that Papa?' Esme asked hopefully.

'It could be,' I said. The display showed an international number.

'Hello?'

'Cathy Glass?' a man with a slight accent asked.

'Yes.'

'I'm Hugo, Esme's father.'

'Hello, nice to hear from you. Esme is with me now.'

'How is she? I've been so worried.' I could hear the anxiety in his voice. 'The relief when I got that call this morning to say she'd been found was unbelievable. Can I talk to her, please, and then perhaps we can talk?' I saw my chances of eating disappear.

'Yes, of course.'

I passed the phone to Esme. 'It's your father,' I said.

She pressed the phone to her ear. 'Papa!' she cried, delighted. 'Where are you? When are you coming to get me?'

I couldn't hear his reply. Bobbie hadn't asked me to put the phone on speaker and monitor the call as I'd had to with Rachel and Damian. But Paula and I stayed in the kitchen-diner with Esme as she listened to what her father was saying. Sometimes she looked serious, sometimes she smiled, occasionally she nodded and said, 'Yes, Papa,' and, 'No.'

After about five minutes or so Esme said, 'I love you too,' and passed the phone to me. 'Papa wants to talk to you.'

'Thanks, love. You have your dinner with Paula while I speak to him.'

Leaving them in the kitchen-diner, I took my phone into the living room.

'My adult daughter, Paula, is with Esme,' I told Hugo. 'I've left them having dinner.'

'Sorry to interrupt your meal. How is Esme? I spoke to her briefly this morning, but she didn't say much. She used to be such a chatterbox. The social worker said she was quiet.'

'She's had a traumatic day,' I said. 'And she's only just arrived here. She seems to be coping remarkable well, considering. Try not to worry. We'll take good care of her until you arrive.'

'Thank you. I don't know how much you have been told but I have legal custody of my daughter.'

'Yes, the social worker said.'

'Esme's mother and I separated four years ago when she got herself involved in a religious sect. She calls herself Serenity but her real name is Mary. She changed it when she joined the sect. She's filled Esme's head with a lot of silly nonsense. I had regular contact with Esme to begin with and she lived with me every other week. But when her mother took her to live in the cult with her it grew less and less, and I had to take her to court to have it reinstated. Since then, it's been a continuous battle of court cases, not helped by all the lockdowns and restrictions. I was finally granted full custody towards the end of last year and that's when they disappeared. I thought they might be in England. Esme's mother is from the UK. Without the pandemic I think she would have been found sooner. I haven't seen my daughter in nearly eight months. It's been horrendous.'

'I can imagine,' I sympathized. 'But Esme is safe now.'

'I need to keep telling myself that. I'd like to see her tomorrow. The social worker said I could video-call. Do you have Skype?'

'Yes. I'll text you my details. Roughly what time tomorrow?'

'Shall we say ten a.m.? Is that all right for you?'

'Yes, fine.'

'I'd like to say goodnight to Esme, then I'll leave you to have your dinner in peace. Please call me day or night if you have any questions. I'm a musician but my work has dried up during the pandemic, so I am at home a lot. I'm missing Esme so much. The social worker said she didn't have any clothes with her.'

'Just what she is wearing, but don't worry, I have spare clean clothes for her. Tomorrow we'll go shopping and buy what she needs. I'll put her on now so you can say goodnight.'

'Thank you, Cathy.'

I returned to the kitchen-dinner where Paula and Esme were sitting at the table, having just finished eating. Their plates were empty.

'Your father wants to say goodnight, then he will video-call tomorrow,' I told Esme, and passed her my phone.

She listened and then said, 'Night, Papa, I love and miss you too.' She blew a kiss down the phone before handing it back to me.

'Night,' I said to Hugo.

'Night. Thanks again. Remember to call me if you need to.'

'I will.'

Esme was looking a bit brighter now.

'Would you like some pudding?' I asked her as she sipped her drink.

'No, thank you,' she replied politely.

I checked the lateral flow tests and they were all negative, which was a relief. I then texted my Skype details to Hugo. He replied straight away. *Thank you. I'll call tomorrow at 10 a.m.* I had the feeling he wouldn't be late.

'Can I go to bed now?' Esme asked. 'I'm very tired.' She looked it.

'Come on, love, I'll take you upstairs.'

She left the table. 'Night, Paula,' she said, and offered her cheek for kissing.

I guessed it was what she was used to. As foster carers we take the cue for how much physical contact the child wants from them. Some children can be very tactile, some inappropriately so, when we have to put in place boundaries following our safer-caring policy. Other children may not want a hug or kiss for a long time – some never, although that is rare.

Esme and Paula cheek-kissed and then Esme came with me down the hall, where I paused to show her the front room before taking her upstairs. I showed her into her bedroom where I'd already set out nightwear that would fit her. I'd also put a fresh towel, toothbrush and toiletries in the bathroom for her.

'Is this my bed?' she asked, touching it.

'Yes, love.'

'We didn't have beds at the farm.'

'No? What did you sleep on?'

'Mats on the floor. Mama said it was better for our bodies. But I had a bed at Papa's and I liked it.' I'd fostered children before who hadn't slept in a bed, but that was usually a result of poverty, not because it was considered better for their bodies, which I doubted. Later, when I wrote up my log notes I'd include what Esme was telling me.

'It's usual to sleep in a bed; we all do here,' I said. 'Were there other children at the farm?'

'Yes, six of us. Mama said they were my brothers and sisters, but I know they weren't really.'

I assumed the social services were aware of the children living on the farm, but I'd inform Bobbie and include it in my notes just in case. I showed Esme where Paula and I slept, and then we went into the bathroom.

'Do I have to have a shower?' she asked. 'I'm very tired.'

'No, love. Just have a good wash and you can shower in the morning.'

She looked relieved. 'We always had to shower at night at the farm, even if it was late. We had to take turns and sometimes I was waiting for ages. But we had to. Axel said it was to wash off the sins of the day.'

Something else to add to my log, I thought.

'We shower or have a bath every day like most people to keep our bodies clean,' I said. I don't think Esme really believed it was to wash away sin; she was repeating what she'd been told. I was starting to understand her father's comments about her mother filling her head with a lot of nonsense, but I wouldn't be criticizing her. Esme had spent a lot of time with her mother and would love her regardless.

This was confirmed a short while later when, having had a wash and brushed her teeth, I saw her into bed.

'Do you think Mama is all right?' Esme asked. Many children in care worry about their parents and need to be reassured.

'Yes. Your social worker has spoken to her and will make sure she's all right.'

'Do you think she's angry with me?'

'No, love. She'll understand.'

'I love Mama and Papa, but I think it's better if I live with Papa,' Esme said. I'm often taken aback by the maturity and wisdom of children. 'That's what the judge said too.'

'Yes, love. Were you happy living with your father?'

'I was. Papa says I will be able to see Mama once we're home.'

'Good.'

Esme got into bed, snuggled down and looked comfortable.

'Have you got everything you need?' I asked.

'Yes, thank you,' she said sweetly. I thought that whatever the parents' differences, they had done some good parenting.

'Call me in the night if you need me,' I said. 'Would you like your curtains open or closed?' I went to the window. It was still light outside; the sun was just starting its descent.

Esme thought for a moment. 'I don't know. We didn't have curtains at the farm. Mama said it was good to see the stars and moon God had created.'

I smiled. 'It's up to you, love.'

'I have a blind in my room at Papa's and he closes it a bit at night.'

'I'll draw the curtains a little then,' I suggested. 'Like this.' It's important a child feels comfortable at night, as it will help them sleep. I drew the curtains so there was a gap in the middle. 'How's that?'

'Nice, thank you. Will you kiss me goodnight like Mama and Papa did?'

'Of course, love.'

I kissed her forehead, told her again to call me if she needed me and then came out, leaving the door ajar so I would hear her.

As I returned downstairs my concerns were not so much with Esme, who was safe now, but the other children at the farm. Before I did anything else I emailed

Bobbie, stating what Esme had said, then I began my log notes for Esme while it was all still fresh in my mind. There was a lot to write.

CHAPTER TWENTY-THREE

ESME

I never sleep well when there is a new child in the house. I'm half listening out in case they wake up frightened, not knowing where they are and in need of reassurance. As it turned out I needn't have worried. I checked on Esme before I went to bed at around 11 p.m. and she was sleeping peacefully, her long hair spread out on the pillow like an angel. As soon as I woke at 6 a.m. I looked into her room again and she was still fast asleep. I quietly closed her door, had a coffee, then showered and dressed. It was 9 a.m. when Esme woke, by which time Paula was working in her bedroom. I heard Esme get up to use the toilet and I went upstairs.

'All right, love?' I asked her when she came out. 'You slept well.'

'I did. Has Papa phoned?'

'Not yet, love. In about an hour.'

'I need to shower and dress so I'm ready,' she said.

'There's plenty of time. Here are your clothes, all nice and clean.' I'd washed and dried what she'd been wearing yesterday as I thought she'd feel more comfortable in her own clothes rather than those from my spares.

I went with her to the bathroom where I showed her how to use the shower and checked she had everything she needed. I came out and closed the door, but waited on the landing until she'd finished, just in case she needed anything. When she came out she was towel drying her hair, having washed it in the shower.

'Do you want a hairdryer?' I asked.

She thought for a moment. 'Yes, I used one at Papa's.'

'But not at the farm?'

'No. We had to let our hair and bodies dry naturally. The adults said it was more natural, but it was cold in winter.'

'I can imagine.' I fetched my hairdryer from my bedroom.

'Can you dry it like Papa used to?' Esme asked.

'I'll try.'

She stood in front of the mirror in her bedroom while I brushed and dried her long, shiny hair, drawing it off her forehead.

'Papa used to do it like this,' she said when I'd finished, and twisted some strands of her hair.

'In a plait?' I asked.

'Yes, can you do that?'

'I'll do my best. One plait or two?'

'One, at the back.'

'OK. Wait here and I'll get a band.'

I had a good selection of hairbands, clips and braids from all the years I'd been fostering. I kept them in a box in a drawer in my bedroom. I hadn't had to do a plait for a long time, but I thought that, like swimming or riding a bike, it wasn't something you forgot. I returned with a suitable band and Esme watched me in the mirror as I

253

concentrated on plaiting her hair and secured it at the end with the band.

'Just like Papa does it,' she said, pleased.

'Great. Let's get you some breakfast before he calls.'

As we went downstairs Esme asked where Paula was and I explained she was working in her bedroom and she'd see her later. In the kitchen I showed her what I had in the cupboards for breakfast, and she said she'd like bread and butter with honey on it.

'We made our bread at the farm,' she said. 'I used to help.'

'This is from the shop, but it's organic wholemeal, so healthy,' I said.

I let her butter the bread and put on the honey; she seemed very self-sufficient. She asked for a glass of milk, and as I poured it she said they had a cow at the farm that they milked, and lots of chickens that laid eggs. Some of their lifestyle practices seemed very healthy, almost idyllic, while others I felt were obsessive, even bizarre. How far these practices met the needs of the children there would be for the social services to decide.

As Esme ate she told me they all had their meals together at the farm. I said we ate dinner together and sometimes breakfast and lunch. I could see the time ticking towards 10 a.m. so I fetched my laptop ready for her father's video call. Esme was just finishing her milk when it came through. I knew from the Essential Information Form that Hugo was thirty-seven, but he looked younger, boyish, with a mop of black hair and dark eyes just like Esme's. He appeared to be in a living room, with bookshelves lining the wall behind him.

'Good morning, Cathy. Is Esme there?' he said, as impatient to see her as she was him.

'Good morning, Hugo. Here she is,' I replied, and angled the laptop so they could see each other.

'Papa!' Esme screamed, setting down her glass and jumping for joy. 'Papa! Papa!'

Sammy, who'd been sitting by the table hoping for a titbit, was scared by the noise and shot off.

'Esme, my love. It's so long since I've seen you,' Hugo said.

'So long, Papa. A long time. But you're at home? I thought you were coming to get me.' Her face fell.

'I am coming as soon as I can, Esme, but countries have lots of rules and regulations that I have to follow, even more with Covid. Do you have your passport?'

Esme looked at me and I moved so I was in Hugo's view.

'Not as far as I know,' I said. 'She doesn't have it here.'

'I thought not – the social worker said Esme was just holding the piece of paper with my phone number on it when she escaped. I wanted to check with you, but I will fast-track a new one. Unless her mother can be persuaded to hand it over.'

'I don't know,' I said.

'Axel has our passports, not Mama,' Esme said. 'He took Mama's phone too.'

'Axel?' Hugo queried.

'I think he's the leader of the group where Esme has been living,' I said. 'You'll need to speak to Bobbie to see if there is any way of getting it back.'

'I will, but I'll start the fast-track for a new one; it will probably be quicker.' He returned his attention to Esme and I moved to one side. 'So, my wonderful daughter, it won't be long.'

'How long, Papa?'

'Days, maybe a week. I'll make everything happen as quickly as I can. You were so brave to run away, and well done for keeping that piece of paper with my mobile number on it.'

Esme smiled weakly. 'I love you, Papa. Have you spoken to Mama?'

'No.'

'I think she will be upset and angry that I ran away.' Clearly Esme was worrying about her mother as she'd said something similar yesterday.

'It's me who should be angry with her,' Hugo said, but without malice. 'She took you away when she had no right to. It caused me a lot of worry and expense. I have so many legal bills to pay, and more to come.'

'Am I worth it?' Esme asked innocently.

'Of course. I will give anything to have you safely back here. So tell me, what is Cathy's house like? I know you have your own bedroom – the social worker said.'

'Yes, Papa. It's a nice room, not like at the farm. I slept well and Cathy has done my hair like you do.'

'I can see. It looks good.'

'Hugo,' I said. 'Sorry to butt in – would you like to see Esme's bedroom? We could give you a virtual tour of the house.'

'There's no need,' he replied. 'The social worker said you will look after Esme well until I arrive.'

'Can I see my bedroom there?' Esme asked.

'Yes. It's exactly as you left it. Well, I tidied it, but that's all.'

I watched the screen with Esme as Hugo carried the device he was using from the living room, down a short hall and into Esme's bedroom. She gave a gasp of delight, and for good reason. It was a lovely bedroom decorated in lilac with a white wooden bed, matching wardrobe, chest of drawers and bookshelves. The floral duvet cover matched the pillowcase and the blind at the window, which Esme had spoken of last night. Cuddly toys sat on the bed, the chair and the shelves, lodged between books and other toys. How different to the farm Esme had described, I thought. But the reminder of home was bittersweet and too much for Esme.

'I want to come home,' Papa,' she said, her eyes filling.

'I know, but don't upset yourself,' Hugo said, visibly moved. 'You have been found, that's all that matters. You are safe. The time will soon pass.' He returned to the living room. 'What are you doing today?' he asked, but Esme was still looking sad and didn't reply. 'Cathy told me she is taking you shopping to buy you new clothes, so that will be nice,' he tried.

Still Esme didn't reply.

'I think you will need new clothes here as well,' Hugo said. 'Those in your wardrobe will be too small. What else have you planned for today?' he asked, trying to brighten her mood.

Esme shrugged despondently, so I replied.

'The social worker suggested I do some home tutoring with Esme as she isn't going to school, and it's a fine day so we'll go in the garden.'

'Esme didn't go to school when her mother took her to live in the cult there, but she went to school here.'

'Mama said we learnt from nature and what is around us,' Esme said, defending her mother.

'But you also need lessons in school for a wide education,' Hugo said.

'Will you tell Mama I'm sorry?' Esme said.

'There's no need,' Hugo replied. But I was thinking that Esme needed some reassurance about her mother, even contact, and I'd mention it to Bobbie when we next spoke.

'I don't want Mama to be in trouble,' Esme said. 'I just want to come home.'

'I know, my love, and I promise I will bring you home as soon as I can,' Hugo said. 'Papa doesn't break promises, does he?'

'No,' Esme replied quietly.

'Grandma and Grandpa send their love and are looking forward to seeing you again.' These were Hugo's parents. Esme's maternal grandmother was a widow and lived in the UK. 'Julian next door is looking forward to seeing you again too,' Hugo said. 'I told him and his mother you'd been found. They send their love and say they will have a party when you come back.'

Esme brightened a little.

'Your class at school will be pleased to see you again,' Hugo continued. 'They sent a lovely card when you left. I've told the Headmistress you've been found.'

'I liked my school,' Esme said quietly.

'I know, and you will go there as soon as you can. The schools break up in two weeks' time here for the summer holidays, so I'm hoping you will be able to join them for the last week.'

'That's good, Papa.'

And so their conversation continued for about twenty minutes, with Hugo reminding Esme of her life there and what they would do when she returned. Every so often Esme made a comment about her mother, which her father glossed over, but I could see how worried she was. The call ended with Hugo and Esme blowing each other kisses and Hugo saying, 'I'll call at the same time tomorrow. Is that all right with you, Cathy?'

'Yes.'

Esme was looking sad as the call ended so I decided we'd go shopping straight away to take her mind off it.

'Here's our shopping list so far,' I said, passing her my handwritten list. 'Can you think of anything else?'

I'd included sandals and shoes as her flip-flops weren't practical for everyday use, day clothes, underwear, socks, nightwear and a lightweight jacket or raincoat.

'I can't think of anything else,' she said without much enthusiasm, and handed it back.

'It won't be long until your papa can come,' I reassured her, and gave her a hug.

She was quiet in the car, looking out of her side window as I drove to the shopping centre, but once we were there, among the brightly lit shops, she cheered up a little. I guessed she hadn't been shopping much since arriving here, if at all. At her age she didn't have to wear a face mask in public places, but many children were now so I gave her a disposable one. We shopped for an hour and a half and then I suggested we had a drink and a snack in the department store's café. She asked for a hot chocolate, which she said was like the ones she'd had with her father, but she didn't want anything to eat. When we finished we went into a bookshop and chose some home-schooling workbooks in maths, science and English.

'You can be my teacher,' she said with a small smile.

We were shopping for nearly three hours in total and, once home, I made us a late lunch. Paula had already had hers. After we'd eaten we unpacked the bags and hung her new clothes in the wardrobe in her bedroom. We then sat in the garden where we began some of the lessons in the books I'd bought. Thankfully, the answers were in the back as some of the science questions had me flummoxed. We worked for an hour and then I suggested a game of badminton. Esme played, but I could tell her heart wasn't in it; it was in another country with her dear papa.

Just before 4 p.m. Bobbie phoned my mobile. We were still in the garden and I moved slightly away from Esme so I could speak freely. Bobbie asked how Esme was and I told her she'd had a good night and was eating well, and what we'd been doing. Then I repeated what Esme had said about her life on the farm and that there were other children there. Bobbie said they were aware there were other minors living there and it was being investigated. I told her how contact with her father was going – the phone call last night and the video call this morning – and that he was going to Skype each morning at ten o'clock. I also said that Esme was worried about her mother, and I wondered if there were any plans for her to have some telephone contact.

'Not at present, but I shall be visiting the farm with a colleague later this week when I hope to meet her mother. It's very difficult getting in touch with anyone there as they don't have phones. If they need to make a call, they use the payphone in the village. I read what you said in your email about Axel, thank you.'

Bobbie then asked to speak to Esme so I passed her the phone. They didn't talk for long; Bobbie would have been making sure Esme was all right and had everything she needed. Esme replied 'yes' a few times and said she'd spoken to her papa. When they finished Esme handed back my phone and asked if she could watch some television now as they didn't have one at the farm.

We went in through the patio doors where I showed her how to work the remote. Five minutes later Joy phoned and I told her more or less what I'd told Bobbie. I'd copied Joy into the email I'd sent to Bobbie, and she had access to my log notes. She would normally visit within a week of a child arriving and said she'd set up a Zoom call for Friday afternoon, assuming Esme was still with me, which we thought she would be. Nothing was said about me stepping back from fostering and I didn't mention it again. However, before I began making dinner, I texted Adrian and Lucy and brought them up to date:

Hope you are OK. Am fostering Esme for a short while until her father can collect her. Love Mum xx

Lucy replied with a thumbs-up emoji, and Adrian texted, *Thanks for letting me know. We're good x*

I also texted Lara to see how she was. I told her I was looking after Esme and that she wasn't in school so I probably wouldn't be able to visit her this week.

No problem x, she replied.

Paula finished work at 5.30 and the three of us ate together at the table in the kitchen-diner where we usually took our meals. Esme asked Paula what sort of work she did, and Paula explained.

'Did you go to college?' she asked.

'Yes, to get a degree.'

'Papa wants me to be a musician like him, but I'm not sure,' Esme said. 'Sometimes he has to work very late and I have a babysitter.'

'Do you play a musical instrument?' I asked as we ate.

'I can play the piano and violin a little, but I prefer to sing.'

'That's lovely. I'm afraid I don't have a piano or a violin for you to practise on, but do please sing, any time.' My children had all had some music lessons with various instruments but none of them had continued.

'I'll sing when Papa comes,' Esme replied wistfully.

My heart went out to her, and I could see Paula looking at her compassionately. Esme was a lovely child who came across as intelligent and sensitive. I hoped what had happened to her didn't blight her future happiness, although I thought it would take some time for her to get over it, even when she was home with her dear papa. I didn't know the details of how she'd been taken from her father's custody and brought here, and I wasn't going to question her. I guessed it had been pretty traumatic, especially when she'd found out she wouldn't be able to see her father, with whom she clearly had a very strong bond.

After dinner (Esme ate well and had a dessert of yoghurt and fruit), I suggested she might like to choose some games from the toy cupboards, which we could play. I opened the cupboard doors to show her the shelves brimming with board games, puzzles, card games and boxes of toys, accumulated from years of fostering. I pointed out some board games that I thought she might

like, but her attention went to a box of dolls and dolls'
clothes.

I helped her lift it out and we took it into the living
room. Paula said she was going to her room for a while
and would be down later. Esme spent the next hour
completely absorbed in dressing and undressing the dolls,
combing and styling their hair and playing with them – a
small child again.

Paula came down around 7.30 and we showed Esme
how to play Uno. We had a few games, then Esme said,
'I'll go to bed now so the time for Papa to phone will
come more quickly.'

She kissed Paula goodnight and gave her a hug. I went
upstairs with Esme and waited on the landing while she
was in the bathroom. She came out in her new nightwear,
and I saw her into bed.

'I hope Mama is all right,' she said again as I tucked
her in.

'I'm sure she will be. Bobbie is going to see her this
week.' I didn't mention that I'd asked Bobbie about
phone contact as I didn't want to raise Esme's hopes and
have them dashed if she couldn't speak to her mother.

I hugged and kissed her goodnight, and her last words
before I left her room were, 'Be certain to wake me in
time to speak to Papa.'

'I will, love, don't worry.'

CHAPTER TWENTY-FOUR

AN ANXIOUS WAIT

Esme was up earlier than the previous day, just before
8 a.m., having slept well. She showered and dressed
in her new clothes, then I brushed and plaited her hair.
We had breakfast with Paula and then she went to work
in her bedroom. As 10 a.m. approached I fetched my
laptop and set it at the table in the kitchen-diner. The
light seemed just right in here for the best screen image.
Esme sat beside me and at ten o'clock the video call from
Hugo came through. I clicked the mouse to connect the
call and then moved aside.

'Papa, you are still at home!' Esme said reproachfully.
'When are you leaving to collect me?'

'As soon as I can, my love, but the forms take time to
be processed. Everything takes so much longer now.' I
heard him sigh. 'I telephoned the embassy twice yesterday and already again this morning. I will try again later
today. They are very busy. It's not like it used to be before
Covid when you could just buy a ticket and get on a train
or a plane.'

I knew that countries had different rules and
restrictions on travel and were unlocking at different
rates. I had no idea what was involved in Hugo

coming to England and then returning home with his daughter.

'So tell me what you've been doing. Is Cathy there?' he asked.

'I'm here,' I said, and moved into view. 'Try not to worry. Esme is doing very well. I know it will take time and I am keeping her occupied.' Then to Esme I said, 'Tell your papa what you've been doing.'

'Cathy took me shopping and I've got some new clothes,' she said, and stood to show him.

'Very smart.'

'I've been doing schoolwork,' she continued. 'Cathy bought some workbooks.'

'I'm pleased.'

'And I've been watching television and playing in the garden and talking to Paula. She's Cathy's grown-up daughter.'

But it wasn't long before her conversation turned again to when she could go home. Hugo reassured her he was doing all he could to make it happen as quickly as possible, and said she needed to be a 'big girl'.

'I don't want to be a big girl,' Esme said, and she began to cry.

Hugo looked close to tears himself. I put my arm around Esme and comforted her, then fetched a tissue and dried her eyes.

'Be happy for your father,' I told her.

'I'll try,' she sniffed.

They talked for a while longer, but it was difficult for them both, then Hugo wound up and said he'd phone again tomorrow. After they'd said goodbye and I'd closed my laptop, I had a little chat with Esme and said it would help her papa if she could try to be happy during the calls. She said she would, bless her.

We completed a few pages from her workbooks and then I suggested we walk to our local park. I was trying to keep her occupied so she wouldn't fret for her father. Because it was a school day there were just a few very young children in the park. Esme had a swing and I showed her the duck pond. She talked a bit about the park near where she lived, and how she and Julian went there. I learnt that as well as living in the apartment next to hers, Julian was in her class at school and they'd been friends since nursery.

We returned home and had lunch with Paula. When Paula went to her bedroom to work again Esme said she wanted to do some more schoolwork so Papa would be pleased. I sat with her and helped her as necessary. Later in the afternoon she played with the dolls again. That evening after dinner, as it was still warm outside, Paula suggested they played badminton. But then just after 7 p.m. Esme said she wanted to go to bed so it wouldn't be too long until Papa called. It was strange fostering Esme, different. I was really just biding time keeping her as happy as possible until her father arrived. Usually, I could plan ahead and get involved with the child and their school and make a difference to their lives, but only Esme's father could do that.

At bedtime Esme grew tearful again. 'I think Papa has forgotten me,' she said as she climbed into bed.

'Of course he hasn't forgotten you,' I replied. 'He loves you more than anyone else in the world. He's doing everything he can to come here as soon as possible.'

I'm sure Esme knew that, but, feeling sorry for herself, she needed to hear it.

'It was wrong of Mama to take me with her,' Esme said.

'I think it was an unwise decision,' I said carefully.

'Mama said it was for a holiday and Papa wouldn't mind. Then she wouldn't talk about it.'

I nodded.

'But I want to see her again,' Esme added.

'I understand – she's your mother – but we will have to leave that to your social worker and father to sort out.'

Like many children whose parents separate, Esme had divided loyalties, made more complicated by her mother's actions.

I sat on the edge of Esme's bed. The small window was open on another warm June evening. Through it came the sound of someone playing the flute, the plaintive notes dream-like and delicate. I'd never heard it before and I wondered which of my neighbours or their children was playing.

'I know that tune,' Esme said.

'So do I.' It was 'My Heart Will Go On', its haunting melody immortalized in the film *Titanic*. I could hear the lyrics in my head as the tune continued, magical and so emotive.

Esme broke our silence. 'Julian can play this on his flute,' she said in a whisper, and gave a small smile.

'What a lovely coincidence.'

We continued to listen in silence until the piece ended. We waited but there were no further tunes. It had arrived in the still of the evening, borne on the warmth of the night, a reminder of home and a message of reassurance and hope for Esme's safe return.

'We weren't allowed to make music or sing at the farm,' Esme said, when we were sure no more tunes would follow. 'We had to chant and hum. Mama said it relieved stress and encouraged inner peace. But it went on for ages and was boring.'

'What sort of chanting and humming?' I asked, thinking I'd better add this to my log, alongside the other disclosures Esme had made.

'It was like this,' Esme said, and she began to make a noise that sounded like a fly trapped in a glass bottle – such a contrast to the soulful flute that had just been playing.

I felt sure it wasn't as bad as Esme suggested, and I was aware that some chants and humming can be soothing, but whether it was right to insist a child participated and to ban them from singing, I doubted.

I sat with Esme until she was ready to go to sleep, then I kissed her goodnight and came out. Downstairs, I checked my phone and saw a text message from Hugo: *Thank you for looking after Esme. This is all taking longer than I expected. Hugo.*

I replied: *Don't worry, I'll look after Esme for as long as necessary.*

I checked my emails and found one from Joy, sent only an hour before, cancelling the virtual visit she'd booked for tomorrow. She apologized for the short notice and said she'd be in touch to arrange another visit next week and to have a good weekend.

Esme slept well and woke looking forward to her father's video call when she felt sure he would have the good news she was waiting for. He didn't and spent a very long time reassuring Esme that he was doing all he could to hurry it along. After the call Esme did some 'schoolwork', as we were now calling it, and then she took a book from the bookshelf and began reading it. We had lunch with Paula and after that I took Esme for a walk into our High Street for a change, and then back through the park. Anything to keep her occupied. We made some cakes in the afternoon and that evening at dinner I suggested that tomorrow – Saturday – we went out for the day, after her father's video call, of course. Paula agreed that it was a good idea and Esme asked if there was a boating lake like the one near where she lived, where her papa took her in the summer with a picnic. I knew of something similar about half an hour's drive away. I texted Lucy and Adrian to see if they wanted to join us there, but it was too short notice; they were both busy. Lucy suggested we met on Sunday afternoon in the park near her and I replied that we would.

As the Zoom call Joy was going to arrange was no longer happening, the day passed in much the same way as the previous one. I phoned Adrian in the evening and also spoke to Kirsty, who said she was feeling fine; she had no morning sickness but was permanently hungry. She said Adrian was being very attentive and looking after her well, which I was pleased to hear. I reminded them to let me know if there was anything I could do.

On Saturday Paula and I made a picnic while Esme spoke to her father – he had nothing new to tell her – then we went to the boating lake for the day. On Sunday we met Lucy, Darren and Emma in the park. Esme was very good with Emma and told us that Julian had a little sister she played with. That night Esme asked if I'd heard anything about her mother and I said, honestly, I hadn't. I was hoping that Bobbie would have some news when she phoned.

On Monday morning Esme woke in a bit of a bad mood. 'It's a week tomorrow and Papa still isn't here!' she said crossly.

I reassured her that her father was doing his best, but I appreciated that a week is a long time in a child's life, especially when waiting for something big to happen. Esme ate her breakfast with a bit of a sour expression. When her father video-called she got annoyed with him and repeated what she'd said to me – that it had been a week now and he was taking too long. Poor man.

'I'm waiting for your new passport,' Hugo said lamely.

'So ask Mama for the old one!' Esme demanded rudely.

'I can't, my love. She doesn't answer her phone.'

'I told you, Axel has it!' Esme snapped. 'You have to go to the farm and find it!' Annoyed, she slammed down the laptop lid.

'Esme, that's not going to help,' I said. I lifted the lid and Hugo was still there.

'Sorry, Papa,' she said.

'I'll phone the social worker,' Hugo said. 'Perhaps she can help find your passport. I thought it would be quicker to get a new one, but now I'm not so sure.'

I really couldn't add anything so I prompted Esme to tell her father what she'd been doing, including how we spent yesterday afternoon in the park with Lucy and her family. He always took an interest in what Esme told him and they talked a bit about Emma and then Julian's sister. The conversation ended with Hugo saying, 'I'll phone the social worker now. But, Esme, if I have no news tomorrow, please do not be angry with me. I'm doing my best.'

'I know, Papa. I promise I won't be angry.'

'Good girl.'

They blew each other a kiss and the call ended.

'Let's do some schoolwork,' I said. I'd no sooner arranged the workbooks on the table when Bobbie phoned. I knew Hugo hadn't had time to speak to her yet. I stayed with Esme as I took the call.

'I didn't have a chance to call you on Friday,' she began. 'It was in my diary, but events took over.' Bobbie would have about twenty-five cases, possibly more, all requiring her attention. 'How is Esme?'

'She's doing all right. A bit frustrated that it's taking so long. Her father just video-called and now we're going to do some schoolwork.'

I was about to continue in more detail when Esme asked, 'Is that Bobbie, the social worker?'

I nodded.

'Can I talk to her?'

'Yes.' Esme had a right to speak to her social worker when she wished, as do all children in care. 'Esme would like to talk to you,' I told Bobbie.

'Put her on.'

I passed my phone to Esme. 'Can you go to the farm today and ask Mama for my passport?' she said to Bobbie. 'Papa is taking too long to get me a new one.'

I couldn't hear Bobbie's reply, but I knew from Esme's face it wasn't the news she wanted.

'Where is she?' Esme asked after a few moments, now shocked. She listened some more and then, looking very worried, handed the phone back to me. 'Mama's gone.'

'It's Cathy,' I said. 'What's happened?'

Bobbie told me that when she and a colleague had visited the farm last week to check on the other children there, Esme's mother had already left, without leaving a forwarding address or saying where she was going. I asked Bobbie if she'd taken their passports or her mobile phone but she didn't know, and she didn't have Esme's mother's mobile number. She said she'd ask Esme's father. I looked at Esme as I told Bobbie she was worried about her mother and had been asking to speak to her – there was no reason why Esme shouldn't hear this. Bobbie said she'd let us know if her mother got in touch. Mary knew Esme was in the care of the local authority and could easily find their number and contact them if she wished.

'I need to go now, Cathy,' Bobbie said. 'Esme's father is trying to phone me.'

I said goodbye and put my phone down.

'Mama's gone,' Esme said anxiously.

'I know, love.'

'Where can she be?'

'I don't know.'

'Do you think she's in this country?'

'I honestly don't know, but she's an adult and will be able to look after herself, so try not to worry.' I thought Esme's mother, Mary, who was calling herself Serenity, must be reasonably streetwise as she'd made it here with Esme during the pandemic.

'But Mama hasn't got any money,' Esme said. 'We had to give it to Axel when we first got to the farm.'

'Your mother can go to the social services for help.'

'Or Papa can help her.'

'Yes.' I thought that, despite everything, Hugo would probably help Mary if she got in touch with him. He seemed a nice guy.

'Shall we phone Papa and tell him?' Esme asked.

'He's calling Bobbie now so she'll tell him.'

I tried to distract Esme with her workbooks, but she wasn't in the mood to study. Her worries had now shifted from how quickly her papa would arrive to her mother being missing.

'Where is Mama?' Esme asked every so often. 'Where can she be? … Where has she gone? … Do you think she has called Papa?' And so on.

I told Esme I was sure her mother was safe and if she phoned either Bobbie or her father, they would let us know. But the day passed without hearing anything further. That evening I texted Hugo, although I didn't tell Esme.

Bobbie phoned this morning and said Esme's mother had left the farm. Is there any news?

Hugo replied: *I called Bobbie and said I'd let her know if Mary contacted me.*

From which I deduced there was no more news.

Children often worry about their parents more than adults realize, even in secure, stable, loving families, sometimes imagining dreadful things happening to them, possibly them dying. It's part of a child's vulnerability – the fear of being left alone in the world, unable to fend for themselves. Although Esme had me looking after her and knew her father would be on his way as soon as possible, it didn't stop her from worrying that something dreadful had happened to her mother. This continued throughout the following day, when there was no more news. Then on Wednesday morning, when I woke and checked my phone I found a voice message from Hugo, sent during the night, saying Mary had been found. I was so relieved. Hugo said she'd borrowed a phone and called him. Her phone, money, passports, watch and other valuables were still at the farm but she was going to try to get them. He said he'd transferred some money to see her through and ended by saying, 'Please tell Esme her mother is safe. I'll video-call this morning as usual.'

CHAPTER TWENTY-FIVE

ESME SINGS

Of course, Esme was delighted her mother had been found; I told her as soon as she woke. She told Paula at breakfast. In fact, Esme could talk about nothing else, but she had plenty of questions for me that I couldn't answer. I replayed her father's voicemail so she could hear what he'd said and knew everything I did.

Paula went to her room at 9 a.m. to work and Esme wandered around the house unable to settle, waiting for her father's video-call. At 9.50 I set my laptop on the dining table, ready. Esme sat in front of it watching the screen. I joined her just before 10 a.m. but unfortunately Hugo was five minutes late, which seemed an eternity to Esme. When he did appear Esme, having forgotten her promise not to be angry with her father, said, 'Papa! I've been waiting ages for you!'

'I'm so sorry,' he said, running his fingers through his hair. 'I've had little sleep and a busy morning.' He looked tired and slightly dishevelled.

'Where is Mama? Can I talk to her?' Esme asked impatiently.

'I don't know when you will be able to talk to your mama, but I've spoken to her twice. She's going to the farm where you were staying today to try to get her belongings.'

'Why did she leave?' Esme asked, which I'd wondered too.

'She told me she didn't want to stay there without you.'

'Will she come home with us?' Esme asked hopefully.

'Not to live with us, no. Where she decides to live is up to her. Your mama has a lot of thinking to do to work out what is best for her in the future and what sort of life she wants. It will be her decision.'

'Will Mama get my passport?' Esme asked, hardly pausing to take a breath between questions.

'She may, but there is no need. It's been cancelled and your new passport arrived this morning.' He smiled and held it up for Esme to see.

Esme squealed with delight. 'Papa has my new passport! When are you coming to get me?'

'I've booked my ticket,' Hugo said with another smile. 'That's why I was late calling you.'

'Papa's coming!' Esme cried, so loudly she didn't hear the rest of what her father was saying so he had to repeat it.

'I land late on Saturday afternoon. I have to fill in a travel locator form, so I need to book a hotel, and Covid tests, one to fly and another on day two when I get there. There's a lot to do so it will be Tuesday before I see you.'

'But, Papa, that's nearly a week!' Esme exclaimed.

'I know, my love, but that's how it is now with all the Covid rules and regulations to follow. You must help Papa and be patient. I will call every day, but I have a lot to do.'

'All right, Papa, I will be patient.'

'Good girl.'

'Is Bobbie aware of these arrangements?' I asked. 'She needs to know.'

'She is on my list of people to phone,' Hugo said. Then to Esme, 'I have many calls to make so tell me what you are planning to do today and then we'll say goodbye, and I'll speak to you again tomorrow.'

Esme looked a bit disappointed. 'I'm going to do some of my schoolwork and then play. Will you talk to Mama today?'

'It's possible.'

'Can you tell her I love her?'

'I will, but I'm sure she already knows.'

They finished by blowing kisses to each other before Hugo ended the call. I was relieved that Esme's mother had been found safe and well and that Hugo was helping her. But as he'd told Esme, her future was hers to decide. I assumed if she stayed in this country Esme wouldn't see her very often.

While l shared Esme's relief and happiness, I quietly retained a degree of caution. So often in fostering happy endings are delayed and sometimes don't happen at all. While I was sure Esme would be reunited with her dear papa, I harboured some doubts on when this would be. The pandemic had caused a lot of uncertainty, which had made planning ahead very difficult. All it needed was another sudden lockdown in either of our countries and Hugo's arrival and Esme's return home would be delayed indefinitely. I kept that thought to myself.

Esme managed to complete a few exercises in her workbooks, but her concentration kept wandering to

Mama and Papa and what they were doing. She told Paula at lunchtime her papa had her passport and was coming on Saturday but she wouldn't see him until Tuesday. Paula was naturally pleased for her and said Tuesday wasn't that far away.

After lunch, when Paula had returned to her bedroom to work, I suggested to Esme we went out for a while, but she said she'd rather sit in the garden and read her book. She told me about the courtyard at the rear of her father's apartment where she sometimes sat reading a book or playing if he was busy and needed to concentrate. It was enclosed and had palm trees in large blue pots. If you looked up you saw other apartments; they had balconies with window boxes where flowers grew. She said her father could see her from the window while he worked, and she could see him. It sounded like a lovely arrangement.

Esme and I spent most of the afternoon in the garden. When she'd had enough of reading she helped me with some gardening. She said the courtyard at home didn't have weeds because it was mainly paving but there were lots of weeds at the farm and they used to eat them. I suggested those weeds might be crops, but she said they made soup out of dandelions and nettles, which I had heard of, as well as other plants I hadn't.

Neither Bobbie nor Joy called that day, but in the evening Paula and I heard Esme sing for the first time. She had said she would sing when her father came to collect her, so I assumed buying his ticket was good enough. Esme was in the bathroom getting ready for bed. I was downstairs working at my computer as I waited for her to finish, when I would go up and see her into bed. To begin with I thought Paula was listening to music in her bedroom, then I realized it was coming from the bathroom.

I left my computer and went upstairs as the song continued and my heart filled. Note perfect, Esme was singing 'Hallelujah', her sweet yet powerful voice seeming to illuminate the house. Tears sprang to my eyes. It's such an emotive song anyway, and hearing it sung by a young girl, who was thankful for good news, made it even more evocative. I stood on the landing, my eyes glistening, and listened. Paula quietly opened her bedroom door and joined me. I could see she was as moved as I was. We stood there in awe, blinking back tears.

When Esme finished and the bathroom door opened we both clapped.

'That was lovely,' I said, still choked up.

'Beautiful,' Paula added.

Esme looked embarrassed. 'Thank you. I sing at night in bed. That's one of Papa's favourites. He says I sound like an angel and it's a pity I don't always behave like one.'

I smiled. 'You have a lovely voice. Please sing some more.'

'I'll try, but it has to come from within me. Papa says music is from the soul, and I sort of know what he means. Sometimes he cries when I sing.'

'I'm not surprised,' I said. 'It's very moving.'

Esme wouldn't sing for us while we were watching her, so Paula said goodnight and I saw Esme into bed, leaving the door open a little as usual. A while later she began singing 'Amazing Grace', then 'What a Wonderful

World' and 'All Through the Night'. I kept stopping what I was doing just to listen. It truly was from her soul and it touched mine. Eventually she sang herself to sleep. She was a beautiful, spiritual child and I thought it was a pity she hadn't been allowed to sing at the farm for all those months. She would have found it comforting, and I'm sure others would have enjoyed it. It seemed strange that a cult that was supposed to be about peace and inner tranquillity didn't allow singing. I think music, whatever form it takes, lifts us from the everyday and connects us with something much higher and enriching. Clearly Esme's father had nurtured this in Esme. What sort of person her mother was I had no idea, as I knew so little about her.

On Thursday when Hugo video-called he told us he'd completed all the forms for travel to England, had booked their Covid tests and their hotel, and had emailed Bobbie with the details. He hadn't received a reply from her yet and asked me if I'd heard from her. I said I thought she was probably very busy but I'd phone her tomorrow if she didn't call me. Apart from anything else, I needed confirmation from her that Esme could go with her father next Tuesday.

Esme asked her father about her mama and he said she'd gone to the farm and had got all her belongings apart from her money, which had been used towards the running of the farm. He reassured Esme that he'd sent her mother some money, so she'd be all right. He'd also told her that Esme's old passport wasn't valid any more and she could destroy it.

'Where is Mama now?' Esme asked.

'I don't know exactly. But she has enough money to pay for lodgings.' Which satisfied Esme for the time being.

Esme sang herself to sleep again that night; she'd been singing quietly to herself on and off all day. Knowing her father was on his way had allowed her to relax and be happy again.

On Friday when Hugo video-called he talked a bit about what they would do when Esme got home. He said his and Esme's return flights were booked for next Friday to allow time for their return Covid tests. That was the last day of the school term so Esme wouldn't be home in time to join her class, but Hugo said that as many of her school friends lived nearby she'd see them during the long school holidays. He also said that he didn't think he'd be able to Skype tomorrow morning as he'd be on his way to the airport. He'd text or phone as soon as he landed, then video-call from his hotel room.

On Friday afternoon Bobbie phoned and confirmed the arrangements: that Esme would go with her father on Tuesday, assuming his Covid test was negative. She asked me to test Esme that morning and have her bags packed ready, as she'd arranged to meet Hugo at my house at 10.30 a.m. If either Esme or her father tested positive for Covid then their departure would be delayed and Esme would stay with me until they both tested negative. I asked about Esme's mother and Bobbie said she hadn't been in touch with the social services so it was unlikely that Esme would see her before she left, after which contact arrangements would be for her parents to sort out. Bobbie then spoke to Esme to make sure she understood what was happening and, wishing her a nice weekend, said goodbye and she'd see her on Tuesday.

Esme was so looking forward to her father's arrival that she could hardly finish her dinner that evening, then she wanted an early night so it would soon be morning and Papa would be on his way. She knew that he wouldn't be video-calling on Saturday morning so I suggested we went shopping. I wanted to buy her a little keepsake, a memento of her time with us, and she said she wanted to buy her papa a gift. I'd given her the allowance she was entitled to, plus a bit more.

Although Esme was in bed early, it was late before she fell asleep. I heard her start little songs, then lose concentration and stop, her thoughts clearly elsewhere. I went into her room and asked her if she was all right.

'Yes, I'm happy and thinking of Papa,' she said, and she looked it.

The following morning when I checked my phone there was nothing from Hugo, so I assumed all was going to plan. I wasn't expecting to hear from him until he was at the airport.

Esme was awake early despite not going to sleep until late. Naturally she asked about her papa and I reassured her. She managed a little breakfast and we left the house shortly after 9 a.m. to go shopping, leaving Paula to have a lie-in at the weekend. Face masks on, we browsed the department store where Esme spent time choosing a gift for her father. She eventually settled on a bone-china mug that she said her father could drink his tea from. It had a very ornate picture on the side of an English country garden, which Esme told me looked like my garden.

I wish! I thought. I asked her if she might like a matching one for herself – my gift to her – and she said she would. I paid for both and told her to keep her allowance to spend at the airport. As the assistant wrapped the gifts Esme couldn't resist telling her one was for her papa and they were going on a plane. The assistant added extra packaging so the china travelled safely.

As we left the shopping centre my phone bleeped. It was a text message from Hugo saying he was at the airport and the flight was due to leave on time. I replied: *Have a good journey. See you soon.*

That afternoon was all about keeping Esme occupied as her father travelled. Paula, as usual, was a big help and baked cakes with Esme, then played ball games and did some skipping and so forth in the garden. Just after 5.30 p.m. I received another text from Hugo saying he had landed and was waiting for his luggage. I showed Esme the text and I replied: *Great! Thanks for letting us know.* Then three hours later he phoned from his hotel. I put Esme on and they spoke for a while. I couldn't hear what he was saying but Esme kept smiling and saying, 'Yes, Papa.' He ended by telling her he'd video-call tomorrow at 10 a.m. Esme had another early night, but this time she went off to sleep quite quickly, softly singing 'Unchained Melody'. She certainly knew how to pull at my heart strings!

The following morning, at five minutes to ten, Esme and I were in front of my laptop at the dining table ready for Hugo's video call. Paula had taken toast and tea to her room as she didn't have to be up for work. Dead on ten o'clock, Hugo's video call came through and there was Hugo in a hotel room.

'Is that where I'm going to stay?' Esme asked excitedly.

'Yes, just for a few days until our Covid tests are back,' he replied, then he panned the device around his room so she could see. It was a family room with a double and single bed.

'I have something to tell you,' Hugo said, setting the device in front of him again. 'Your mama has asked to talk to you, so I've given her Cathy's number. Is Cathy still there?'

Having said hello, I was now sitting slightly to one side, so I moved into his line of vision.

'I hope that's OK,' Hugo said to me. 'Mary needs to speak to Esme.'

Strictly speaking, it wasn't OK to give out my number. Hugo should have checked with the social services or me first, but I'd experienced worse breaches of confidentiality during my fostering career. I suppose he just hadn't thought about it.

'You didn't give her my address?' I asked. Mary had snatched Esme once, and for this reason Bobbie had said she wouldn't be told where I was living.

'No, just your phone number. She's hoping to call this afternoon,' Hugo said, oblivious to any oversight on his part.

'All right. Do you know what time?'

'No. She just said this afternoon.'

'Is Mama going to leave too?' Esme asked.

'I don't know. That will be her decision,' Hugo replied, as he had before.

The conversation went to Hugo's flight, his self-isolation while waiting for his Covid test results, Esme's schoolwork and returning home. Esme told her father she had bought him a present but he couldn't open it until they were home because the lady in the shop had wrapped it in lots of tissue paper so it wouldn't get broken.

'That's nice, thank you, but having you home will be the best present,' Hugo said.

They talked for about half an hour and then Hugo wound up and said he'd video-call again at the same time tomorrow.

It wasn't long before Esme's thoughts of seeing her father again after eight months were overridden by the knowledge that her mother was going to phone that afternoon. She kept mentioning it and asking what time she would call, which I didn't know. I'd already made the decision that I would put my phone on speaker so I could listen to and monitor the call. Had it not been the weekend I would have phoned Bobbie for advice. In an emergency I could have called the duty social worker, but this wasn't an emergency. Often in fostering the carer has to make a snap decision based on experience and common sense.

Esme didn't want to go out in case she missed her mother's call, although I told her I always took my mobile with me. We did some schoolwork – her father had asked her how it was going – then after lunch we went into the garden, but Esme couldn't really settle to anything.

It was two o'clock when my mobile rang from a number not in my contacts list.

'Is that Mama?' Esme cried, rushing to my side.

I put the phone to my ear as I answered. 'Hello?'

Then came a woman's voice, so quiet and indistinct that I nearly missed what she was saying.

'I'm Serenity, Esme's mama. I'm sorry to disturb you. Could I talk to her, please?'

CHAPTER TWENTY-SIX

MARY

I'd built a picture in my mind of Serenity, real name Mary, as self-centred and irresponsible, someone who'd put her own needs first at the expense of her child. But as she and Esme talked, with my phone on speaker, I realized that she was more likely naive, impressionable and easily influenced – like many of the mothers of the children I'd fostered. Esme kept telling her off and Mary repeatedly said she was sorry and agreed she'd been wrong in taking Esme and bringing her to this country. I formed the impression that she'd been persuaded, even brainwashed, into believing that life in a cult for her and her child was much better than one in the outside world. Every criticism and accusation of wrongdoing Esme threw at her mother – and there were plenty – Mary agreed with and apologized for. She knew I was listening as I'd told her at the start of the conversation, but I don't think her contrition was for my benefit. She was artless and hadn't thought through the implications of taking Esme, and now accepted that it was very wrong. Apart from the heartache she'd caused Esme and Hugo, she'd defied a court order that had given Hugo custody of Esme and would now have to face the consequences.

'Is Papa angry with you?' Esme asked at length.

'Your papa doesn't get angry with anyone, but he's disappointed in me,' Mary said remorsefully.

I saw no need to interrupt the conversation or change its direction as it continued. There was a lot that needed to be said. Esme was angry with her mother, had questions that needed answering, and Mary accepted this.

Eventually, Esme asked, 'Are you going to leave when Papa and I leave?'

'Do you want me to?' her mother asked in a small voice. 'After everything I've done?'

'Of course, but Papa says you won't be able to see me alone again.'

'I know.'

'So are you going to leave then?' Esme demanded.

'I don't think I have enough money for the fare.'

'Papa will pay,' Esme replied. 'Ask Papa.'

'All right, I'll try.'

'Phone him now,' Esme persisted.

'I will.'

They'd been on the phone for nearly an hour and I thought this was probably a good time to stop. My phone battery was dying; I could have plugged it into the charger, but I felt that perhaps the conversation needed to be wound up now. A lot had been said and Esme needed to process it all. I suspected her mother did too; she sounded exhausted. I assumed she'd phone again if she wanted.

'The battery on my phone is about to go,' I said. 'Do you want to say goodbye and phone another time?'

'Yes,' Mary said. 'Thank you.'

'Call Papa now,' Esme said, clearly wanting her mother to return when they did.

'I will. I promise.'

They said goodbye and the call ended as it had begun, with Esme's mother apologizing.

Esme fell silent for a while and then began talking about her mother, going over all she'd said, and how she was sorry, and that Esme still loved her even though she'd caused her and Papa a lot of hurt. Esme said that there were times at the farm when she'd thought she'd never be able to leave and see her papa or her real home again. I said I thought her mother had acted impulsively and hadn't stopped to consider the consequences, but that she loved her.

That night when I wrote up my log notes I included Esme's mother's call and paraphrased what she'd said. I also emailed Bobbie with an update, copying in Joy. I hadn't heard from Joy since she'd cancelled her virtual visit. If she didn't reschedule it for Monday, it would be too late as Esme was leaving on Tuesday.

Although Esme hadn't been with us long, because of her nature and the circumstances in which she'd arrived Paula and I felt close to her, a part of her life, and with a vested interest in her future happiness. Hugo video-called as usual at 10 a.m. on Monday and his joy at being able to collect Esme the following day was obvious. Esme told him about her mother's call, but he knew already as Mary had phoned him straight after. He said she had decided to return home, so he'd bought her a ticket rather than giving her money. She was booked on the same flight as they were. Esme was ecstatic.

'But,' Hugo continued, 'we have agreed she won't phone you again until we have returned and sorted out contact arrangements.'

'I understand, Papa. Then I will be able to see her.'

'Yes.'

When they'd finished I checked my emails. Bobbie had replied to my last email, thanking me for the update and confirming she'd be at my house by 10.30 a.m. tomorrow.

Esme then helped me pack her belongings, leaving out her nightwear and fresh clothes for tomorrow. She'd arrived with nothing and now had a suitcase of belongings. She couldn't settle to much after that and in the end watched some children's films on television. She would have gone to bed straight after dinner if she'd had her way. But it was another warm evening and Paula said she was in need of some exercise, having been sitting at her laptop all day, and suggested we walk to our local park. It didn't close until late in summer. As we set off Esme said this would be the last time she'd come to our park.

'Perhaps you'll come to visit us?' I suggested.

'Yes. I'll tell Papa, and you can come to us too.'

The café was still open so we all had an ice-cream, which we ate while wandering around the park. I took a photograph of Esme – one for the collection I would email to Hugo. Esme wanted one of us all so I took a selfie of the three of us in the park – our last evening together.

On Tuesday morning Esme was up, washed and dressed by 7.30 a.m., as was I. I put her night clothes and what she'd been wearing yesterday in the washer-dryer so she would leave with no laundry. I thought it would help

Hugo as they were staying in a hotel for the rest of the week. Bobbie had asked me to give Esme a lateral flow test, so I did that before breakfast. Then, to be on the safe side, I tested myself and Paula when she was up. Thankfully, the tests were all negative. At 9 a.m. Paula went to her room to work but said to call her when Esme was due to leave so she could say goodbye.

I packed the last of Esme's clothes and put her bags in the hallway, ready. From what Bobbie had said she wouldn't be coming in and Hugo would have a cab running, so I guessed neither of them would stay for long. Esme and I sat in the living room talking about all that had happened. I thought she'd be talking about it for a very long time as she slowly came to terms with and recovered from her ordeal.

At little before 10.30 the doorbell rang and we both went to answer it. It was Bobbie wearing a face mask. I took a couple of disposable masks from the hall stand and passed one to Esme.

'Good morning,' Bobbie said. 'All set?'

'Yes.' I stood aside so she could see Esme's bags – the suitcase and hand luggage.

'Is Papa here?' Esme asked hopefully.

'Not yet,' Bobbie replied.

Esme put on her shoes and went down the path and watched for her father's arrival.

'Did you test Esme?' Bobbie asked me as we waited.

'Yes, negative. I've uploaded the test results.'

It was another warm morning, but not sultry and uncomfortably hot. A few minutes passed and then a cab pulled up. The moment it stopped the rear door opened and Hugo jumped out.

'Papa! My papa!' Esme cried, and flew into his arms.

'Oh, Esme, at last,' Hugo said, his voice breaking.

They hugged and hugged as though they would never let each other go. I swallowed the lump rising in my throat. Hugo was wearing a mask, but joy and love shone in his eyes.

'Shall we get the bags out?' Bobbie asked me practically.

'And I need to fetch Paula to say goodbye.'

I went indoors. Paula had heard the doorbell and was already on her way downstairs. We took a bag each and carried them out to the pavement. Bobbie came with us but kept her distance.

'This is my daughter, Paula,' I said to Hugo.

He paused from hugging Esme. 'Thank you both for everything,' he said, and shook our hands warmly. He then reached into the cab and presented us with a magnificent bouquet of flowers.

'That is nice of you,' I said, really appreciating the gesture.

'They're beautiful,' Paula added.

'Thank you for all you've done for Esme,' Hugo said again. 'We will never forget your kindness.'

The cab driver, having seen us bring out the bags, now got out and put them into the boot of the car.

'I'll set up a virtual visit for tomorrow,' Bobbie told Hugo, clearly needing to leave.

'And when you have a moment please call and let us know how you are,' I said to Hugo.

'Of course we will. Thank you again.'

I put the bouquet of flowers down on the pavement while I gave Esme a big hug. Paula hugged her too, then

Esme and her father got into the back seat of the cab. Hugo closed the door and lowered the window.

'Thanks again,' he said.

'You're very welcome. Take care.'

They both waved and smiled as the cab drew away. I picked up the bouquet of flowers.

'That's a nice way to end a placement,' Bobbie said, and headed for her car.

'Yes, it is,' I agreed. 'Very nice indeed.'

EPILOGUE

The days were flying by and I seemed to be as busy as ever. I was helping more with Emma, writing, and supporting Lara and Arthur as well as other young people. I'd also begun redecorating, with the intention of working through the house. Paula helped at weekends. Details of induction courses and training arrived, for which the fostering team would 'appreciate my input'. I confirmed I was happy to attend, and I began preparing the sessions – at present online.

I began doing some respite fostering, but that's another story. As well as wanting to spend more time with my family, I'd become increasingly frustrated with the system. Social care provision for children and young people in the UK is among the best in the world, but there's still room for improvement, as there is in many countries.

At the time of writing two shocking cases have hit the news in England where parents have been found guilty of torturing and murdering a child in their care. That is shocking enough, but social services had been visiting these families so there must have been missed opportunities to rescue the children. Sadly, it's happened before, as it has in other countries. There will be inquiries into what went wrong and hopefully lessons will be learnt. When I think of cases like this and those like Rachel's I sometimes wonder if the wrong children are in care, but judging when a child can be safely supported at home and when they should be removed is a fine line to tread.

I am still in contact with many of those I've fostered – by phone, social media and in person. Foster carers never forget the children they've looked after. For updates on the children in my books please visit https://cathyglass.co.uk/updates/

If you are interested in fostering, please check out the information and links to organizations on my website. I know many have been drawn to fostering through reading my books. Please let me know how you get on.

SUGGESTED TOPICS FOR READING-GROUP DISCUSSION

_____

Was it appropriate for Ryan to play hide-and-seek with Becks? Was it appropriate for him and his sister, Evie, to rough and tumble at their age?

After the investigation, Tash and her family resign from fostering. What are your feelings about this?

Cathy talks about the vulnerability of foster carers. Why might a young person make an unfounded allegation against a carer or one of their family?

What could be added to a family's safer-caring policy to help keep all family members safe?

Cathy continues to support Lara and others she has fostered. Why might this be important?

Lara asks Cathy if Joel can stay at her home for the night. Why does Cathy refuse?

How was Troy able to ingratiate himself into the lives of Rachel and her family?

Based on what we know, do you think Rachel's children should have been taken into care?

How has the pandemic affected fostering practices?

At what point does Cathy start to consider the possibility of scaling back from fostering? What are her reasons/thought process?

Anne says that three children is too much for a single carer. Do you agree?

Esme has run away from a cult. Cathy and Paula are surprised to learn that cults exist in the UK. Were you? What do you know about cults?

CHRONOLOGY

If you would like to read, or re-read, my books in chronological order, here is the list to date:

Cut	*Hidden*
The Silent Cry	*Mummy Told Me Not to Tell*
Daddy's Little Princess	*Another Forgotten Child*
Nobody's Son	*The Child Bride*
Cruel to be Kind	*Can I Let You Go?*
The Night the Angels Came	*Finding Stevie*
A Long Way from Home	*Innocent*
A Baby's Cry	*Too Scared to Tell*
The Saddest Girl in the World	*A Terrible Secret*
Please Don't Take My Baby	*A Life Lost*
Will You Love Me?	*An Innocent Baby*
I Miss Mummy	*Neglected*
Saving Danny	*A Family Torn Apart*
Girl Alone	*Unwanted*
Where Has Mummy Gone?	*Unsafe*
Damaged	

The titles below can be slotted in anywhere, as can my Lisa Stone thrillers: http://lisastonebooks.co.uk/:

The Girl in the Mirror	*Happy Adults*
My Dad's a Policeman	*Happy Mealtimes for Kids*
Run, Mummy, Run	*About Writing and How*
Happy Kids	*to Publish*

This list is also on the books page of my website: https://cathyglass.co.uk/true-stories-cathy-glass/

Cathy Glass

One remarkable woman, more
than **150** foster children cared for.

Cathy Glass has been a foster carer
for 30 years, during which time she has
looked after more than 150 children, as well
as raising three children of her own. She was
awarded a degree in education and psychology
as a mature student, and writes under a
pseudonym. To find out more about Cathy
and her story visit **www.cathyglass.co.uk**.

The care system
failed Lara.

Will she fail
her own child?

CATHY GLASS

THE MILLION COPY BESTSELLING AUTHOR

Unwanted

Unwanted

**Lara was seven when she was put
into foster care after her mother died
from a drug overdose**

The care system failed Lara and
now she is failing her son . . .

A Family Torn Apart

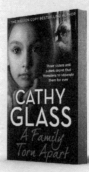

Angie and Polly are loved and looked-after by their parents, so why are they brought into foster care?

But as they settle with Cathy, and start to talk of life at home, it becomes clear something is badly wrong.

Neglected

The police remove Jamey from home as an emergency and take him to foster carer Cathy

But as Jamey starts to settle in and make progress a new threat emerges, which changes everything.

An Innocent Baby

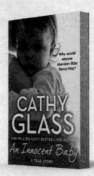

Abandoned at birth, Darcy-May is brought to Cathy with a police escort

Her teenage mother wants nothing to do with her, but why? She is an adorable baby.

A Life Lost

Jackson is aggressive, confrontational and often volatile

Then, in a dramatic turn of events, the true reason for Jackson's behaviour comes to light . . .

A Terrible Secret

Tilly is so frightened of her stepfather, Dave, that she asks to go into foster care

The more Cathy learns about Dave's behaviour, the more worried she becomes …

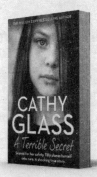

Too Scared to Tell

Oskar has been arriving at school hungry, unkempt and bruised. His mother has gone abroad and left him in the care of 'friends'

As the weeks pass, Cathy's concerns deepen. Oskar is clearly frightened of someone – but who? And why?

Innocent

Siblings Molly and Kit arrive at Cathy's frightened, injured and ill

The parents say they are not to blame. Could the social services have got it wrong?

Finding Stevie

Fourteen-year-old Stevie is exploring his gender identity

Like many young people, he spends time online, but Cathy is shocked when she learns his terrible secret.

Where Has Mummy Gone?

When Melody is taken into care, she fears her mother won't cope alone

It is only when Melody's mother vanishes that what has really been going on at home comes to light.

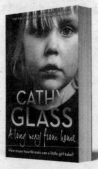

A Long Way from Home

Abandoned in an orphanage, Anna's future looks bleak until she is adopted

Anna's new parents love her, so why does she end up in foster care?

Cruel to be Kind

Max is shockingly overweight and struggles to make friends

Cathy faces a challenge to help this unhappy boy.

Nobody's Son

Born in prison and brought up in care, Alex has only ever known rejection

He is longing for a family of his own, but again the system fails him.

Can I Let You Go?

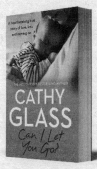

Faye is 24, pregnant and has learning difficulties as a result of her mother's alcoholism

Can Cathy help Faye learn enough to parent her child?

The Silent Cry

A mother battling depression. A family in denial

Cathy is desperate to help before something terrible happens.

Girl Alone

An angry, traumatized young girl on a path to self-destruction

Can Cathy discover the truth behind Joss's dangerous behaviour before it's too late?

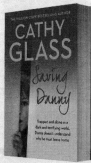

Saving Danny

Danny's parents can no longer cope with his challenging behaviour

Calling on all her expertise, Cathy discovers a frightened little boy who just wants to be loved.

The Child Bride

A girl blamed and abused for dishonouring her community

Cathy discovers the devastating truth.

Daddy's Little Princess

A sweet-natured girl with a complicated past

Cathy picks up the pieces after events take a dramatic turn.

Will You Love Me?

A broken child desperate for a loving home

The true story of Cathy's adopted daughter Lucy.

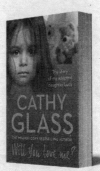

Please Don't Take My Baby

Seventeen-year-old Jade is pregnant, homeless and alone

Cathy has room in her heart for two.

Another Forgotten Child

Eight-year-old Aimee was on the child-protection register at birth

Cathy is determined to give her the happy home she deserves.

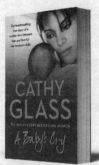

A Baby's Cry

A newborn, only hours old, taken into care

Cathy protects tiny Harrison from the potentially fatal secrets that surround his existence.

The Night the Angels Came

A little boy on the brink of bereavement

Cathy and her family make sure Michael is never alone.

Mummy Told Me Not to Tell

A troubled boy sworn to secrecy

After his dark past has been revealed, Cathy helps Reece to rebuild his life.

I Miss Mummy

Four-year-old Alice doesn't understand why she's in care

Cathy fights for her to have the happy home she deserves.

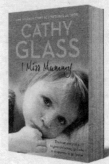

The Saddest Girl in the World

A haunted child who refuses to speak

Do Donna's scars run too deep for Cathy to help?

Cut

Dawn is desperate to be loved

Abused and abandoned, this vulnerable child pushes Cathy and her family to their limits.

Hidden

The boy with no past

Can Cathy help Tayo to feel like he belongs again?

Damaged

A forgotten child

Cathy is Jodie's last hope. For the first time, this abused young girl has found someone she can trust.

Run, Mummy, Run

The gripping story of a woman caught in a horrific cycle of abuse, and the desperate measures she must take to escape.

My Dad's a Policeman

The dramatic short story about a young boy's desperate bid to keep his family together.

The Girl in the Mirror

Trying to piece together her past, Mandy uncovers a dreadful family secret that has been blanked from her memory for years.

About Writing
and How to Publish

A clear, concise practical
guide on writing and the best
ways to get published.

Happy Mealtimes
for Kids

A guide to healthy eating
with simple recipes that
children love.

Happy Adults

A practical guide to achieving lasting
happiness, contentment and success.
The essential manual for getting
the best out of life.

Happy Kids

A clear and concise guide to
raising confident, well-behaved
and happy children.

THE DOCTOR

How much do you know about
the couple next door?

STALKER

Security cameras are there to
keep us safe. Aren't they?

THE DARKNESS
WITHIN

You know your son better than
anyone. Don't you?

Be amazed
Be moved
Be inspired

Follow Cathy:

/cathy.glass.180

@CathyGlassUK

www.cathyglass.co.uk

Cathy loves to hear from readers and reads
and replies to posts, but she asks that no plot
spoilers are posted, please. We're sure
you appreciate why.

MOVING
Memoirs

Stories of hope, courage and
the power of love . . .

Sign up to the Moving Memoirs email and you'll
be the first to hear about new books, discounts,
and get sneak previews from your
favourite authors!

Sign up at

www.moving-memoirs.com